The EcoEdge

Urgent design challenges in building sustainable cities

Editors: Esther Charlesworth and Rob Adams

Routledge
Taylor & Francis Group

LONDON AND NEW YORK

First published 2011
by Routledge
2 Park Square, Milton Park, Abingdon, Oxon OX14 4RN

Simultaneously published in the USA and Canada
by Routledge
270 Madison Avenue, New York, NY 10016

Routledge is an imprint of the Taylor & Francis Group, an informa business

British Library Cataloguing in Publication Data
A catalogue record for this book is available from the British Library

Library of Congress Cataloging-in-Publication Data
Charlesworth, Esther Ruth.
  The EcoEdge: urgent design challenges in building sustainable cities/Esther Charlesworth and Rob Adams.
  p. cm.
  Includes index.
  1. City planning–Environmental aspects. 2. Sustainable urban development. I. Adams, Rob (Rob John) II. Title. III. Title: Urgent design challenges in building sustainable cities.
  NA9053.E58C49 2011
  711'.4–dc22   2010034684

ISBN: 978-0-415-57247-7 (hbk)
ISBN: 978-0-415-57248-4 (pbk)

Typeset in Dante
by Wearset Ltd, Boldon, Tyne and Wear

Printed and bound in Great Britain by TJ International Ltd, Padstow, Cornwall

The EcoEdge

'Greenspeak' is increasingly central to the discourses of the architectural design and planning professions. However, constructed examples of the principles in practice, of designers, planners and urban politicians actually walking the sustainability talk into action are not nearly as common ...

This book presents the experiences of design practitioners who have implemented sustainable design projects rather than just theorized about them. Presenting diverse case studies of contemporary sustainable urban practice from Europe, Africa, India, South America, the USA and Australia, this book offers the reader a fantastic wealth of practical material from a range of internationally renowned authors. It includes:

- 14 global case studies which act as benchmarks and inspirations for transformation;
- voices and experiences of developing economies such as India and China, heard on equal footing with those from Europe, North America and Australia;
- an exploration of urgent design challenges such as population density, recreating infrastructure that supports carbon neutral or low carbon (emission) intensive urban activities, and retrofitting for sustainability;
- a clear structure: divided into 3 parts, each part is introduced by a thematic overview essay by an internationally respected design scholar, on sustainability and their field of practice. These essays provide insight into each case study chapter that follows; locating practical themes explored and pointing out where further work is needed in policy, planning, design and research.

Well-illustrated, thematically focused and with superb global coverage, this book presents the reader with a multi-voiced and yet highly cohesive reference for anyone interested in green issues in urban design and architecture.

Dr Esther Charlesworth is the founding Director of Architects without Frontiers (Australia), a design non-profit organisation committed to working with communities in need. She is currently Senior Research Fellow in Architecture at RMIT University, Melbourne. After working as an architect and urban designer in Melbourne, Sydney and New York, Esther lectured in architecture at QUT, Brisbane, the University of Melbourne and at the American University of Beirut between 2000–2002. Between 1995 and 1999 Esther was Senior Urban Designer with the City of Melbourne and there founded the CityEdge International Urban Design Series. She has published widely on the theme of social responsibility and architecture including: *CityEdge: Contemporary Case Studies in Urbanism* (2005), *Architects Without Frontiers, War, Reconstruction and Design Responsibility* (2006) and *Divided Cities* (2009).

Professor Rob John Adams AM is Director City Design at the City of Melbourne. Rob Adams has over 36 years' experience as a practising architect and urban designer consistently producing design-research based urban projects and strategies receiving over 100 state and national awards for excellence. In 2007 Rob was awarded an Order of Australia in recognition for services to urban design, town planning and architecture, and in 2008 named as the Australian Prime Minister's Environmentalist of the Year at the Banksia Awards.

Contents

List of figures   vii

List of tables   x

Notes on contributors   xi

Acknowledgements   xiv

List of abbreviations   xv

The EcoEdge   1
Esther Charlesworth

Part I
Urban design and a sustainable city   5

Overview   7
Melanie Dodd

Air in the city: The place of work   12
Scott Drake

Assassination in the sustainable city: The Netherlands and beyond   20
Wim Hafkamp

Reprogramming cities for increased populations and climate change   30
Rob Adams

Sustainability for survival: Moving the United Kingdom beyond the zero carbon agenda   39
John Worthington

Chaos and resilience: The Johannesburg experience   50
Chrisna Du Plessis

Part II
Infrastructure and a sustainable city   61

Overview   63
Ralph Horne

Sustainable drinking water and sanitation: Two Indian cases   70
Shantha Sheela Nair

Sustainable Savannah   81
Scott Boylston

Ecopolis: Small steps towards urbanism as a living system   90
Paul Downton

The green edge: China between hope and hazard   103
Neville Mars

Part III
Architecture and a sustainable city   115

Overview   117
Leon van Schaik

A landscape framework for urban sustainability: Thu Thiem,
Ho Chi Minh city   121
Dennis Pieprz

Networks cities in China: Sustaining culture, economics and the
environment   133
James Brearley and Qun Fang

The responsive city: London South Bank experiences   148
Alex Lifschutz

Small-scale sustainability: Parasite Las Palmas and beyond   158
Mechthild Stuhlmacher

Sustainable subtropical city: An architecture of timber-framed
landscapes   171
Brit Andresen

Beyond the EcoEdge   184
John Fien and Esther Charlesworth

Index   191

Figures

3.1   Part plan showing mixed mode space in National Australia Bank,
      Docklands, Melbourne   16
3.2   Mixed mode space showing operable windows   17
4.1   View from soccer stadium showing, right, an apartment building
      that houses a cogeneration plant providing electricity and heat to the
      neighbourhood   25
4.2   Major international highway A2 cutting through Maastricht
      residential neighbourhoods   26
4.3   Resident support for architectural heritage in the Indische Buurt,
      Amsterdam   28
4.4   Neighbourhood renovation is no 'cure all' for a multicultural
      society   29
5.1   Green AXO map   34
5.2   Set of assumptions   35
5.3   Maribyrnong Road: before and after   36
6.1   Cambridge City plan provides park-and-ride gateways to the
      historic university core at key areas for intensification: the
      university land to the north-west, Addenbrookes Hospital and
      Medical Research Park to the south, the airport to the east, and
      Cambridge Science Park and the proposed Chesterton station to
      the north   44
6.2   Cambridgeshire subregional expansion strategy, showing the
      proposed transport network, green grid and new communities at
      Northstowe and Cambourne   45
6.3   Parklands spatial framework, an environment and landscape
      strategy for the Thames Gateway, east of London   46
6.4   Design for London's proposed Green Grid for the east of London
      provides a range of formal and informal recreation spaces and
      landscapes and helps East London adapt to climate change by
      reducing flood risk and enhancing surface-water management   47
7.1   South Africa's greatest urban consolidation   52
7.2   Beggar selling jokes   53
9.1   Sources of drinking water for Chennai city   71

9.2	Changes in groundwater levels for Chennai (1983–2007)	72
9.3	Four examples of rainwater harvesting systems	74
9.4	Collecting street rainwater to recharge wells	74
9.5	A newly built EcoSan toilet in Musiri	77
9.6	An EcoSan toilet under construction in Musiri	78
9.7	Saliyar Street ECCT, Musiri Town Panchayat, the 'Use and Get Paid Toilet…'	79
10.1	Starland Lofts	83
10.2	Fellwood rendering	85
10.3	Frogtown	85
10.4	Poetter Hall	86
10.5	SCAD buildings in Savannah	87
11.1	Ecological building. Key: (1) Abiotic substances: basic elements and compounds of the environment; (2) Producers: autotrophic (food-making) organisms; (3) Consumers/macroconsumers: heterotrophic (food-eating) organisms; (4) Scomposters/microconsumers: heterotrophic organisms, chiefly bacteria and fungi, that reduce 'waste' to simple substances useable by producers	91
11.2	Paper-wasps' nest: the wasps cannot procreate and survive without building these extensions of their physiology	92
11.3	Roof garden at Christie Walk: an artificial living system depending on, and supporting, its inhabitants and users	95
11.4	Section through the intensive roof garden	97
11.5	Christie Walk organizational chart	98
11.6	Site plan of Christie Walk	99
11.7	Peak day power consumption: Christie Walk compared with Mawson Lakes and average South Australian consumption	100
12.1	Tianjin CBD: a compact grid system around a green ring, natural water filtering system and subway connections lay the infrastructural foundations of a green CBD	109
12.2	The People's Urbanity of China	110
12.3	The L-building (hybrid *hutong*) concept	111
12.4	L-building sketch	111
12.5	D-rail: a major transportation project designed to bridge Beijing's ring-road network and promote interactive mobility over existing walls of congestion	112
12.6	The E_Tree offers shadow, uses sunlight and hides parking lots	113
13.1	Overview	116
14.1	The Thu Thiem urban design plan	122
14.2	Urban design strategy	123
14.3	Urban design plan	124
14.4	Integration of canals and wetlands	126
14.5	Canal district	127
14.6	High density along Crescent Boulevard	129
15.1	General arrangement plan	136
15.2	City detail plan	137

15.3	Green network plan	138
15.4	Networks diagram	138
15.5	Green network	139
15.6	Commercial network	140
15.7	Rural and urban networks	141
15.8	3D urban	141
15.9	Four cells	142
15.10	Urban heat island programme	142
16.1	The cleared Coin Street sites	152
16.2	Coin Street housing	153
16.3	Thames Riverside Walk looking towards the Oxo Tower	154
16.4	Hungerford Bridge	156
17.1	Parasite Las Palmas, Rotterdam	159
17.2	Private house under construction	162
17.3	091 Plans of private house	163
17.4	Private house, west façade, during construction	164
17.5	Private house, west façade	164
17.6	House No. 19, Utrecht	166
17.7	De Kamers, Amersfoort, exterior	166
17.8	De Kamers, ground floor	167
17.9	De Kamers, first floor	168
17.10	De Kamers, interior	169
17.11	De Kamers, theatre space house for culture	170
18.1	Mooloomba City: architecture of timber-framed landscapes for the future subtropical city	174
18.2	Mooloomba House: timber-framed house and landscape	174
18.3	Mooloomba House: transparency in house and landscape	175
18.4	Mooloomba House: permeable tectonic structure with people and landscape scale	175
18.5	Mooloomba House: axonometric drawing of belvedere timber construction	176
18.6	Mooloomba House: exterior view of belvedere timber with landscape	176
18.7	Mooloomba House Studio: transverse section study – early sketch	178
18.8	Mooloomba House: view from sitting room 'cave' to studio 'bower'	180
18.9	Mooloomba House: longitudinal section study – early sketch	181
18.10	Mooloomba House: longitudinal section	181
18.11	Mooloomba House: studio room in the afternoon	182
19.1	Lifelong learning and the triple bottom line of sustainability	188

Tables

11.1   Comparison between Christie Walk and conventional
        development (based on an actual example)   101
14.1   Planned land uses for Thu Thiem   130
19.1   Tools for deliberative democracy   189

Contributors

Rob Adams, University of Melbourne Professorial Fellow, and Director of Design and Culture for the City of Melbourne. His seminal work as an architect and urban designer, including his role in revitalizing Melbourne, was recognized with an Order of Australia in 2007 for services to urban design, town planning and architecture. In 2008 he was named the Prime Minister's Environmentalist of the Year (Banksia Awards).

Brit Andresen was awarded the RAIA Gold Medal for 2002 in recognition of her outstanding achievements as an academic and design architect in Australia and overseas. Andresen is Director of Andresen O'Gorman Architects and Professor of Architecture at the University of Queensland.

Scott Boylston is Professor of Graphic Design at Savannah College of Art and Design, Georgia. He wrote the acclaimed *Designing Sustainable Packaging* (Lawrence King Publishers 2009) and has published short stories and poetry on environmental degradation. His poster designs have featured in international shows on prison reform, immigration rights, globalization and governmental hypocrisy.

James Brearley, Adjunct Professor at RMIT University, Melbourne, and **Qun Fang** established the Shanghai branch of BAU Brearley Architects + Urbanists in 2001. BAU and Steve Whitford won first prize in the 2001 Invited Urban Design Competition for a 25 km² extension to Xin Yu City. They attribute their success and thoroughness to an interdisciplinary approach to architecture, landscape, urban design and planning.

Esther Charlesworth, Senior Lecturer in Architecture and Design, RMIT University, Melbourne, is founding director of Architects Without Frontiers (Australia). She researches the roles of design professionals in community development, particularly post-conflict and natural disaster. Publications include *Architects without Frontiers: War, Reconstruction and Design Responsibility* (Elsevier 2006) and *Divided Cities: Beirut, Belfast, Jerusalem, Nicosia and Mostar* (University of Pennsylvania Press 2009), co-written with Jon Calame.

Melanie Dodd is an architect and head of the Architecture programme at RMIT University, Melbourne. She is a member of the international art and architecture collaborative Muf, and founder member of Mufaus, a multidisciplinary and research-based practice. Muf has been exhibited and published at the Carnegie Museum in Pittsburgh, Van Allen Institute in New York and the Design Museum in London. Melanie was the Creative Director of the 2010 National Architecture Conference in Sydney – 'Extra/Ordinary'.

Paul Downton is Principal Architect, Urban Ecologist and Director of Ecopolis Architects (Adelaide, Australia). A prize-winning architect and urbanist, he is best known for his futurist concepts of 'ecopolis' and 'urban fractals', incorporating ecological architecture, eco-city design and bio-urbanist strategies. Editor and primary author of the Australian government's highly successful *Your Home Technical Manual*, his most recent work is *Ecopolis: Architecture and Cities for a Changing Climate* (Springer Press/CSIRO 2009).

Scott Drake is a Senior Lecturer in Architecture, Building and Planning at the University of Melbourne, the principal author of *The Elements of Architecture: Principles of Environmental Performance in Buildings* (Earthscan 2009), and author of *The Third Skin: Architecture, Technology and Environment* (UNSW Press 2007).

Chrisna Du Plessis is Principal Researcher at the Council for Scientific and Industrial Research (CSIR), South Africa. With a BArch and MArch in sustainable development (University of Pretoria), a PhD in urban sustainability science (University of Salford) and an honorary doctorate in Engineering (Chalmers University of Technology), she prepared the *Agenda 21 for Sustainable Construction in Developing Countries* for UNEP and CIB.

John Fien, Professor of Sustainability in the Innovation Leadership programme at RMIT University, is responsible for supporting research on social, environmental and economic sustainability across the university. With interdisciplinary experience in education and training, natural resource management, public participation and sustainable consumption, he has a broad sustainability agenda, developing partnerships between university researchers, business, industry, government, NGOs, schools and communities.

Wim Hafkamp is Scientific Director, Nicis Institute in The Hague. He was Professor of Environmental Studies and Head of the Erasmus Centre for Sustainable Development and Management (Erasmus University, Rotterdam). A specialist in modelling the economic effects of sustainable environmental policies, he has been a member of the Dutch Advisory Council on Housing, Spatial Planning and Environment and Council for Transport and Infrastructure.

Ralph Horne is the Director of the Centre for Design and a Professor at RMIT University, Melbourne. He is a specialist on environmental assessment and design in the UK and Australia. Recent research has centred on eco-design and social context, especially with respect to affordable housing, product and packaging eco-design, consumption, life-cycle assessment, carbon-neutral communities and sustainable household practices.

Alex Lifschutz worked at Foster Associates (1981–1986) on the forty-three-storey Hong Kong and Shanghai Bank headquarters and then co-founded Lifschutz Davidson. Alex is active in all the practice's projects and initiates research and development on new systems of construction and adaptable structures. Since 2002, he has been an elected member of the Architectural Association Council.

Neville Mars, a Dutch architect, is Director of the Dynamic City Foundation (DCF) in Beijing and engaged in research and the design of China's rapid urban development. His research on long-term design solutions related to hyper-speed market-driven development and China's formulated goal to build 400 new cities by 2020 resulted in *The Chinese Dream: A Society under Construction* (010 Publishers 2008).

Shantha Sheela Nair is in charge of India's rural sanitation, which is just one of her responsibilities as the Secretary, DDWS, Ministry of Rural Development for the Government of India in New Delhi. A leading figure in sustainability debates in India, she seeks to ensure that sanitation is given a high priority at all levels of government and ardently promotes rainwater harvesting.

Dennis Pieprz, Sasaki's President, plays a leading role in the firm's design practice, including urban design and regeneration, and interdisciplinary teamwork. He led the design of Sasaki's prize-winning Olympic Green, the urban design plan for the main site of the 2008 Beijing Olympics, and has been the design principal for over thirty national design award-winning projects.

Leon van Schaik, Innovation Professor of Architecture at RMIT University, Melbourne, was awarded an Order of Australia in 2006 for services to architecture. He has developed a model postgraduate architecture programme. Publications include: *Mastering Architecture: Becoming a Creative Innovator in Practice* (Wiley 2005), *Design City Melbourne* (Wiley 2006), *Spatial Intelligence: New Futures for Architecture* (Wiley 2008) and *Procuring Innovative Architecture* (Routledge 2010).

Mechthild Stuhlmacher (and Rien Korteknie) founded Korteknie Stuhlmacher Architects in 2001. The firm deals with residences, experimental housing, public buildings for education, sports and culture, commercial buildings, urbanism and art in public spaces. Stuhlmacher is a founding member of the Parasite Foundation, an organization focused on high-quality temporary building. She has taught architectural design at Delft University of Technology since 1997.

John Worthington, co-founder of leading international strategy and design consultancy DEGW, is the Graham Willis Professor in Architecture at the University of Sheffield and Director of Learning for the Academy of Urbanism. He has been a chairman of CABE/RIBA Building Futures (2003–2006), a board member for the London Thames Gateway Development Corporation (2006–2009) and wrote *Reinventing the Workplace* (Architectural Press, 2nd edn 2006).

Acknowledgements

This book would not have been possible without the sustained support from the City of Melbourne who had the vision to host the original EcoEdge conferences during 2005 and 2008. Special thanks also go to Anitra Nelson and Frans Timmerman for their patience and skill in assisting the editors of this book. Finally thanks to Francesca Ford for her encouragement of the *EcoEdge* concept between 2008 and 2010.

We are grateful for permission to reproduce images from the following copyright holders.

BVN Architecture (Figure 3.1), John Gollings/National Library of Australia (Figure 3.2), City of Melbourne (Map 5.1, Figures 5.1 and 5.2), Melaver, Inc./Lott Barber (Figure 10.2), Ian Lambot (Figure 16.4), Michael Barnett (Figure 18.2), Anthony Browell (Figures 18.3 and 18.4) and John Gollings (Figure 18.6).

Every effort has been made to contact and acknowledge copyright owners. If any material has been included without permission, the publishers offer their apologies. The publishers would be pleased to have any errors or omissions brought to their attention so that corrections may be published at later printing.

Esther Charlesworth and Rob Adams
June 2010

Abbreviations

BAU	Brearley Architects and Urbanists
BREEAM	Building Research Establishment Environmental Assessment Method
CABE	Commission for Architecture and the Built Environment
CAS	complex adaptive system
CBD	city or central business district
CCP	Chinese Communist Party
CEF	Chatham Environmental Forum
CSCB	Coin Street Community Builders
DD	dynamic density
EcoSan	ecological sanitation
ECCT	EcoSan community compost toilets
FAR	floor area ratio
ICA	Investment and Construction Authority
IfS	Institute for Sustainability
LDS	Lifschutz Davidson Sandilands
LEED	Leadership in Energy and Environmental Design
MUD	market-driven unintentional development
OGC	Office of Government Commerce
PUC	People's Urbanity of China
SCAD	Savannah College of Art and Design
SES	social-ecological system
SOHO	single occupant home office / small office home office
UEA	Urban Ecology Australia
UPI	Urban Planning Institute
URI	Urban Renaissance Institute
VVD	Volkspartij voor Vrijheid en Democratie (People's Party for Freedom and Democracy)

The EcoEdge

Esther Charlesworth

> At a design level, we need to be able to test and interrogate alternative scenarios. What is it like to live in a climate change resilient city? What does that mean for urban places, other than simply engineering solutions? How much will we want to live by the water if it's cut off from us by levy walls? And if higher housing densities around public transport aren't going to be our sole solution to reducing emissions, what will be? And what would a retrofitted suburb be like to live in? And how do you negotiate all of this with communities, and make it happen?
>
> (Stalker 2007: 4)

EcoEdge stories

This book was inspired by debates and dialogue at the regular CityEdge International Urban Design conferences hosted by the City of Melbourne (Australia). The popularity and impact of the CityEdge series on both the audience and speakers – many of them urban design politicians, architects and urban designers responsible for shaping the form of a large number of global cities – indicate an increasing desire amongst both design practitioners and academics to learn from, and build on, the sustainable urban design stories of their international peers.

The fourteen case studies in this book are inspiring benchmarks for the transformation of cities of both the North and the South, including China, India, South Africa, Vietnam, the UK, Denmark, the Netherlands, the USA and Australia. These case studies highlight the urgent design challenges of population density, infrastructure, carbon-neutral (or at least low-carbon) urban planning, and retrofitting for sustainability. Each author has addressed the emerging 'green' issues of their chosen city and offered solutions, where applicable, to implement visions of what a sustainable design practice might look like across a range of urban scales and cultures. Many of the contributors have also examined the often conflicting responsibilities and opportunities for designers and urban policy makers working in the challenging realms of sustainable urban design, planning, architecture and building technology. For example, bringing together a group of urban designers to develop a master plan based on carbon-neutral planning principles for a new or old urban centre is one part of the journey towards delivering a sustainable future to communities; actually securing political and financial support to deliver on the promise of that plan is a much harder and rarer achievement.

The case studies in *The EcoEdge: Urgent Design Challenges in Building Sustainable Cities* are organized around three major fields of practice in the quest for urban sustainability: (1) urban design, (2) infrastructure and (3) architecture. Each of these three sections of the book is introduced by an overview essay by an internationally respected scholar of design and sustainability. These essays offer insights on the significant principles and lessons in the case studies they introduce.

Greenspeak or greenwash?

'Greenspeak' is increasingly central to the discourses of the design and planning professions. However, constructed examples of the principles in practice, of designers, planners and urban politicians actually *walking* the sustainability *talk* into *action*, are not nearly as common. *The EcoEdge: Urgent Design Challenges in Building Sustainable Cities* presents the experiences of design practitioners who have implemented sustainable design projects rather than just theorized about them. Many architects and designers have been successful at implementing sustainability at the scale of the individual product or building through the use of passive solar design and innovative construction technologies. Likewise householders across the globe are increasingly playing their part in the eco-revolution, installing water tanks, solar panels and worm farms in their own backyards. And yet the scale that will contribute exponentially to a reduction in greenhouse gases and rising sea levels is not necessarily the one of *individual* action or individual buildings but rather the one of *collective* political and design collaboration in tackling emissions from the city and its resultant sprawl. Sadly, despite the media scrum created by the Kyoto, Copenhagen and climate conferences, this attention to the physical manifestations of environmental policy on metropolitan regions (through strategies of urban consolidation and increasing public transport) seems to have been put in the 'too hard' basket for politicians invested with the power and funds to actually reduce the likely impacts of climate change.

Designer denial

Projected to us every hour, every day through a barrage of media sources, the commonly accepted scientific facts of climate change are that urban centres in the future will become hotter, dryer and more vulnerable to intense storms, cyclones and flooding, with coastal centres experiencing even greater and often disastrous storm surges, rising sea levels and population displacement. Though it is now common knowledge that cities create most of the planet's greenhouse gas emissions, as *EcoEdge* author Ralph Horne tells us, the gap between the empirical data on global warming and realizable design visions for solutions for compact cities with a low-carbon future has never been greater.

Esther Charlesworth

With most metropolises from Mumbai to Melbourne expected to double in size in the next twenty to forty years, the time has come for the design profession to develop – with 'military urgency', *EcoEdge* author Paul Downton suggests – sustainable urban design models built on policy decisions on the construction and investment in critical regional infrastructure (transport and employment) hubs. Without such design visions, politicians are left with climate change policies galore but no means to ever implement them. Without attention to the perilous physical consequences of urban vulnerability wrought by global warming, urban designers will likewise be left with sophisticated master plans with little demographic relevance and perhaps little future employment.

Avoiding silos

The many intersecting and overlapping themes in the fourteen case studies are discussed in the 'epilogue' in this book. However, if one overarching theme is to be highlighted here, it is that the urgent challenge of urban sustainability cannot be solved, as Albert Einstein once said, 'with the same thinking we used when we created them'. The disciplinary chauvinism of traditional design practices, for example architecture that privileges aesthetic form over social justice or environmental sustainability, is central to many urban problems. So architects, urban designers and planners must heed the lessons of the case studies in this book and engage in much more dynamic and proactive ways with their colleagues from science, urban sociology, commerce and politics. As *EcoEdge* author, Wim Hafkamp, argues:

> The design challenge is no longer about urban form, the built environment per se, or the quality of public space, but about shaping interactions between all those involved: residents, teachers, employers, housing corporations, youth workers and police, through to politicians and ministers.

Reference

Stalker, C. (2007) 'Design in the age of climate change', paper presented to *Urban Design Australia Conference*, Canberra, September. Online: www.urbandesignaustralia.com.au/images/Docs/Papers/CarolineStalkerDes%20in%20the%20Age%20of%20Climate%20Change.pdf; accessed 12 December 2009.

Part I

Urban Design and a Sustainable City

Overview

Melanie Dodd

Cities are as much a manifestation of systems of behaviours and overlapping sociologies as they are configurations of built forms and spatial juxtapositions. But this emphasis is often forgotten or at least becomes abstracted in the emergence of lines on the page, and consequent built fabric, that constitutes the discipline of designing the city. The detached gaze of the urban planner all too frequently omits aspects of time and the rhythms of everyday life, perhaps not surprisingly because they are difficult to pin down and draw out using conventional tools of representation. If we cannot draw the life of the city, how can we design it? The invisible realm of daily habits and routines are an integral but slippery parallel to the physical spaces and buildings that we inhabit, and are frequently marginalized from urban design as practised in local governments and corporations.

Perhaps we have never properly lost our sense that urban design emerged from the problems of nineteenth-century city growth and the need to attend to the difficult infrastructural tasks of sanitation, water supply and delivery and transport of food: matters of engineering and technology. Yet in early periods of city growth, there was a fantastically close and symbiotic relationship between daily life and urban form. This was a golden age of urban ecology (Reid 1993). In cities like London and Paris in the seventeenth century, for example, rubbish (largely organic waste from kitchens and human effluent or 'night soil') was dumped in the street, promoting micro-economies of collectors or 'muckrakers' collecting and supplying as valuable compost to adjacent market gardens that supplied food to the masses. In fact, the profound way in which the rhythms of eating food have shaped our cities (Steele 2009) reveals a more humble history from which we should draw inspiration, especially since in our post-industrial cities we have copious examples of hard (engineering) infrastructure, now paradoxically detrimental to our quality of life. We seem to have come full circle. Once again we are suffering from issues of sustainability in urban conurbations, this time from a surfeit of technological solutions rather than a lack of them. From damaging car-dependence to dominating agro-corporation logistics to air conditioning, we have multiple urban 'mechanisms' that are rapidly draining our dwindling resources.

An understanding of how we can effect a fundamental shift in urban design practices could more usefully draw on the softer infrastructural domain of human behaviour rather than technologies of form (Landry 2000) or hard infrastructures. In seeking to establish more sustainable urban ecosystems, perhaps we need to focus on the complex notion of human agency and the associated social and cultural values implicit in how we behave and act in our daily life. Drake touches on this paradox in his study on the values of air in the city, which he concludes may have more to do with pleasure than health: more sociology than technology. An apparently technical study of the value of fresh air actually reveals that people use the 'space' of fresh air for more reasons than clean oxygen alone might provide them – including the opportunity for long views, refreshment opportunities and food, as well as a social chat. We might recognize this as a phenomenologically defined typology of space; one less concerned with the measurable versions of air than the qualitative and lateral associations that a broader definition – 'taking the air' – might imply.

Sociological examinations of human habit and everyday life make a compelling case for a different evaluation of how we might work towards urban sustainability. The notion of how we are 'somehow captured and held in thrall by predatory habits' (Shove 2009) – over-heating our domestic spaces, ubiquitous provision of en-suite bathrooms – means we can envisage 'tweaking' and manipulating behavioural habits to have a more profound effect on our energy consumption. This is less at the scale of built form, and rather more at the level of the messy realities of daily life. Similar sociological consideration of everyday domestic systems (Manzini and Jégou 2003), such as production, consumption and waste cycles, can allow us to rediscover sustainable micro-ecologies of daily life that can seed the ground-up ecology of the city.

The limitations of an environmentally dominant approach to sustainable development in the city is articulated even more forcefully by Hafkamp, who points out the relevance of the socio-political dimensions of the city. Increasing numbers of instances of racial intolerance in contemporary society in the Netherlands contextualizes an argument that our cities are not neutral vessels capable of being acted on by top-down policy towards sustainability. They are places of diversity and difference with profound socio-economic disadvantage, where sustainability agendas that focus on climate change have even less traction. An insidious fear of the stranger, the outsider and the extremist represents a type of global paranoia that has been predicted by political theorists (Bauman 1996) as an unfortunate side effect of global democracy after the fall of communism. The issue for multicultural cities is less about arrangements of built form and more about the 'daily negotiation of difference' (Amin and Thrift 2002) that is necessary. City building professionals have identified that there are significant practical and policy questions about managing and enhancing co-existence in shared spaces in the city (Sandercock 2003). It is acknowledged that a new urban condition exists: one in which difference, fragmentation and plurality prevail and are inevitable outcomes of our multicultural and transitory city lives. Planning and urban design with multiple publics requires a new type of process: more participatory and more agonistic processes that can acknowledge conflict and dissension. A focus at the level of the specific neighbourhood, 'shaping interactions' and the daily negotiation of difference, is critical if we are to manage changing regimes.

Adams presents us with more conventionally accepted dilemmas for the sustainable city and how it might be designed, referring to the statistical realities of population growth in Melbourne. Nevertheless, the assertion that we can accommodate a doubling of the population within the existing city boundaries returns us to similar territory. Adams focuses on systemic transformations – incentives and regulatory leadership, advocacy and financial mechanisms – that are necessary to stimulate a shift in societal expectation and behaviour towards denser infill living. The research offers compelling data that intensification and density need only occur on 6 to 10 per cent of the existing city (urban corridors and activity centres) to achieve this doubling of capacity. But the dilemma remains, how can behavioural norms and entrenched habits be modified? The capacity for policy initiatives alone to persuade people to live more densely is questionable. Theoretical possibilities will be achieved, as Adams states, only if most of the population begins to alter their current expectations for large detached houses on single lots. This is even more difficult where the private market dominates housing development, and offerings are tailored specifically to the status quo, well connected to domestic property inflation and investment realities that benefit the homeowner. It is an interesting observation that some of the most innovative and successful initiatives in urban sustainability have been forced on cities by circumstance. The influential urban agriculture movement in Cuba has spawned over 2700 state-run urban vegetable gardens, developed in vacant city lots, part of an effort by the socialist government to ease food shortages and nutritional problems specifically caused by import sanctions and blockades by other countries. Although one might not recommend such desperate measures, it is salutary to note that sociological shifts of the scale required for a doubling of density requires more than ordinary incentive to be effected.

Clearly managing behavioural 'change' is emerging as a primary concern for those considering urbanism and design for sustainability. Worthington concludes exactly this, and correctly characterizes cities as in constant flux: 'change is the norm.' He critiques the instrumentally driven approach to urban planning that privileges the achievement of measurable outcomes and generic values to the exclusion of other social, cultural and economic complexities with all their specificity and particularity of context. Rather than a zero carbon agenda, he advocates integrating approaches that are locally initiated and driven – as with the Cambridge Futures Initiative – as much through community from the ground up as via policy from the top down.

In fact the final chapter in this part, by Du Plessis, brings us full circle, and provides a framework in which to situate a common and compelling agenda for urban designers and architects in their consideration of city design and sustainability. Du Plessis concurs that the issue is not one of applying control through regulation and rigid 'blueprints' for performance. Twentieth-century urban design polemics have been progressively discredited because of the fixity of their ideological approaches, which have sought to ameliorate the ills of the chaotic city, resulting in fixed and irreparable outcomes for the future. Rather there is a need to reconceptualize the city as a complex 'ecosystem' of barely balanced chaos and flux. The cities of developing nations and the global south offer useful exemplars for constructing a more radical framework for how we conceive and manage the city as an adaptive system where 'daily life requires constant negotiation of both social and spatial boundaries'. The philosopher Michel de Certeau (1988) refers to the dialectical relationship between tactics and strategies. He links *strategies* with institutions and structures of power, while *tactics* are seen as a tool of contingency, utilized by individuals to respond to issues and constraints on the ground as they arise as a sort of self-organizing behaviour. These tactical responses to daily circumstances are opportunistic adaptations that actually drive the ecosystem of the city. Du Plessis asks precisely the right question when she speculates about how we can practise sustainability in a complex adaptive system. What she defines as 'socio-ecological systems' (SES) crucially consist of 'human' agents, their actions and behavioural patterns, which are subject to social, cultural, political and economic specificity. A 'systems' way of thinking is fundamentally different from the rationality and ordering tendencies manifested in most urban design, which is commonly understood and practised as an 'acting upon' and ordering of artefacts (the city). Such control is the pitfall of twentieth-century urbanism (Koolhaas and Mau 1998). A more sophisticated interpretation is that, in working with 'active matter' or people (De Landa 1997), the designer cannot impose preconceived notions into designed spaces. In fact this marks a fundamental shift in the acknowledged role of the designer of cities (Kaliski *et al.* 2008) to one that is far more defined as an agent or facilitator, or orchestrator of potentials and opportunities arising constantly, and over time.

Of course, architecture and urbanism have started to rise to the challenge of redefining themselves in line with a systems way of thinking. Certainly the idea of the urban designer as omnipotent creator has been exposed, and design processes that acknowledge the power and effect of human agency have arisen, whether through the political aspects of participatory design, the strategic approach of loose-fit infrastructures or, with the advent of computer technology, methodologies of simulation, prediction and optimization techniques. Whichever the direction, the challenge is not to fetishize the technique, but rather to uncover the local constituencies of place and allow these particularities to inform an approach to urban change that is inspired and sensitive to sociological and behavioural routines, and which accommodates necessary adaptive shifts towards sustainability objectives.

By acknowledging the inherent instability of the cities ecology, we can actually learn to value the 'imperfect' aspects of urbanity, and formulate a way forward to manage adaptation and adjustment over time: a matter of managing the chaos, rather than cleaning up the mess.

References

Amin, A. and Thrift, N. (2002) *Cities: Reimagining the Urban*, Cambridge: Polity Press.
Bauman, Z. (1996) *Alone Again: Ethics after Certainty*, London: Demos.
Certeau, M. de (1988) *The Practice of Everyday Life*, Berkeley and Los Angeles: University of California Press.

Melanie Dodd

De Landa, M. (1997) *A Thousand Years of Non-Linear History*, New York: Zone Books.

Kaliski, J., Chase, J. and Crawford, M. (2008) *Everyday Urbanism*, New York: Monacelli Press.

Koolhaas, R. and Mau, B. (1998) *S M L XL*, New York: Monacelli Press.

Landry, C. (2000) *The Creative City: A Toolkit for Urban Innovators*, London: Earthscan.

Manzini, E. and Jégou, F. (2003) *Sustainable Everyday, Scenarios of Urban Life*, Milan: Edizione Ambiente.

Reid, D. (1993) *Paris Sewers and Sewermen*, Cambridge, Mass.: Harvard University Press.

Sandercock, L. (2003) *Cosmopolis II: Mongrel Cities in the 21st Century*, London: Continuum.

Shove, E. (2009) 'Habits and Their Creatures', unpublished, Lancaster University.

Steele, C. (2009) *Hungry City: How Food Shapes Our Lives*, London: Random House.

Air in the City

The Place of Work

Scott Drake

The modern city can be seen in large part as an assembly of technologies for dealing with population density. While there are concerns about the long-term viability of current levels of material, water and energy use, it is important to recognize that these are not aberrations caused by Western consumer culture, but necessary techniques for dealing with city life. No doubt the sustainability of urban systems can be improved, but doing so will involve an unravelling and rebuilding of the very foundations of cities and their infrastructure.

This chapter discusses some of the design implications of urban water demand and then the challenges involved with adding a 'refresh' space to the workplace. This simple example of changing the way we deal with air in buildings offers lessons for changing the way we deal with energy and water, namely that the innovations needed are not simply technological but are fundamentally typological.

Urban water demand and supply

The environmental effects of strategies to deal with population density are most evident in the material composition of the modern city. The high level of embodied energy invested in concrete and steel enables the creation of durable building surfaces that are tolerant to weathering and resistant to human use and abuse (Brand 1994; Leatherbarrow and Mostafavi 1993). Concrete, bitumen and stone are used to create pavements and roads necessary to cope with the volume of traffic, both wheeled and pedestrian, which would turn city streets into mud and dust otherwise. This leads to adverse environmental effects, most notably water run-off from paving and the urban heat island effect from the reduced albedo of city surfaces relative to their surroundings. These effects can be mitigated in part by changes to drainage systems or increasing urban plantings through green roofs and walls. However, plantings are not easily accommodated within the existing building fabric, as they require significant changes to the structure and design of buildings to accommodate the soil, water, drainage and maintenance needed to keep them alive.

Cities are not yet designed to be green but they are designed to be clean. It is easy to overlook the role of water in the design of cities, and the way it reflects early modern strategies for human health and hygiene. The first great advances in urban hygiene came with the mechanization of the textile industries at the beginning of the Industrial Revolution, increasing the availability of cotton for clothing and beds (the term 'Manchester' (centre of the English cotton industry in the eighteenth and nineteenth centuries) is still used today for bed sheets). The second great advance in urban hygiene came late in the nineteenth century, with the growing realization of the link between water and health, first through the work of epidemiologists such as Dr John Snow and later through the work of microbiologists, especially Louis Pasteur and Robert Koch. The fact that modern city dwellers now use several hundred litres of water each day is a testament to the effectiveness of these strategies of avoiding the epidemics that threatened early city dwellers through the contagious effects of high-density living.

I have read with interest that ants have far more advanced antibiotic systems than humans do, but still marvel at the ability of human ingenuity in externalizing the fight against disease through the creation of the bathroom and the laundry, and the normalization of their attendant rituals (Douglas 1966; Vigarello 1988; Goubert 1989; Shove 2003). Such rituals, of course, soon develop into forms of sensory pleasure, with the daily shower providing the sort of hydrotherapy once only accessible through travel to spa towns or natural springs. The use of water for pleasure also reveals a largely untold story, namely its role in thermoregulation. Even after the emergence of centralized heating and air-conditioning systems, water remains an immediate and highly effective way to heat or cool the body through conduction. Its use in gardens, while often dismissed as purely ornamental, can still provide physiological benefits of cooling and cleaning the air through evapo-transpiration.

The current trend towards localized collection and use of water was originally avoided in favour of the quality control and economies of scale offered by centralized systems. Such systems were originally designed to replace 'in-series' use from rivers with parallel, single-use fixtures connected to both supply and drainage pipes. With centralized systems now reaching the limits of their capacity and maintenance regimes, 'sustainable' design has initiated local collection and use of rainwater, and encourages the re-use of water through grey-water and black-water treatment plants. For these to work successfully, planning laws need to accommodate practices such as the watering of parks from the rooftops of nearby buildings. But they also require economic incentives, making them viable as a supplement to centralized supply.

Energy use

Perhaps the most significant means of coping with population density is the appropriation of energy, which has become fundamental to human physiology and culture. The use of energy began with the harnessing of fire, enabling high-calorie cooked diets and freeing time for social and cultural activities, and then accelerated with the harvesting of surplus through agriculture (Wrangham 2009). While the calorific economy of cities remains important, it is the appropriation of stored solar energy in the form of fossil fuels that has enabled them to flourish (Tainter 1988). Strategies for energy use have been so successful that humans in modern cities are able to consume energy in multiples of up to 100 times the amount needed for basic metabolism (Boyden 2004). Urban populations use energy for transport, industrial processes and, most significantly here, for the construction and operation of buildings. One benefit of the high level of energy use in cities is the avoidance of manual labour by humans or by large populations of pack animals (Latour 1991; 1992). Energy use has facilitated the shifting work patterns of the modern city from blue-collar to white-collar work, from machine labour to symbolic manipulation, from factory to office.

It can be argued that the characteristic building type of the twentieth century is the high-rise office tower (Martin 2005). It is often claimed that buildings account for up to 40 per cent of the energy used in cities. Of course, the building is merely a means for delivering that most valuable of commodities, habitable space. The elevator inverted the previous logic whereby space closest to the ground, or raised slightly above it on the *piano nobile*, was the most valuable. This contributed to the transformation of space into a tradable commodity, bringing with it speculative excesses that continue to this day (Willis 1995). While elevators are significant, the major source of energy use in such buildings is to create artificial environments in deep-plan spaces lifted high off the ground. Before the development of air conditioning, even the tallest buildings had their floor-plate dimensions constrained by the need for daylight and natural ventilation. Combined with the fluorescent tube, used to replicate daylight within these large towers, air conditioning helped to separate the interior from the environmental functions of the external façade (Abalos and Herreros 2003).

The innovations of Willis Carrier and others that made air conditioning possible were originally intended for manufacturing processes and food transport, but soon found application in the high-density spaces of the city: theatres, department stores and, eventually, the office. What makes air conditioning particularly relevant to office space is the narrow temperature range needed for keeping sedentary workers productive, i.e. warm enough to use their hands all day but not so hot as to mark documents with sweat. The artificial environment, combined with the reinforced concrete frame and the glass curtain wall, create the dominant typology of the modern city – the centre-core, steel and glass office tower.

For all its pervasiveness, it is surprising how little research has been done about the suitability of air-conditioned office space as an environment for human habitation. One reason for this may be the popular wisdom regarding the Hawthorne Effect, namely that management attentiveness was the most important environmental condition of the workplace (Gillespie 1991). This may well be true, but it does not exonerate building designers or owners from creating healthy and habitable buildings. Only with the emergence of ideas about 'New Workplace' design by Frank Duffy (1997) and John Worthington (2006) in the late twentieth century was the value of the workplace in encouraging a better workplace realized. By then, of course, there had been significant changes in the technology of work, with mobile phones and computers giving portability, and management practices were no longer hierarchic but relied instead on the initiative and motivation of the worker. These changes have coincided with the sustainability movement, with sometimes overlapping and intersecting effects. For example, reducing space requirements by more effective and efficient design of the workplace will reduce energy use without any changes to building performance. Another benefit is the move away from centre-core towers to linear floor-plates with open work areas, allowing innovations such as chilled beam ceilings and displacement ventilation, which improve indoor air quality and occupant comfort.

Mixed mode

One largely unexplored consequence of new workplace practices is the prospect of new models of thermal comfort that are not based on static work conditions and the new models of thermal control that they might inspire. The steady-state models developed by Ole Fanger in the 1970s rely on sedentary work populations requiring minimal distraction from the environmental systems of the building. But what happens when employees can move around the workplace throughout the course of a working day? Might they seek relief from the constant temperatures of air-conditioned space to enjoy a cool breeze or a warm patch of sunlight? And, if so, might that lead to more sustainable building typologies that rely less on air conditioning and more on passive means of environmental control?

In the study of a breakout space in the National Bank building at Melbourne's Docklands, designed by James Grose and colleagues at Bligh Voller Nield (Drake 2005), we are attempting to develop such a model (see Figures 3.1 and 3.2). The building was completed before the Green Building Council of Australia had fully developed its Greenstar model and was not designed explicitly as a sustainable building. However, a key innovation of this project is the inclusion of a series of mixed-mode spaces along the northern façade, facing the waters of Victoria Harbour. Natural ventilation is achieved using an air-intake at floor level along the external façade, complemented by an exhaust stack rising through the atrium on the opposite side. The spaces, which contain kitchen facilities for staff, also have operable windows and (in some cases) doors to external balconies. The natural ventilation operates when outside conditions are favourable, and is automatically switched over to air conditioning if temperatures outside become too high or too low, or if set levels of rain or wind are exceeded.

In a project funded by the Australia Research Council, we expected to find that the use of these spaces would correlate with external conditions, i.e. being used most frequently when natural ventilation was operating. Instead what we have found is that the spaces are used throughout the day regardless of external conditions, that the patterns of use have more to do with the need for a break *from* internal conditions than a need to connect to the outside. Questionnaire responses indicate that visitors are primarily there to get away from their desk or to prepare and consume food and drink. Interestingly, environmental reasons are the third-most frequent response. Visitors are also

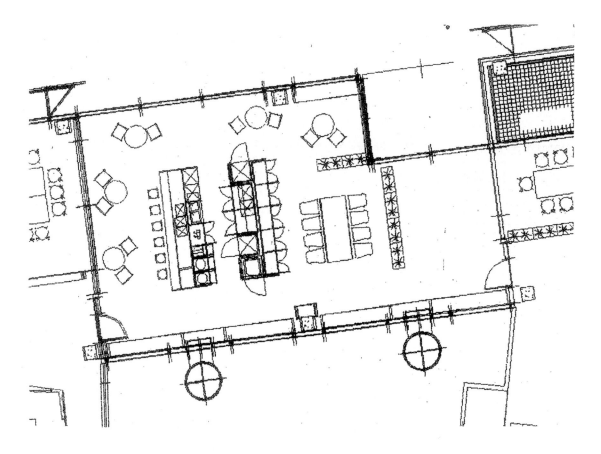

3.1

Part plan showing mixed mode
space in National Australia
Bank, Docklands, Melbourne

Source: BVN Architecture

there to enjoy the sunlight, view, fresh air or variation in temperature relative to the rest of the building. The frequency of visits is surprising too, with some staff using the space up to six times a day.

Natural ventilation is not the primary reason for workers to visit the space, nor should it be. In fact, the key innovation lies in recognizing that the kitchen is a social space, not a service space; that it belongs near the windows with the best view and not tucked away in the service core next to fire stairs and toilets. Having placed the kitchen in the best part of the floor-plate inspired us to enhance the connection with external conditions using operable windows and natural ventilation. This gives people a chance to breathe fresh air at the same time as they are ingesting water or food. From this study I contend that breathing fresh air is as fundamental a physiological need as drinking or eating, that people can cope without it if it is not available but will do it regularly when it is. In a fully air-conditioned building, the only way to do this is to go outside, with breaks for eating, shopping or smoking providing an excuse to escape the monotony of the indoor environment.

I am not against air conditioning per se, merely contending that it needs to be used judiciously and thoughtfully if cities are to be made more sustainable. The ability to control temperature and air flow to any space has had an enormous impact on the shape of cities. It has led to the sort of density that is praised by proponents of sustainability by building to

Scott Drake

3.2
Mixed mode space showing
operable windows

Photo: John Gollings 2004, National
Australia Bank building, water-view
consultation rooms, Docklands,
Melbourne [National Library of
Australia, Bib ID 3822130]

boundary lines, making use of awkward or difficult sites and reducing
transport costs. It has provided protection for workers from the adverse
conditions of the modern city, keeping the noise, dust and odours confined
to the streets where they are created.

But, what if city streets were quieter, cleaner, greener? What if
pedestrians and trees, electric vehicles and public transport rather than diesel
trucks and private cars dominated them? The quality of air in cities is both an
urban and an architectural problem, and needs to be dealt with accordingly.
Urban projects to reduce traffic and increase vegetation must be measured in
terms of their contribution to the environmental quality of individual
buildings and, conversely, the air-handling systems for individual buildings
ought to be designed with consideration for their interaction with urban space.
Like the ingenious legislation requiring industries to take in water downstream
from their own outlets, we need to find ways to integrate private and public
interest in protecting and using urban air.

For the sake of convenience I will call the sort of space described above a
'refresh' space, combining the benefits of 'refreshment' in terms of food or
drink with the ability to 'refresh' the body and mind with sunlight, views or
outside air. The lesson here is that natural ventilation ought not to be
considered independently of building function, and that its inclusion is best
achieved with an element of stealth, attaching it to other, necessary spaces
within a building. However, including such a space is no easy task.

For natural ventilation to work properly, it requires openings on at least two, preferably opposite, sides of a space. In the case of the National Bank building, the space is located between the external façade (including air intakes) and the internal atrium, where the air is exhausted through the rather dramatic stainless steel stacks. This strategy can readily be adopted in new buildings or included in the refurbishment of older offices with narrow floor-plates. However, such spaces are much harder to incorporate into centre-core, deep floor-plate office towers, which remain the dominant typology in most cities. And, like most typologies, they have a momentum that is difficult to redirect. That momentum is partly due to existing practices (how things are done) and partly due to available sites for innovation, literally places where new typologies can be tested. The sort of plot consolidation undertaken to create such towers means that the shape of most inner-city sites, and the buildings that surround them, encourages the typology to be perpetuated. This momentum is further compounded by the aversion to risk of the real estate and banking industries, and will no doubt be made worse by the recent difficulties encountered (and encouraged) by property trusts.

So, what seems like a simple suggestion – adding a 'refresh' space to the workplace – is difficult to achieve in practice. The reason for discussing the problem here is that changing the way we deal with air in buildings offers lessons for changing the way we deal with energy and water, namely that the innovations needed are not simply technological but are fundamentally typological. Strategies such as localized collection and use of energy, or the capture and recycling of water, or the introduction of green walls or roofs, require entirely new solutions to buildings and the way they interact with their surrounds in both environmental and urban terms. For the architects I talk to in practice, who are eager to make buildings more sustainable, the challenge is not technological – they know how to do it – but involves convincing commercial and institutional clients to undertake the risk that goes along with innovation. Only by taking such risks will we be able to discover the new typologies needed to deal with population density without relying on the artificial environments of modernism, and lead to cities that enjoy a greater interaction between the built and the natural environment.

References

Abalos, I. and Herreros, J. (2003) *Tower and Office: From Modernist Theory to Contemporary Practice*, Cambridge, Mass.: MIT Press.

Boyden, S. (2004) *The Biology of Civilisation: Understanding Human Culture as a Force in Nature*, Sydney: University of New South Wales Press.

Brand, S. (1994) *How Buildings Learn: What Happens after They're Built*, New York: Viking Penguin.

Douglas, M. (1966) *Purity and Danger: An Analysis of Concepts of Pollution and Taboo*, London: Routledge & Kegan Paul.

Drake, S. (2005) 'National @ Docklands', *Architecture Australia* 94/1, January/February, 62–69.

Duffy, F. (1997) *The New Office*, London: Conrad Octopus.

Gillespie, R. (1991) *Manufacturing Knowledge: A History of the Hawthorne Experiments*, Cambridge and New York: Cambridge University Press.

Goubert, J.-P. (1989) *The Conquest of Water: The Advent of Health in the Industrial Age*, trans. A. Wilson, Princeton, N.J.: Princeton University Press.

Latour, B. (1991) 'Technology is society made durable', in J. Law (ed.), *A Sociology of Monsters: Essays on Power, Technology, and Domination*, London: Routledge & Kegan Paul.

Latour, B. (1992) 'Where are the missing masses? The sociology of a few mundane artifacts', in W. Bijker and J. Law (eds), *Shaping Technology/Building Society: Studies in Sociotechnical Change*, Cambridge, Mass.: MIT Press.

Leatherbarrow, D. and Mostafavi, M. (1993) *On Weathering: The Life of Buildings in Time*, Cambridge, Mass.: MIT Press.

Martin, R. (2005) *The Organizational Complex: Architecture, Media, and Corporate Space*, Cambridge, Mass.: MIT Press.

Shove, E. (2003) *Comfort, Cleanliness and Convenience: The Social Organization of Normality*, Oxford: Berg.

Tainter, J.A. (1988) *The Collapse of Complex Societies*, Cambridge: Cambridge University Press.

Vigarello, G. (1988) *Concepts of Cleanliness: Changing Attitudes in France since the Middle Ages*. Cambridge: Cambridge University Press.

Willis, C. (1995) *Form Follows Finance: Skyscrapers and Skylines in New York and Chicago*, New York: Princeton Architectural Press.

Worthington, J. (ed.) (2006) *Reinventing the Workplace*, Oxford and Burlington, Mass.: Architectural Press.

Wrangham, R. (2009) *Catching Fire: How Cooking Made Us Human*, New York: Basic Books.

Assassination in the Sustainable City

The Netherlands and Beyond

Wim Hafkamp

The 'sustainable city', as we have come to know it from the 1990s scientific, policy and activist literature, gets energy from renewable sources and has no air or water pollution. Material flows are managed through global supply chains and 'cradle to cradle' industrial ecology. People move on foot, by bicycle, or share cars. They eat organic food, preferably from regional producers and community-supported agriculture. Every day in professional domains from urban planning, housing and transportation to public policy and education, we work to make this ideal a reality.

Therefore, practice and policy, as well as theory, on sustainable cities are generally concerned with the environmental dimension of sustainability. Long-term visions, medium-term plans and short-term action programmes are dominated by initiatives towards making a city climate proof, achieving sustainable water use, creating green public spaces, putting the ability to walk and cycle first, applying the 'cradle to cradle' principle to industrial parks and strengthening public transport to 'reduce car dependency'. This list is not exhaustive. Typically, this is also what dominates the programmes of conferences such as EcoEdge, Green Cities. The importance of the economic and the social dimensions is often acknowledged, without visible implications, however. In cities with a booming economy and a stable social climate, this need not be a problem. But, in cities that are experiencing economic decline, with high unemployment rates, high numbers of people living in poverty, where the population feels unsafe in large parts of the city, or where high immigration rates cause integration problems and religious strife, it may be the main reason why the drive towards sustainability fails.

Recently, the context for working towards a sustainable city has changed in the Netherlands. Urban issues on the political agenda have been redefined to give priority to ethnic and religious tension and dysfunctional neighbourhoods. These issues focus on safety in streets, crime, multi-problem households, language deficits among migrants, school drop-outs, civic participation, poverty and unemployment.

The key challenge is to design new approaches to sustainable urban development covering these social and economic concerns along with environmental ones. The design challenge is no longer about urban form, the built environment per se, or the quality of public space, but about shaping interactions between all those involved: residents, teachers, employers, housing corporations, youth workers and police, through to politicians and ministers.

The turning point: urgence emerging

The assassination of Pim Fortuyn in May 2002, at the peak of the election campaign for the Dutch parliament, shocked nearly sixteen million people nationwide, and many well beyond. This was the first politically motivated murder in the Netherlands since the hanging of the De Witt brothers in a political conflict in 1672. Fortuyn had started his own political movement less than a year before and participated in the election campaign as 'List Pim Fortuyn' with a political programme dominated by stopping immigration, integration by assimilation, restoring safety and opposing Islam. This resonated with large parts of the electorate, while Fortuyn himself was very charismatic. His assassin was an animal-rights activist. When asked why he had done it, he simply said, '[Fortuyn] constituted a danger to the country.' A few weeks later in the elections, List Pim Fortuyn scored more than one-sixth of the votes, giving them twenty-six seats in a parliament of 150. Just weeks after Fortuyn's funeral, his party joined the new coalition government.

Just two years later, in November 2004, the filmmaker Theo van Gogh was murdered even more brutally than Fortuyn. Van Gogh was a successful director and a high-profile, provocative newspaper columnist, and often appeared on television talk shows. In his columns and public appearances he would antagonize, vilify and confront his opponents. He rejected all types of fundamentalism, especially religious fundamentalism, whether Muslim or Christian. However, that was not what made Samir A. decide to kill him. He did that because of the movie van Gogh had produced based on a script by Ayaan Hirshi Ali, a Somali immigrant and member of parliament for the conservatives. The movie denounced violence against women as expressed in the Koran by showing graphic images of texts projected on a naked/veiled female body.

Both murders shocked a nation because they tore at a central value in the national identity: tolerance. The Dutch, whether in the era of 'the seven provinces', the republic or the modern parliamentary democracy cum monarchy, had always seen tolerance as essential. Tolerance had always been their way of coping with the differences between Catholic and Protestant, progressive and conservative, immigrant and native. Respect for, and some understanding of, their 'otherness' had always been the foundation for institutional ways of dealing with these differences, in the school system, health care and political representation. That tolerance had eroded to indifference, and underlying conflicts had been stoked to boiling point.

The Dutch are proud of their polders, the land reclamations that had taken place throughout many centuries. And they had been proud of their verb 'to polder', which referred to their way of dealing with conflicts and difficulties: all parties around the table, discussing issues, seeking solutions beneficial or at least acceptable to all. Quite a few successes on the environmental dimension of sustainability are actually the results of poldering: the Oosterscheldedam, the first water-permeable dam in coastal defence works of a river estuary in the 1970s, successful environmental policies in the 1980s and 1990s based on negotiated agreements between government and industry, and initiatives between government, housing corporations and the construction sector on sustainable housing, to name just a few. By 2002, however, poldering had come to refer to endless talks without results. In the next section I will discuss how that came to be.

Dissatisfaction and conflict: urgence explored

It is not easy to understand the dissatisfaction and the roots of the conflicts that characterized Dutch society in the late 1990s. For one thing, the economy was booming, and had been booming since the Gulf War. Growth figures were higher for the Netherlands than for most other European countries. By the end of the 1990s many, not just in the Netherlands, were quite sure that economic recession had been mastered. Unemployment levels were at an all-time low, around 3 per cent. Everybody had to be happy, but was not. The issues of immigration and integration did not just surface at the end of the 1990s, they had been current since the late 1970s and throughout the 1980s. Initially, immigrant workers and their families were newcomers (mostly from Turkey and Morocco), along with immigrants from (former) Dutch colonies (Surinam and the Netherlands Antilles). In the 1980s and early 1990s the number of immigrants grew, largely because of the influx of refugees from various parts of the world (from, among others, Somalia, Sierra Leone, Afghanistan and the former Yugoslavia).

In the media, politicians, journalists and opinion leaders called regularly for stopping immigration, integration by assimilation and no preferential treatment. Some argued that the sheer level of immigration had become critical. The rapid increase and the concentration of immigrants in low-income neighbourhoods with poor housing stock was, at core, an 'us' versus 'them' conflict. Others claimed that only populist politicians like Fortuyn had the ability to force the issue. Add to that the gap between 'politicians in The Hague' and the liberal media professionals, none of whom live in the destitute neighbourhoods, and we can understand the revolt among the voters.

Whatever the explanation, one thing is clear: the sustainability agenda I described in the first section of this chapter no longer has a fruitful reception in large parts of our cities. Many people can't read and, if they can, they can't read Dutch or they don't read the local house-to-house weekly paper. And, if they do, they don't feel invited to these evening neighbourhood meetings where everyone may 'polder along' on the renovation plan for the neighbourhood, the new *structuurplan groen*, or the 're-profiling of the street'. I have attended many of these evenings and afternoons, as a participant, a moderator or an environmental economist. The constant element is that the participants are predominantly Dutch natives over the age of forty. A significant part of the population is absent in the dialogue on the sustainable city.

Sustainability off the agenda

Environmental issues had been one of three key popular concerns for over three decades. By late 2001 that was no longer the case. In his election campaign Fortuyn spoke clearly about climate change as 'a confabulation'. The 2002 parliamentary elections led to the formation of a coalition government that actively decided not to have an agenda on the environment or sustainability. In fact, this was the first coalition government since the 1960s that did not have an environment minister; a junior minister now held this portfolio. Environmental spokespersons in parliament, from whichever political party, had always been held in high regard, inside and outside parliament. Now, for the first time, they were hissed at by their parliamentary colleagues: 'Environment is out!' Four issues now dominate the new agenda: safety, immigration, integration and Islam. I will discuss each of these four below, though without doing so in full.

Safety came to rank highest on the agenda, even though the data on crime (petty crime, violence, drug-related crime and organized crime) had not given rise to this, there were related phenomena that had. People's perception of safety became more and more important. At the same time, police performance was increasingly criticized, up to the point where the police were accused of allowing the existence of 'no go' areas, where groups or even gangs of youngsters were in charge. Similarly the justice department and the public prosecutor came under attack. As a result, the measurement of police performance and police performance goals became central to government policy. Also, with Rotterdam in the lead, a system of indicators was developed to track safety, both perceived and recorded, at the neighbourhood level, and report quarterly and yearly on improvements.

Immigration came on the agenda largely because of dissatisfaction with immigration figures in the 1990s. Due to the political process in the late 1990s, with the conservatives in a social-democratic government coalition, immigration had already been curbed sharply. Regulations on immigration became even sharper under the new government, for example, requiring potential migrants to learn Dutch before coming to the Netherlands, and to prove they had a job that would give them a certain minimum income.

Regulations on *integration* became more stringent as well, with an integration law that forced all non-Dutch residents to prove they were able to speak sufficient Dutch. All had to take an integration course, learn about Dutch culture and history and take a written test. Rita Verdonk, who was a member of the Dutch neo-liberal Volkspartij voor Vrijheid en Democratie (VVD, or People's Party for Freedom and Democracy) and the Minister for Integration and Immigration who had instituted the new legislation, did not return in the new government formed in 2007. She started her own political movement, Proud of the Netherlands (TON, Trots Op Nederland). Rotterdam required, and was given, a legal basis for its policy to refuse low-income tenants, mostly immigrants, to move into dwellings in certain neighbourhoods that already have a high percentage of residents from an immigrant background (the 'Rotterdam law').

It was the murder of Theo van Gogh, and the movie he made with Ayaan Hirshi Ali, that put *Islam* very firmly on the agenda. The construction of new mosques became ever more contentious, not least because the funding of these mosques appeared to come from Islamic fundamentalist political organizations abroad, rather than from local Muslims. A political vacuum came to exist after the demise of Fortuyn's political party in the elections of 2006, and after the departure of Ayaan Hirshi Ali from the Dutch parliament. She was expelled from the country after the responsible minister, Verdonk, acted on the finding that Hirshi Ali had not spoken the truth when she applied for refugee status in the Netherlands on first entering the country. Another member of parliament, Geert Wilders, quickly filled the vacuum. Like Hirshi Ali and Verdonk, Wilders, also a member of the VVD, started his own political movement.

Early in 2010, weekly polls indicated that support for populist right-wing movements amounted to one-third of the electorate. This was higher than at the peak of the 2002 elections. None of these movements is a political party in the conventional sense: they have no members and no internal democracy.

The traditional advocates of sustainability need to respond. It is urgent that they seek a new point of departure, and re-articulate the concept of sustainable development, in particular in cities. They must consider all of their target audiences, create a new rapport with them and engage in a dialogue on sustainability and courses of action. This means acknowledging, first of all, that sustainable development is about development, about bringing out the potential in people. Sustainable development in its full meaning has social and economic dimensions as well as an environmental dimension. This takes the sustainability agenda well beyond the one we see in most sustainability plans or vision documents. Cities are almost by definition about migration, from rural to urban, between countries and within or across networks (Castell's cities of flows) in a globalizing world.

Solutions and ways forward

The key challenge is to design new approaches to sustainable urban development covering these social and economic concerns along with environmental ones. The design challenge is no longer about urban form, the built environment per se, or the quality of public space, but about shaping interactions between all those involved: residents, teachers, employers, housing corporations, youth workers and police, through to politicians and ministers.

In this section I discuss four urban (re)development projects in which sustainability is taken beyond the environmental dimension. There is no space to introduce each of these projects in full, but I will discuss the ways in which these projects make a difference.

Ajax soccer grounds, Amsterdam
Strong resident participation from day one in a new 'vital coalition' (consisting of a housing corporation, a project developer, a real estate agent, a construction

4.1
View from soccer stadium showing, right, an apartment building that houses a cogeneration plant providing electricity and heat to the neighbourhood

Photo: Wim Hafkamp

company and the city of Amsterdam) resulted in a project with strong social values (mixed population across socio-economic strata, social cohesion, mixed use) and strong environmental aspects: the blue-green ribbon of rainwater capture and vegetation, which is also a green buffer; pedestrian and cyclist friendliness; off-street parking; plus a cogeneration unit integrated in one of the housing blocks, producing heat (for district heating) as well as electricity, yielding an extremely high energy efficiency. All dwellings are well insulated, not just for energy efficiency, but also for comfort and quality. To the full satisfaction of all residents the project has a very high density of over 600 dwellings on 6 ha of land. A strong sense of identity has been created by relating the architecture, ornaments and names of streets and bridges to the soccer history of the grounds.

Traffic artery tunnel project, Maastricht

The congested international freeway cutting through a residential neighbourhood in the city of Maastricht had become an anachronism. What was designed in the 1950s as a boulevard for urban and regional automobile traffic had turned into a freeway with horrific noise screens. The freeway acted as a physical barrier, creating disconnected, insular neighbourhoods where the

4.2
Major international highway A2
cutting through Maastricht
residential neighbourhoods

Photo: Wim Hafkamp

residents suffered from excessive noise levels day and night, as well as high levels of air pollution (especially particulate matter and nitrogen oxide).

This joint initiative by the City of Maastricht and the Dutch national public works service aims to arrive at a solution that meets the three dimensions of sustainable development. On the economic dimension, by creating a transport capacity that is in proportion with the transport system of the region and the nation and that anticipates road pricing. Again on the economic dimension, by providing an investment impulse in the neighbourhood economy and employment that strengthens the urban economy of the entire urban field. On the social dimension, by restoring and enhancing the social fabric of the neighbourhood. And finally, on the social and environmental dimensions, by setting right a matter of environmental injustice.

The initiative constitutes an innovative public tender in which consortia prepare a bid in three rounds. Unlike in most public tenders, it is not the lowest bidder who wins here, but the best bidder. The tenderer makes available a sum of money estimated to cover almost, but not fully, the cost of constructing a tunnel nearly 3 km long. The consortia prepare a bid to design, build and operate the tunnel, as well as to redevelop the land on top of and around the tunnel. In this case, we speak of nearly 300 ha on which around 1100 dwellings and 200 000 m^2 of office and retail space will be built. A large part of this area is a protected area under stress (from pollution and fragmentation) and the project will have to relieve that stress and secure the protected area. The area is also part of a highly valued historical landscape, which is to be protected through the project. In their bid the consortia demonstrate how they will meet minimum requirements in seven groups of criteria, including environment (air, noise, ground water, water quality, etc.), walkability and cyclability, traffic safety and fluidity, quality of public space and urban design/architecture. For each of the seven groups of criteria the tenderers also developed 'ambition levels'. They know that it will not be possible for consortia to attain the ambition levels on all seven groups of criteria, but challenge them to do their best.

The public tender is done in three rounds. In the first round, consortia develop their rough plans, with sketches and initial analyses. At the end of the first round, the number of consortia is reduced from five to three. In the second round the three remaining consortia elaborate their plans in detail, after which there is a round of extensive public consultation. In the final round, the tenderers adapt their plans to the results of public consultation in the previous round, and submit a 'hard' tender. After this final round, an external jury prepares an assessment and identifies the consortium that most closely meets the ambition levels. It should be added here that public consultation takes place not only at the end of the second round in this process, but also in the design of the process itself. That was done with extensive public consultation, with respect to both the bidding process and the minimum requirements and ambition levels. Furthermore, all tenderers were encouraged to consult the public and bring in new partners. The process is just as much about bringing out creativity and ingenuity in design and planning as it is in linking urban agendas and generating support.

Restoration of the Dapperbuurt, Amsterdam

The Dapperbuurt ('Brave Neighbourhood') in Amsterdam was mostly built in the very early years of the twentieth century by housing corporations that had only recently been established to provide respectable, healthy and affordable housing to low-income workers and their families. These early housing blocks exude a social-democratic pride, with their acknowledged architectural qualities. The dwellings were more than adequate 100 years ago, but not any more. They are small by today's standards, of an awkward design, with too many small rooms. Initially they had no toilets or showers (these were installed in post-war remodelling projects). The living comfort in these dwellings is limited because they are so poorly insulated, and many are eroded by intensive use: the dwellings are often inhabited by families that have grown larger over time, through birth or immigration. And on top of that is a lack of maintenance.

In present-day neighbourhood restoration, the worst part of the housing stock is demolished while the better part, with the highest historical and architectural value, is renovated. As a result there will be a mixed stock of old and new housing, but all dwellings will be suitable for the present tenants for decades to come: well proportioned, well insulated and connected to district heating. In the same process, the public space in the neighbourhood is redesigned, providing room for children to play and for adults to sit, read and play '*jeu de boules*'. Old public buildings, with their own recognized historical and architectural qualities, are renovated. Public schools, churches and municipal offices now become cultural centres, youth hostels, neighbourhood

cinemas and restaurants, bringing new economic and social life to the neighbourhood. The preparation of a process like this takes many years, involving the municipality, housing corporations, schools, residents and local shopkeepers and merchants.

Multiculturalism in the Dapperbuurt, Amsterdam

The Dapperbuurt went through a similar restoration process as the Indische buurt ('Indies Neighbourhood') in the 1980s and 1990s. This project shows that physical interventions at the neighbourhood level are not a 'cure all' for the problems of a society. The participation rate in the labour market is low: in about 60 per cent of households there is no income from work, which means that social exclusion remains high. Drug trade and drug use are no longer visible in the streets, but they have not diminished. With its multicultural appearance, the social balance is very fragile. The mixed population that characterized the neighbourhood by the end of the twentieth century tends to remain poor: those who can afford it move out, and those who are too poor to find a good place to live move in. There is a sign of hope: students and young professionals looking for an affordable place to live accept that the neighbourhood does not have eminent standing. However, gentrification will have its own implications.

Conclusion

Close to half the population of major Dutch cities has a non-European background, largely first- or second-generation immigrants, living in mostly poor neighbourhoods in which the economic and social problems of cities

4.4
Neighbourhood renovation is no 'cure all' for a multicultural society

Photo: Wim Hafkamp

accumulate. It is vital that our thinking about sustainable cities, and the actions proposed, include this social and economic dimension. A limited, environmentalist approach to sustainable development is not sufficient, as it is not very useful to ask residents to use energy-efficient light bulbs and dual-flush toilets if they are pestering their neighbours out of their home, or if they are the victims of pestering.

With the above cases in mind, successful urban sustainability programmes must be:

- drafted and adopted from the bottom up with residents and other actors in neighbourhoods;
- addressing all concerns brought into the process, in new coalitions formed by them;
- linking agendas, from energy, climate and air pollution to those of safety, education, work and income;
- articulating, when relevant, a 'design challenge' and addressing it; and
- building on the local, historical identity of place and people.

Reprogramming Cities for Increased Populations and Climate Change

Rob Adams

Today, we are part of a new revolution, the 'urban revolution' cities, which housed 200 million people, or 10 per cent of the world's population in 1900, now accommodate 3.5 billion people, or 50 per cent of the world's population. By 2050 cities are predicted to accommodate 6.4 billion people or over 70 per cent of the world's population (Brugmann 2009). Even in a country such as Australia, where more than 80 per cent of the population already live in urban areas, the major cities are projected to double their size in the next forty years. The enormity of the challenge of building in only forty years the equivalent of a capital city and its infrastructure that took 175 years to create is daunting, especially given the constraints imposed by the global financial crisis. Thus, in 2009, Melbourne, a city of four million, saw a 40 per cent increase in the demand for housing at the same time as house starts had declined by 3 per cent.

In addition to these internal dilemmas, cities also have external impacts. For example, cities are directly or indirectly responsible for over 75 per cent of the world's greenhouse gas emissions and, as in the Industrial Revolution in Britain, our cities are slowly choking us to death. However, while the smog, pollution, poor health, loss of landscapes and social difficulties were easily attributed to the form and infrastructure of the industrial city, greenhouse impacts are insidious and less visible. The challenge for our generation is not only to build the equivalent capacity of existing cities, which has taken centuries to develop, but also to do this in only forty years and in a socially inclusive way, while at the same time transforming our existing cities to a low-carbon future.

This chapter examines how the Australian city of Melbourne is seeking to achieve such a transformation. Referring to wider studies, it outlines an alternative approach to urban growth and consolidation to the ones that have been dominant. Examples in Melbourne include an 'early bird' free public transport service, a central city residential movement and plans for an intensification of population and housing densities adjacent to existing rail- and road-based public transport infrastructure.

A new approach

Albert Einstein (cited in Harris 1995) said, 'We can't solve problems by using the same kind of thinking we used when we created them.' This is a good time to heed his advice. The traditional Australian responses of subdividing land and developing on the fringe of our cities will simply exacerbate the existing problems we face. The practice of locating new communities on the fringes is known to increase the financial and social hardship being faced by families far removed from their employment and essential services. The 'vampire studies' carried out by Dodson and Sipe (2006; 2008) on Australia's capital cities indicate that travel and mortgage repayments are creating a poverty trap that is rapidly spreading from the fringe towards the centre of our cities.

In combination, the environmental and infrastructure costs of continuing to build our cities in their current form are becoming exorbitant. Trubka *et al.* (2008) have calculated that building 1000 houses on the fringe of Australia's six capital cities will cost AU$300 million more than building them within existing infrastructure boundaries over a fifty-year period. Thus, in Melbourne, the plan to build 600 000 new houses to accommodate an additional million residents by 2025, with half on the fringe, would cost over AU$100 billion more than if they were all built within the existing city. The challenge we face is not one of building much more of the same but rather one of reprogramming our cities around our existing infrastructure to achieve greater efficiencies than we already have.

We should reflect on the 1960s, as the baby boomers reached university age and imposed an impossible stress on university infrastructure. Their large numbers had not been expected; universities went into overdrive to try to accommodate them. As with our cities today, a common response was to start a rapid building programme that saw many new universities, but options for established universities to expand were limited by the constraints of their locations. One of these was the university I was attending in Cape Town.

The University of Cape Town was located on a confined site on the side of Table Mountain, surrounded by national parks and an established urban fabric. The opportunities for growth were very limited. Apart from a few undeveloped sites and surface car parks within the master plan, developed by Herbert Baker, the campus was already full. The university was forced to look at alternatives to expanding its way out of the problem. A detailed study of the utilization of the existing facilities revealed that many were used for less than 25 per cent of the time. For Cape Town the challenge became one of revising timetables to better use its existing infrastructure.

Returning to Cape Town in 2004, and aware that student numbers had trebled since I left in 1972, I was pleasantly surprised to find that the campus was still familiar. There had been some building on what used to be vacant sites and surface-level car parks, but this only added an intensity and vitality to a campus that had previously been sedate and often boring. The form and spectacular setting of the early plan had been reinforced and complemented, not compromised. In 2050, 70 per cent of urban infrastructure in Australia is still likely to have been established before 2010. Thus, we need to come to a similar realization as my university in Cape Town did in the 1960s.

If we adopt a strategy of consolidation and transformation around existing infrastructure, would the resulting city retain its familiarity, with continuity and change melding together into a vibrant new city that accommodates our burgeoning population? Such transformation would mainly involve rationalization and better utilization of our existing buildings, roads, railways, parks, waterways, energy, communications and fluid distribution systems. All will need to be looked at in a new and open-minded way. Certainly, if we continue to understand, develop and use our infrastructure in traditional twentieth-century ways we are doomed to perpetuate our current problems.

The potential for transformation

Every day we are witnessing the failure, shortcomings and vulnerability of our traditional systems. It is no longer simply an argument about economy of production but increasingly an argument about capacity – the capacity of our cities to withstand the pressures of future population expansion, climate change and outdated modes of operation. Refreshingly, we are also starting to see concrete examples of transformational strategies that clearly illustrate the path out of our current dilemma. One example is a programme currently run by the Victorian Department of Transport. To address the rapid increase in public transport use (60 per cent over five years) and extreme congestion on peak-hour services, the department introduced an 'early bird' service for passengers to travel free of charge before 7 a.m. Launched in March 2008, the 'early bird' service now carries 2600 passengers daily in off-peak travel times on trains that were previously almost empty. The cost benefit of this earlier travel was equivalent to buying five extra trains. Taking into account reduced fares and operating costs, this has saved the government up to AU$85 million (Sexton 2009).

With this in mind, the City of Melbourne decided to test the capacity of the capital not only to absorb its growing population but also to do so in a way that would provide for a more sustainable future. The analysis was informed by previous experiences and work carried out for the European Union by Rob Adams in association with Gehl Architects (2007) and during the last twenty years in Melbourne. The EU study illustrated how twelve cities had turned their fortunes around since the 1980s, such as Glasgow, which, following the Second World War, implemented a strategy of relocating people from the centre of the city to the periphery.

By the 1970s, this strategy had resulted in increasing social isolation and a gradual breakdown of a sense of community. In the 1980s the strategy was reversed. Rather than dispersing the population, the city would in the future work to concentrate its population closer to the centre. Over this same period other European cities transformed themselves using a diverse set of strategies. For instance, Bordeaux concentrated on building a high-quality public realm, a tram network without overhead wires and quality public spaces and buildings, all contributing to improved public confidence and pride in the city. Bilbao used public transport and the Guggenheim Museum to reverse its fortunes, while Copenhagen created quality places for people and high-quality cycling infrastructure to carry over one-third of its population to work.

In Melbourne, twenty-five years of similar initiatives have seen a dying central city move incrementally to become one of the world's most liveable cities, according to the 2009 Economist Intelligence Unit Quality of Life Ranking, among others. Among many strategies and projects, arguably one of the most successful was the creation of a new central city residential population. Following a boom in commercial office buildings, the property market collapsed in the late 1980s, leaving many older buildings empty with little hope of finding tenants. Through a range of financial, regulatory, leadership and advocacy mechanisms, the city attracted over 10 000 new downtown residential dwellings in just eight years, many of them built within converted commercial office buildings. A focus on increasing density, promoting mixed use, increasing connectivity, preserving local character and maintaining a high-quality public realm renewed a declining city centre. This city transformation, mainly utilizing existing infrastructure, shows what is possible if we break out of the mindset that new-build is the only option to expand capacity.

Our recent study *Transforming Australian Cities* (Adams 2009) examined the capacity of the existing city to double its population. It sought to identify the potential for the economic, social and environmental transformation of cities that had been built mainly after the industrial revolution and following the models of the Garden City movement and modernism. The Garden City movement promised us the dream that we could live in the countryside and work in the city, while modernism turned us away from pragmatic locally based solutions and towards international solutions supported by technologies (such as air conditioning) that marginalized 'place influenced design'. Overlay this mindset with an overreaction to the ills of the industrial city and the emergence of the motor car and you have the root causes of the current form of our cities, namely low density, widely spread, activity-zoned cities where the motor car dominates our public realm and marginalizes public transport.

This is not to deny the obvious qualities of the Australian dream of living in a detached house in a well-treed suburb. Dreams are important but ultimately need to be realized sustainably, or they lead to economic, social and environmental disasters. Can we sustain the Australian dream and make it an exemplar for post-industrial cities worldwide? To save the dream we need to genuinely understand the current costs and vulnerabilities of our existing cities and then develop transformational strategies to retain the quality of the lifestyle we desire.

Strategic residential intensification

In exploring the nature of the transformation required, the challenge was to successfully target strategic residential intensification in areas well serviced by existing infrastructure, in particular transport infrastructure, in order to meet the physical demands of a growing population and have the potential to enhance the liveability and sustainability of our cities. Focusing on Melbourne's metropolitan area, we investigated the potential population capacity of three key development areas for encouraging residential intensification according to best practice urban design principles.

The three geographic areas selected for investigation were:

- activity centres, e.g. areas around railway stations;
- urban corridors, along road-based public transport infrastructure;
- productive suburbs in the vast areas of our city.

The understanding was that, over the next decade, these areas would become the most desirable locations for new urban development because of their proximity to existing public transport infrastructure. It was proposed that, by 2050, the key linear road-based public transport corridors would substantially develop into medium-rise high-density corridors connecting all the designated activity centres, providing easy access to high-quality public transport from the adjacent 'productive suburbs' (see Figure 5.1). Developing these corridors would take pressure off the existing suburbs, which could then develop as the new 'green lungs' of our metropolitan areas.

A key task was to look at the potential yield that could accrue from this approach to intensification of the urban corridors. A set of urban design principles was developed in order to inform the study, based on good design practice and experience drawn from local and international examples. These principles formed the parameters at the basis of a GIS model developed and refined to calculate the potential population capacity of transport corridors across metropolitan Melbourne. This approach combined leading urban design with geometrics, translating the qualitative aspects of good urban spaces into quantifiable assumptions that could be applied to physical spaces to test Melbourne's capacity to deliver fundamental transformation. Some assumptions were made in determining the potential for future development along these tram and bus corridors (see Figure 5.2).

Through a process of elimination, the total number of sites deemed available for densification was 12 439 along the tram network and 22 038 along the priority bus routes, providing potential areas of 1418 and 5275 ha respectively.

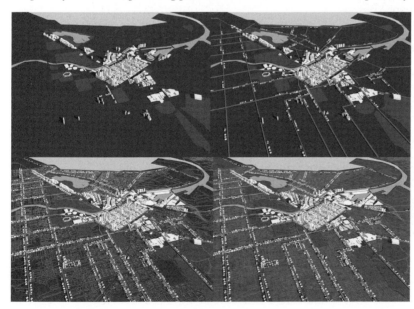

5.1
Green AXO map

Source: City of Melbourne

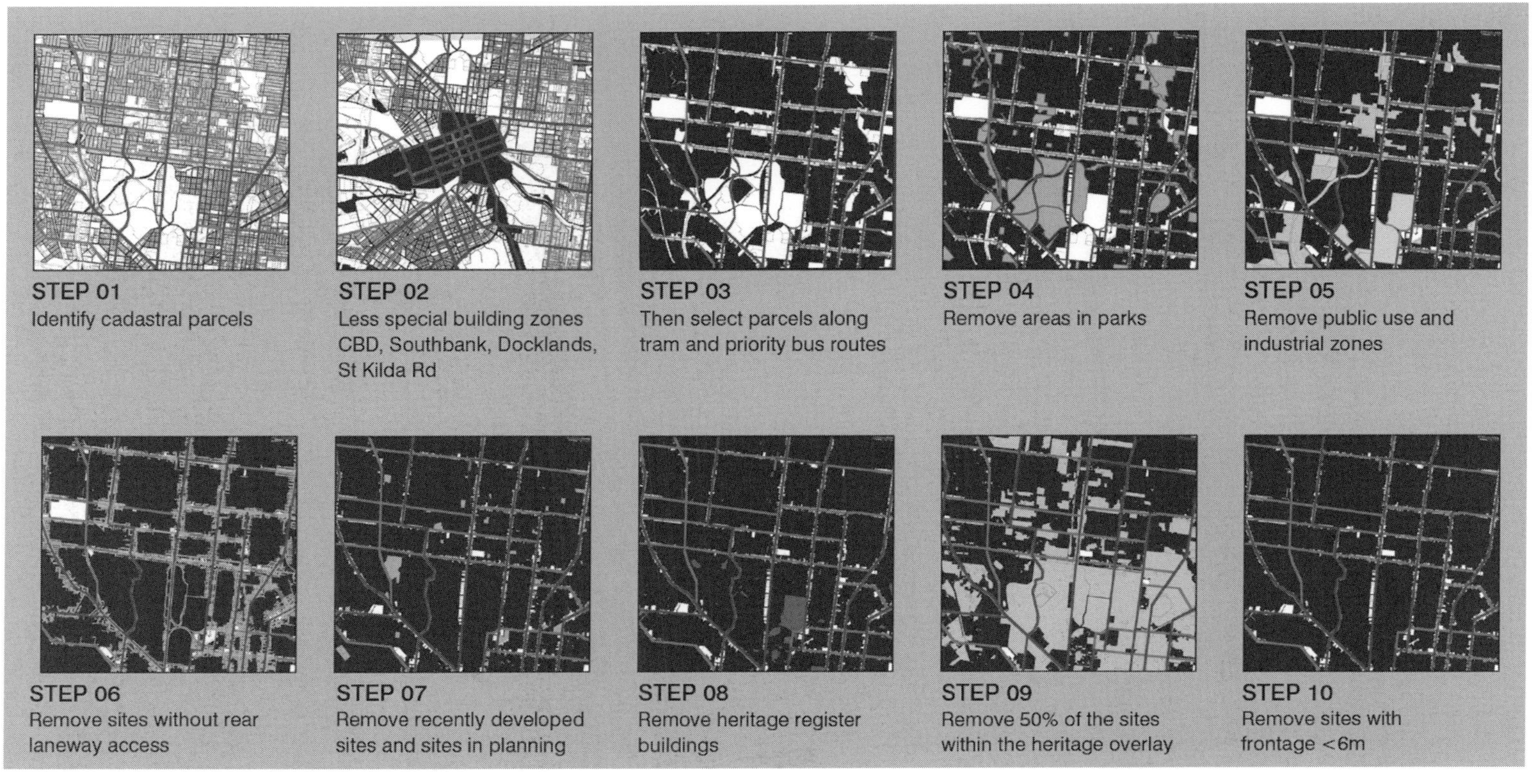

STEP 01
Identify cadastral parcels

STEP 02
Less special building zones
CBD, Southbank, Docklands,
St Kilda Rd

STEP 03
Then select parcels along
tram and priority bus routes

STEP 04
Remove areas in parks

STEP 05
Remove public use and
industrial zones

STEP 06
Remove sites without rear
laneway access

STEP 07
Remove recently developed
sites and sites in planning

STEP 08
Remove heritage register
buildings

STEP 09
Remove 50% of the sites
within the heritage overlay

STEP 10
Remove sites with
frontage <6m

5.2
Set of assumptions

Source: City of Melbourne

The proposed density range of 180 to 450 persons per hectare on identified land parcels equated to developments of three to eight storeys. The findings are compelling. Even when applied conservatively, Melbourne's urban corridors have the potential to accommodate a net population increase of 1 003 950 people in low-density developments of three to four storeys. If a higher-density scenario were applied, similar to the seven storeys found in Barcelona, a net population increase of 2 457 310 is possible. Combined with the potential of activity centres and greyfield sites in the metropolitan area, the city is capable of doubling its population to 8 million while using only 7.5 per cent of the metro area and without further subdivision of fringe land.

Visualizing residential intensification

Alongside the analysis undertaken to quantify the development potential of highly targeted residential intensification in Melbourne, a series of artist's impressions was created to visually explore the application of urban corridor development in specific sites. The resulting suite of images (Figure 5.3) illustrates the urban design principles and clearly highlights that residential intensification does not inevitably equate to high rise.

Transforming public perceptions

Garnering public acceptance is an important prerequisite to the realization of transformations of the scale and significance our cities require. 'Selling' the idea is helped by the reality that similar developments are already, in 2009, starting in many locations around Australia. Equally important is the

Maribyrnong Road, Maribyrnong study area, currently

Possible future

5.3
Maribyrnong Road: before and after

Source: City of Melbourne

realization that, if the land area identified for transformation is 7.5 per cent of the total metropolitan area, over 90 per cent of the city will remain free from the pressures of development. Given the understandable concerns that communities have as a result of the poor development practices of the last fifty years, it is important to reassure them that future development will be of a much higher standard and that low-density suburbs will not be invaded by high-density housing. The work done in Melbourne shows this to be a realistic expectation and, if well articulated and visualized, is likely to allay community fears.

What is needed to make it happen?

There are countless examples of 'good' strategies that were never implemented. Often the gap between policy and reality can be explained by overly complex implementation tools. Planning schemes have become documents produced to defend sceptical communities against development rather than tools to allow easy implementation of well-thought-out development strategies. Given past planning shortcomings, it is understandable that communities become suspicious of development intentions and seek maximum protection through complex (and often voluminous) planning schemes. However, these schemes are so cumbersome now that state governments are consistently overriding them so as to speed up the delivery of much-needed new housing. This developer-led approach is not only producing greater anxiety in communities but also 'cherry picking' and overdeveloping prime sites, often compromising the future development potential of adjacent sites. Often, the result is a vicious cycle of overdevelopment followed by overreaction and yet more pages in the planning schemes.

With the projected rapid expansion of Australia's population, the time has come for simplified sets of urban planning schemes that clearly identify up-front key development areas, areas adjacent to existing high-capacity infrastructure (such as transport routes) where higher-density development is desirable, and areas of stability, historic importance or high local character (such as the Australian suburb) where higher-density development is not appropriate. This simple differentiation up front would allow for more detailed sets of development principles and visions for each area.

Such planning schemes might rid us of the multicoloured-zoning-map approach that served only to simplify our urban experience, and adopt instead the more vital mixed-use approach to cities. By clearly identifying key development areas with 'as of right development' provided certain criteria are met (such as affordability, high environmental standards and quality interfaces with the adjacent streets), we are more likely to produce quality outcomes that incrementally transform our cities to accommodate population increases.

None of these ideas are radical or new. A quick glance at our cities shows that such responsible development is occurring along transport routes, but often only after a lengthy passage through the planning processes. In Melbourne, there is already a shift in preference to well-located higher-density housing, with sixty-four local government areas showing greater sales of apartments than detached houses. There is also clear evidence that improved access to public transport is leading to lower car ownership, thus allowing greater efficiency of use of our valuable road network and reductions in carbon emissions.

If we are to meet the combined pressures of climate change and rapidly increased urbanization, we need to deliver more compact cities that ensure greater utilization of existing infrastructure. As argued here, cities can accommodate low-rise high-density development within less than 10 per cent of the city footprint while preserving and enhancing qualities of those suburbs that are more productive in energy, water and plantings. Cities can retain a familiar feel and much that we admire along with building higher-density areas with greater access to transport and services. In the future cities need to embrace new distributed energy, water-generation and -collection policies to replace large-scale stand-alone facilities that have become increasingly vulnerable to extreme weather events. This way we can also re-establish, within a more sustainable city form, a sense of community, i.e. what has been gradually lost as our cities sprawled indiscriminately over valuable productive farm land and countryside.

History has taught us that continued uncontrolled expansion eventually leads to systemic breakdown followed by decline and failure. With 6.5 billion people, or 70 per cent of the world's population, projected to live in cities by 2050 – cities that will be responsible, directly or indirectly, for up to 80 per cent of the world's greenhouse gases – now is the time to initiate city transformation processes that can produce liveable, financially viable and environmentally sustainable cities.

References

Adams, R. (2009) *Transforming Australian Cities: For a More Financially Viable and Sustainable Future*, Melbourne: City of Melbourne.

Brugmann, J. (2009) *Welcome to the Urban Revolution: How Cities Are Changing the World*, Brisbane: University of Queensland Press.

Dodson, J. and Sipe, G. (2006) 'Shocking the suburbs: Urban location, housing debt and oil vulnerability in the Australian city', Urban Research Program, Research Paper 8, Griffith University, Brisbane.

Dodson, J. and Sipe, G. (2008) 'Unsettling Suburbia: The new landscape of oil and mortgage vulnerability in Australian cities', Urban Research Program, Research Paper 17, Griffith University, Brisbane.

Gehl Architects (2007) *'Baukultur' as an Impulse for Growth: Good Examples for European Cities*, Berlin: Federal Ministry of Transport, Building and Urban Affairs.

Harris, K. (1995) *Collected Quotes from Albert Einstein*. Online. http://rescomp.stanford.edu/~cheshire/EinsteinQuotes.html (accessed 18 November 2009).

Sexton, R. (2009) 'Sleepy commuters doing bit to save state $85 m', *Age*, 27 September.

Trubka, R., Newman, P. and Bilsborough, D. (2008) *Assessing the Costs of Alternative Development Paths of Australian Cities*, Perth: Curtin University and Parsons Brinckerhoff.

Sustainability for Survival

Moving the United Kingdom beyond the Zero Carbon Agenda

John Worthington

Introduction

Life in the twenty-first century is full of paradoxes, no more so than the challenge of building sustainable cities. Vibrant, dynamic, successful cities result from a diversity of functions, ease of accessibility and a variety of choice. Places we enjoy and admire are often 'loose fit', 'sub-optimal', allowing room to manoeuvre. But minimizing the use of scarce resources can often contradict these directions. Planning for a sustainable city and minimizing energy consumption to future-proof against climatic changes are connected but do not always result in the same outcomes. An extreme focus on achieving zero carbon emissions can result in tightly coupled solutions that reduce adaptability, provide marginal additional benefits and may conflict with individual lifestyle expectations.

The growing concern to eradicate risk and foster accountability has resulted in management by checklists and control by performance indicators, which have tended to commoditize the process and reduce sensitivity to local appropriateness. The paradox is that 'zero risk' is highly risky, stifling improvement through innovation and possibly diminishing the very qualities that foster a lasting sustainable future. The most urgent design challenge for our cities might be to reconsider how we define cities, neighbourhoods and places, and to embrace an approach that balances such conflicting demands.

British government policy has addressed the climate change agenda with a plethora of (often conflicting) regulations and initiatives, while the sustainability agenda has often created designs that meet the target of ticking the boxes but do not always respond appropriately to local circumstances. There is much to be commended in current British practice. Selected case studies, primarily drawn from experience of practising in London and the south-east, suggest pointers for policy and its potential design outcomes.

In conclusion it is argued that the characteristics of a sustainable city may be a combination of: more complex systems of government and management; greater flexibility of both infrastructure and thinking; simpler buildings; and the application of hybrid solutions.

Designing for a world of paradox

Change is not a new phenomenon. We can trace the rhythm of change from the period of an agricultural economy, which lasted well over 1000 years, to an industrial economy (200 years) to the service economy (eighty years), where the product is service and assets, infrastructure and institutions, and bureaucrats support a knowledge economy. The product is a process, built on ideas and know-how, institutional communities of practice and assets are networks of knowledge. What is clear is that we live in a world of increasing uncertainty, where change is the norm.

Change can be both incremental and seismic. Gradual, incremental changes can build up to a shift in perception; often an unforeseen event triggers a seismic change in behaviour and organizational structures. The previous economic upheaval was the recession of the early 1990s, which was more than a severe downturn in the economic cycle, but a restructuring of the office service economy. Is the current recession a blip on the radar from which we will return to 'business as usual', or does it signify a major shift in values, and a restructuring of the financial and property investment sector?

In Europe it was perhaps the Boxing Day tsunami followed by Hurricane Katrina that triggered the shift in mass public awareness to recognize our vulnerability to nature's forces and the imperatives of climate change. The disparate agendas of the credit crunch, climate change and ensuring our energy supplies could interplay to create a new set of values and change the climate of opinion (Jupiter *et al.* 2008).

The changes in work practices triggered twenty-five years ago through the impact of information and communications technology (Worthington 2006) is now pervasive, with a change in expectations of how, when and where we can work, with a subsequent impact on lifestyles and urban form (van den Dobbelsteen *et al.* 2009). For city designers and policy makers these changes are forcing a recognition that perhaps it is unrealistic to expect to control the future with precise 'blueprints'. We need frameworks to define limits within which innovation and change can occur. We are moving from a binary world of right and wrong, and a choice of *either* this *or* that, to a world of paradox where the challenge is to allow for *both* this *and* that. Most of the issues we face can be framed as a balance between seemingly conflicting desires. We want to be secure and accessible; private and public; compact and dispersed; independent and communal ... the list is endless.

The zero carbon agenda

Climate change and sustainability are now firmly on most governmental agendas. Too often the words are indiscriminately interchanged. Optimizing energy-saving design features and applying precise-fit spatial solutions may reduce carbon emissions but might hinder long-term flexibility and the agility to respond to future user needs too. The challenge is to balance the very real environmental concerns of climate change with the social and economic demands that contribute long-term holistic sustainability.

In his doctoral thesis on sustainable offices, Andy van den Dobbelsteen (2004) shows how big gains in energy reduction can be made by a combination of organizational, spatial, managerial and technical factors that encompass: rethinking organizational structures; use of space at both the urban and building scale; building design in the choice of depth, configuration and height; timetabling functions over space and time; and technical considerations, such as energy usage and service support. These in turn should be addressed through time and designed for life. However, he recognizes that major step changes in achieving the sustainable office will also require a parallel programme to change expectations, perceptions and behaviour.

Currently the United Kingdom has a plethora of regulations and initiatives, many overlapping and conflicting, with little integration. Dr Bill Bordass of the Usable Buildings Trust has identified the key drivers of the British government's energy policy as:

- political positioning to avoid emissions that are leading to climate change. The United Kingdom accounts for 3 per cent of the world's existing emissions and 15 per cent of cumulative historical ones;
- improving energy security, with North Sea oil and gas running out and potential political uncertainty over world supplies;
- renewing the aged electricity generation and distribution network. This is seen in the context of nuclear and coal installations coming to the end of their useful life, the need to decarbonize and ensure local energy sourcing, and limitations on finance;
- keeping the United Kingdom's economy competitive and 'stopping the lights going out';
- keeping energy affordable and avoiding potential 'fuel poverty';
- demonstrating tangible progress within a context of limited capital.

To meet this broad agenda in the non-domestic construction and property sector, the government has a plethora of regulations, programmes and initiatives driven by different departments.

Bordass argues for clarity and simplicity, finding a balance between regulation, changing behaviour and raising awareness. He proposes applying a multiplier effect, starting with people, through raising awareness, and then being:

- *lean* – halve the demand by reviewing standards, reducing losses, avoiding waste;
- *mean* – double the efficiency by installing more effective equipment, using it efficiently, avoiding system losses and tuning it up;
- *green* – halve the carbon in the supplies with on- and off-site measures.

With such an approach, 'you're down to an eighth of the CO_2'.

The broad sustainability goals in terms of implementation have been expressed as a multitude of separate expectations and actions resulting in a 'tick-box' mentality rather than thinking holistically, which is at the heart of sustainable thinking. Short-term targets often override innovation and long-term improvements. 'Green' has become a useful marketing slogan. Recent research by Fuerst and McAllister (2008) into investment returns has shown that LEED (Leadership in Energy and Environmental Design) and BREEAM (Building Research Establishment Environmental Assessment Method) for excellent commercial office buildings have a 5 per cent uplift in value.

The challenge ahead

The challenge increasingly being recognized by British campaigners, government commissions and forward-looking agencies (such as the Sustainability Development Commission, the government's independent watchdog on sustainable development) is the need to frame the problem and conceive the solution systemically as a process of change through to improvement. The Commission for Architecture and the Built Environment (CABE) has identified five key attributes of a sustainable city (Brown 2009):

- an appetite for change;
- leaders who can think long term;
- working across administrative boundaries;
- freedom to control land and assets;
- complete focus on whole-life value.

These recommendations cross departmental boundaries, start to integrate economic and environmental agendas and place emphasis for action on community ownership. There is recognition that 'preparing towns and cities' for a changing climate is as much about increasing awareness and changing patterns of behaviour as physical actions.

Meeting the challenges of climate change will require a dynamic systems approach. The solution of one problem can trigger an unpredicted problem in another part of the system. CABE's four recommendations, building on good exemplars of past practice and greater integration across government departments, are to:

1 Focus on the neighbourhood scale and locally inspired and implemented initiatives.
2 Use the government's power, both central and local, as an owner, user, procurer and manager of buildings to demonstrate best practice. The Office of Government Commerce (OGC), as the government's procurement agency, with the National Audit Office is providing excellent advice on best practice. The strategic design consultancy DEGW and OGC (2008) show by example how government departments, by rethinking the way they work and the space they need, have reduced their property needs, improved business performance and reduced energy usage.
3 Foster a culture of working together across departments, and thinking holistically to produce integrated planning. CABE's ongoing work advocating the need for an overarching urban design, vision Strud, aims to establish a 'creative collective process of re-imagining a functional urban region ... Which involves debating, refining and agreeing the urban region's identity and story of change ... to facilitate and guide collective decision making, by establishing a relational cross boundary framework' (CABE and URI 2004).
4 Establish a sustainable cities network that provides tailored expert advice, and is

a platform for sharing experience and gaining mutual support. The network www.sustainablecities.org.uk is arranged around seven spatial scales, from the individual building to the region, and linked to six critical themes – energy, waste, water, transport, green infrastructure and public space. The Sustainable Cities programme has drawn together a constituency of cities focused on sustainability, stimulated by CABE's successful 2008 Climate Change Festival in Birmingham. The Forum of the Future's Sustainable Cities Index (which monitors the largest twenty British cities against seventeen attributes organized under three categories of environmental impact, quality of life and future-proofing) provides an authoritative benchmark and a challenge for the selected cities.

Cambridge and its subregion

Cambridge encapsulates many of the dilemmas facing a community engaged in finding a responsible way forward in a world of dramatic economic, social and environmental change. The world-class quality of its university has been the catalyst for success and an engine for growth. Cambridge and its hinterland is the centre for one of the largest concentrations of high-technology industry in Europe. Today there are 1400 high-tech companies in the region, employing 48 000 staff, and attracting 18 per cent of all the venture capital investment in the United Kingdom (www.gcp.uk.net). The challenge facing the city and its subregion is how to allow space for firms to grow, accommodate the housing required at affordable prices and not spoil the quality of environment that has fuelled the city's success.

Ten years ago this dilemma was recognized by the university and the city council and, through a network of far-sighted individuals led by Professor Peter Carolin (2008), then head of the Department of Architecture, Cambridge Futures was initiated. The group had support from academia, local authorities, business and local practitioners, and became an open steering group where all were welcome. Cambridge Futures was a collaborative study outside the statutory planning process, which was able to pose questions and propose options that could potentially be construed as contentious. Seven options were studied, from minimum growth to a self-sustainable 'new town', with intermediate options such as densification, a necklace of satellite villages and 'virtual highways' (Figure 6.1).

Each option was compared in terms of economic efficiency, social equity and environmental quality. The options were presented to the public as exhibition panels, supported by an animated video visualizing the different spatial outcomes. A survey undertaken during the exhibition revealed that:

- 86 per cent of the respondents agreed that more money should be invested in public transport than on roads for cars;
- 81 per cent agreed that it would be bad if only the wealthy could afford to live in Cambridge;
- 78 per cent agreed that the region's high-tech business must be allowed to grow.

Significantly, only 18 per cent agreed that Cambridge and its surroundings should be kept unchanged. DEGW (2001) undertook a study for the Cambridge

6.1
Cambridge City plan provides park-and-ride gateways to the historic university core at key areas for intensification: the university land to the north-west, Addenbrookes Hospital and Medical Research Park to the south, the airport to the east, and Cambridge Science Park and the proposed Chesterton station to the north

Source: UK Crown

City Council on expansion to the east, and a strategy has now been agreed to create gateway development nodes with park-and-ride at the periphery of the city, and implement a guided bus route (Figure 6.1).

Within the region a series of well-connected, self-contained, planned communities are proposed (Figure 6.2). The aim will be to ensure the quality through the Cambridgeshire Quality Charter for growth, which is committed to:

- building a sense of community;
- locating new developments that can benefit from high connectivity;
- tackling climate change;
- creating places of character.

The charter is short and direct. It was prepared with the active engagement of a wide range of stakeholders and is endorsed by local authorities, statutory agencies, utilities, major landowners and private-sector developers (www.cambridgeshirehorizons.co.uk/quality and www.urbed.co. uk). A high level of commitment to the principles and shared understanding has been achieved through study visits, workshops and shared learning. It is an ongoing process that inevitably will be tested through having to adjust to

John Worthington

6.2
Cambridgeshire subregional expansion strategy, showing the proposed transport network, green grid and new communities at Northstowe and Cambourne

smaller budgets for infrastructure. However, the commitment to achieve equitable environmentally sustainable growth that does not compromise quality has been established. As a reflection of this balanced approach, the Cambridge Preservation Society has been reconstituted as Cambridge Past Present and Future.

The Thames Gateway Parklands Vision

The Thames Gateway stretches each side of the estuary from London's heart to the river mouth. An area 30 km across and 60 km long covering 80 000 ha (30 000 of which are brownfield), it has a population of 1.6 million and 700 000 households. It is already the size, in area and population, of many European metropolitan regions, yet is still perceived by many as the 'backyard to London'.

New Labour championed the area as a focus for growth, aiming to provide 120 000 homes and 180 000 jobs by 2016 (Farrell 2008). Sceptics argued that the project was folly: a designated flood area, poorly serviced by public transport and with a low level of skills and educational attainment. Its proponents argued that, with the high-speed rail connection to continental Europe, the stimulus of the development of London Docklands, the second wave of investment for the Olympics in 2012 and the opportunity to develop around a distinctive landscape and cultural heritage resources, energy and imagination should be steered eastwards.

Ten years since the project was begun in earnest, it has myriad agencies, no strong central political leadership and the ambitious housing delivery programme has been stalled by the banking crisis. Today the potential to simplify the decision-making process and reduce the number of agencies is a reality with the formation of the Housing and Communities Agency, a combining of English Partnerships and the Housing Corporation, with the close integration of local regeneration delivery bodies.

The Thames Gateway Parklands Vision, prepared by Terry Farrell, the gateway design champion, provides a clear, logical and inspiring vision under the banner 'One vision – A thousand projects' (www.communities.gov.uk/thamesgateway). Farrell's vision is of one coherent place, composed of the 'brown landscape' of urbanization, the 'blue landscape' of water and the 'green landscape' of food production, learning and recreation-distinctive places within a community parklands spatial framework. Parklands is a brilliant visual representation that gives coherence and expression to initiatives already started. The green grid proposals for South Essex (Landscape Design Associates), London (Design for London) and Kent, when integrated with the different transport programmes, are the basis for a robust strategic planning framework (Figure 6.3).

The historic Medway towns, under the single identity of Medway, are intensifying and regenerating an area of decline. The Institute for Sustainability (IfS) – a consortium of research institutions, private investment, professional organizations and government agencies (www.instituteforsustainability.co.uk) – is working across the Gateway both north and south of the estuary to integrate research initiatives, foster clusters of synergetic industries in the environmental and energy sectors and attract investment. Dagenham Dock Sustainable Industries Park, being developed by London Thames Gateway Development Corporation (www.LondonSIP.com), is planned to enable businesses to share facilities, develop synergies with neighbours and maximize resources and minimize waste (Figure 6.4).

The first three committed tenants – Closed Loop, Cyclomax and the IfS – are already setting new standards for the location and presenting a foretaste of an economy driven by sustainability. The Parklands vision is a big idea that

6.3
Parklands spatial framework, an environment and landscape strategy for the Thames Gateway, east of London

Source: Terry Farrell and Partners

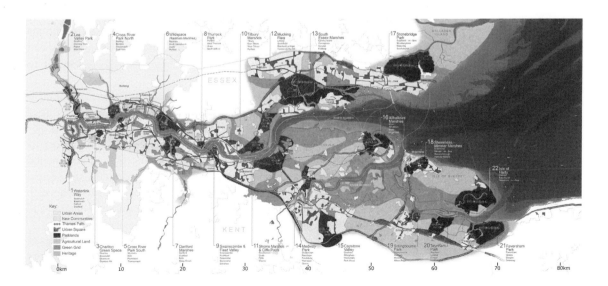

John Worthington

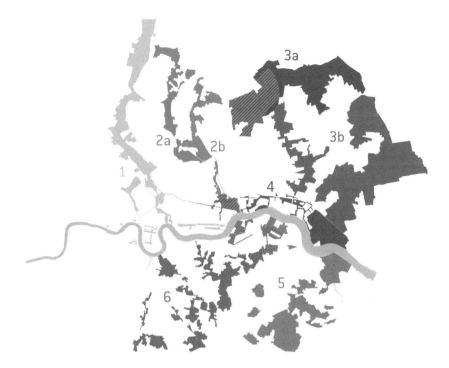

6.4
Design for London's proposed Green Grid for the east of London provides a range of formal and informal recreation spaces and landscapes and helps East London adapt to climate change by reducing flood risk and enhancing surface-water management

can be implemented incrementally, it is underpinned by a sense of the past and strong ecological principles, the aspirations are realistic and the vision is achievable with strong leadership.

A new working environment

One of the clearest exemplars of the sustainable working environment has emerged organically without a grand plan. While the grand plans for the comprehensive regeneration of the railway lands associated with King's Cross and St Pancras stations have been tortuously emerging over the last twenty years, opportunistic small-scale development has been transformative, economically uplifting and bringing vitality to the surrounding areas. Regent Quarter, three blocks east of King's Cross station, is a mixed-use development of new and renovated buildings by P&O Developments.

Following an urban development strategy prepared by Urban Initiatives (2009), the development was undertaken incrementally over five years, with minimum disruption to the area's day-to-day life. The outcome is a lively mix of offices, shops, hotel, bars and living, with young and mature firms, large and small, predominantly in the professional services, creative and media sectors, moving in. Individual building identity is subordinate to the character of the area; there are many doors, small semi-public courts, alleys through and space to meet informally. The area under single management has a buzz and diversity, a locality to be associated with.

Within one of the urban blocks, in a listed industrial shed wedged between two mature consulting organizations, is the Hub (www.kingscross.the-hub.net/

public). The Hub is a network of meeting places, founded as a 'social enterprise to inspire and support', firms with common ethical values, by 'working to create places for people who change things'. The King's Cross building is in a single triple-height space with mezzanines. Its shared and overlapping functions over a sixteen-hour day (as a setting for meeting, working, innovating, learning and connecting) means intensive use. As a model for working, the Hub breaks with most conventions: it uses space more intensely by a factor of ten, selects its customers from those with similar values and uses space rejected by others.

Adjacent to the Regent Quarter is Kings Place. A new development by Parabola Land, with Dixon Jones as architects (www.kingsplace.co.uk/about-kings-place), the site bounded on two sides by canals is a destination and the home of firms such as the Guardian Group, as well as cultural entities such as the Orchestra of the Age of the Enlightenment. The ground and lower floors lit from above are a public attraction with two galleries, concert halls, supporting bars, restaurants and meeting facilities, and offices above. Like the Hub it is intensively used and is a place to meet. It shows how, organically, through the energy of innovative entrepreneurs, a new and dynamic quarter of the city is emerging.

The way ahead

In their paper 'The shape of business: The next ten years', the Confederation of British Industries set out the challenges of operating in a credit-constrained environment. They propose that businesses focus on greater flexibility, a greater willingness to cooperate in joint ventures, and new ways of working, including differing relationships with employees and an acceptance that they will need to question and review many of the processes that have previously been taken for granted: 'Sustainability and ethics will become more integrated into the business mode ... Firms will seek to improve accountability and corporate citizenship further to attract and retain customers and staff.'

Among leading companies, sustainability has become more than public relations 'green wash'. Influential business leaders (Hilton 2009) are recognizing that 'ultimately, companies which talk about action but don't take it will lose competitive advantage'.

The case studies of Cambridge, Thames Gateway and King's Cross, each in their different ways, show that it is both small-scale pragmatic actions and long-term strategic changes in perception, driven by clear, caring and innovative leadership, that will make the changes. Six principles stand out:

1 Establish a context for sustainable action by engaging stakeholders in visits, workshops and forums, so they both see and believe the wider picture.
2 Think holistically while allowing for incremental actions.
3 Embrace a process of evaluation, feedback, continuous adaptation and improvement.
4 Allow for the paradoxes of modern living and balance the conflicting expectations.
5 Review proposed solutions to assess their impact over time.
6 Recognize there is no single 'golden bullet' to provide the instant solution.

Finally, in mature environments such as the United Kingdom, the utopian solution with every facet of the solution an innovation is a dream. The 'installed base' of physical infrastructure and operational, legal and business arrangements may be the greatest barrier to achieving instant large-scale change.

References

Brown, P. (ed.) (2009) *Hallmarks of a Sustainable City*, London: CABE.

CABE and URI (2004) 'Strategic Urban Design (StrUD)', literature and case study review (unpublished), CABE and University of Greenwich.

Carolin, P. (2008) 'Cambridge futures: Enabling consensus on growth and change', in B. Larsson (ed.), *Univer-City: The Old Middle-Sized European Academic Town as Framework of the Global Society of Science – Challenges and Possibilities*, Lund: Sekel Bokforlag.

Confederation of British Industries (2009) 'The shape of business: The next 10 years'. Online: www.cbi.org.uk/pdf/20091123-cbi-shape-of-business.pdf.

DEGW (2001) *Cambridge Expansion*, Report for Cambridge City Council.

Farrell, T. (2008) *Thames Gateway Parklands Masterplan*, London: Department for Communities and Local Government.

Fuerst, F. and McAllister, P. (2008) 'Green noise or green value? Measuring the price effects of environmental certification in commercial buildings', Real Estate & Planning Working Papers rep-wp2008-09, Reading: Henley Business School, Reading University.

Hilton, A. (2009) 'Centre stage for sustainability', *Evening Standard*, 24 November.

Jupiter, T., Elliot, L., Hines, C., Leggett, J., Lucas, C., Murphy, R., Pettifor, A., Secrett, C. and Simms, A. (2008) *A Green New Deal: Joined-up Policies to Solve the Triple Crunch of the Credit Crisis, Climate Change and High Oil Prices*, London: New Economics Foundation.

OGC and DEGW (2008) *Working beyond Walls: The Government Workplace as an Agent of Change*, Norwich: OGC.

Urban Initiatives (2009) 'Review of Tibbalds Prize shortlisted projects: Regents Quarter, Kings Cross, London', *Urban Design* 110.

Van den Dobbelsteen, A. (2004) 'The Sustainable Office: An exploration of the potential for factor 20 environmental improvement of office accommodation', doctoral thesis, TU Delft.

Van den Dobbelsteen, A., van Dorst, M. and van Timmeren, A. (eds) (2009) *Smart Building in a Changing Climate*, Amsterdam: Techne Press.

Worthington, J. (ed.) (2006) *Reinventing the Workplace*, 2nd edn, Oxford: Architectural Press.

Chaos and Resilience

The Johannesburg Experience

Chrisna Du Plessis

Introduction

Like all disciplines with a root in science, town planning, urban design and architecture have been dominated by cultures that valued a particular form of order: linear, rigid, prescriptive and structured by top-down hierarchies and detailed classification. Typologies, regulations and zoning plans were developed to catalogue, order and control both the social and physical environment that constitute human settlement.

Therefore, it is no surprise that this desire for orderliness manifests itself in the language and tools of sustainability. From the basic three pillars of economic, social and environmental sustainability to the many frameworks of sustainability and their many indicators, as much (if not more) effort has gone into finding ways to order, measure and manage sustainability as went into the development of truly alternative solutions to the way things are done. Very few people question whether increased order and management is the right approach to follow or even if we are pursuing the right kind of order.

The South African system of apartheid, and by extension South African cities, provides one of the best examples of the lengths we go to establish order in perceived chaos and uncertainty. However, as pointed out by many scholars (Bonner 1995; Maylam 1995; Bond 2000; Terreblanche 2002), the apartheid era's attempts at ordering the city and society resulted in a false sense of order and security that served only to hide increasing societal chaos and turbulence. After 1994 attempts to re-order the city according to the New South Africa ideals of integration and equity have not been particularly successful (Bremner 2000; Beall *et al.* 2002), and citizen responses to this new uncertainty led to yet further attempts at ordering the city, such as gated communities and City Improvement Districts, that brought their own challenges (Landman 2002; Harrison and Mabin 2006; Peyroux 2006). South African cities hold up a convenient mirror in which we can see how naive human notions of ordering the universe can be.

Finding an appropriate set of concepts to understand sustainability in the context of the South African city provides a particularly thorny challenge as the validity of current theoretical frameworks used to interpret Third World cities is questionable (Parnell 1997). Using the city of Johannesburg as backdrop, this chapter abandons established discourses of urban theory, using complexity and ecosystems theories to explore a different approach to urban sustainability.

Urban experiences in post-apartheid South Africa

A messy continuum of degrees of urbanity stretching across spatial, temporal, economic, geopolitical and cultural boundaries, and straddling watersheds and biomes, South African cities are forever teetering on the brink of social and environmental disasters that are as intertwined as the Gordian knot. The follies of both a shameful past and an idealistic present shape the landscape of a future that hovers in the space between hope and despair. Daily life requires constant negotiation of both social and spatial boundaries created by a diversity of cultures, eleven official languages and the physical and mental fences and tripwires that are the children of apartheid.

South African cities are bursting at the seams, fed by a steady flow of rural migrants and foreigners all looking for the road to riches. Everyday obstacles of a South African city trip up many a well-meaning urban development initiative: sharp economic divisions and armed patrolled electric fences between the 'haves' and the 'also-wants'; sprawling informal settlements and million-dollar-mansion golf estates gobbling up scarce arable land and scarcer water; overburdened or non-existent essential services; high levels of crime and corruption; and dangerous public transport systems.

Yet, for all the despairing talk of disaster, South African cities are vibrant, culturally diverse urban environments teeming with formal and informal economic activity, filled with warm, creative and enterprising people and offering a wealth of greenery and wildlife. This vibrancy is also the result of living in 'edge country', of exploiting the opportunities for innovation and transformation that are found where different systems meet and blend, and where rules are mutable. No South African city illustrates this particularly *Mzanzi* ('South African' in township slang) version of edge-of-chaos urbanization better than Johannesburg.

The metropolitan areas of Johannesburg, Tshwane (Pretoria) and Ekurhuleni, a collection of industrial and mining towns, combine to form the largest urban conurbation in the country (Figure 7.1). Situated in Gauteng Province, which covers only 1.7 per cent of the country's surface area, this small part of South Africa houses almost 20 per cent of the country's population and claims to be the economic powerhouse of Africa. It has the distinction of being one of the world's few major urban conurbations that does not lie on a river, lake or seafront. Being on a watershed, most water is pumped in through some of the world's largest inter-basin transfers. Despite this, Pretoria and Johannesburg are known for their vast urban forests and nature conservancies woven into the structure of the city.

Pretoria reflects the staid orderliness of its Calvinist origins as a *nachtmaal* town, a rural settlement established by pioneer Afrikaner farmers for periodic trading, discussing governance and celebrating communion. In contrast to these origins and Pretoria's bureaucratic culture of a seat of government,

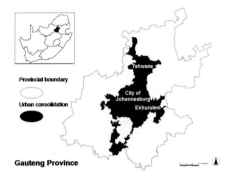

Provincial boundary

Urban consolidation

Gauteng Province

Tshwane

City of Johannesburg

Ekhuruleni

7.1
South Africa's greatest urban consolidation

Source: Chrisna Du Plessis

Johannesburg was forged in the perpetual chaos of a gold rush that proudly endures. Its founding fathers, more intent on making money than keeping order, imposed the bare minimum of organization, allowing the city to evolve according to its own rules. Even during the strictly regulated apartheid years, Johannesburg kept its rebellious nature, spawning 'grey' areas where races mixed despite the law, and fostering the liberation struggle that eventually overthrew apartheid. As a result, for many years it featured on the top of lists such as 'murder capitals of the world' or 'most dangerous cities in the world'.

Despite its fast-paced and perilous lifestyle, there is a richness to Johannesburg life that is lacking in its more sober neighbour. The city has an exciting mix of elite shopping malls stocking designer wares from across the globe, artsy neighbourhoods with lively street cultures, and cultural melting pots. Everywhere people are on the make in whatever space they can find, leading to some interesting juxtapositions and role reversals. Pedlars and refugees from across the continent sell their wares (curios, haircuts, drugs, sex) on the pavement in front of fine restaurants or in the marble lobbies of decaying art deco high-rises hijacked by AK47-wielding slumlords. Beggars at the traffic lights sell jokes and trees and the promise that they are 'crime free' (Figure 7.2), while in the high-security shelter of world-class restaurants a rising black bourgeoisie celebrates dodgy economic empowerment deals with imported cigars and the finest French champagne. Competition is fierce and people act sharp, dress sharp, constantly alert. Every day holds the possibility of a sweet deal and the threat of a gun to the head. But, as in New York, if you can make it in 'Jozi', you can make it anywhere.

Challenge of finding sustainability on the edge of chaos

The anarchic complexity of cities like Johannesburg presents a particularly taxing challenge to sustainable urban planning and management. Current approaches to understanding, measuring and managing urban sustainability rely on mainly quantitative indicator sets often based on two sets developed by the United Nations: the CSD Working List of Indicators (UNCSD 1996) and those developed by UN-Habitat (UN-Habitat 2004: 7). UN indicators have been developed from a politically negotiated understanding of urban sustainability,

Chrisna Du Plessis

7.2

Beggar selling jokes

Photo: Chrisna Du Plessis

the 'development agenda', heavily emphasizing the socio-economic and institutional dimensions of urban development (Alberti 1996: 405). They measure performance against a set of development objectives, rather than the impact of certain actions or development pathways. Another feature of these indicators, whether used for environmental evaluation or track development impact, is their aggregate nature (Alberti 1996; Deakin *et al.* 2002; Finco and Nijkamp 2001).

Aggregate indicator systems break up the problem of urban sustainability into smaller, simpler sub-problems that can then be reduced to specific ratios, e.g. energy use per square metre, people per hectare, or percentage of open space. As Jane Jacobs pointed out in the 1960s, this turns problems of disorganized complexity into 'problems of simplicity' to be resolved in isolation (Jacobs 1992: 438). The suitability of aggregation methods for identifying and assessing different interventions in complex, dynamic systems is questionable (Rittel and Webber 1973; Meadows 1999; Kohler 2002).

However, the key flaw in the measure-to-manage approach to current sustainability initiatives is assuming that there is a way to predict and control urban systems, even though science recognizes that the kind of self-organizing and non-linear behaviour in complex adaptive systems such as cities is inherently unpredictable and leads to uncertainty (Meadows 2002: 2).

Current approaches to understanding and measuring urban sustainability can be criticized for not responding to reality. Following Wolfram Class IV rules (Waldrop 1992: 234; Odell 2003: 48), they are based on a politically negotiated utopian vision of how we would like the world to work and they ignore the reality of cities as dynamic and adaptive complex systems existing at the edge of chaos. To find a realistic approach to urban sustainability, it is necessary to ask how we would understand and practise sustainability in a complex adaptive system.

Solution: reinterpretation in a complex systems approach

Currently we approach cities as if they are entirely manufactured and mechanical objects. However, shaped by organic life forms and organic processes, cities are closer to forests and coral reefs than to machines. So why don't we measure their sustainability as we would that of an ecosystem?

The idea of the city as an ecosystem is not new, but only recently have people begun to ask how this metaphor can be used to provide different, more sustainable approaches to city planning and management. Yet cities are more than ecological systems: they are social-ecological systems (SESs). Anderies *et al.* (2006: 1) describe SESs as integrated living systems consisting of agents (human or otherwise), their actions and behavioural patterns and 'a physical substrate (chemicals, energy, water)', with the interactions among agents and with the substrate generating SESs' dynamics. Du Plessis (2008: 82) has described SESs as consisting of interpenetrating physical (external, tangible, visible) and mental (internal, intangible, invisible) phenomena experienced at individual and collective levels and organized in nested systems across scales of space and time. In addition to this is 'panarchy', holarchic levels of increasing complexity and transcendence represent an 'exterior' created by biogeo-chemical processes (in which humans now play a disproportionate part) and an 'interior' created by and experienced through human psyches and processes of thought, including a 'shared cultural worldspace' (Wilber 2000). SESs are differentiated from simple ecological systems by properties dependent on abstract thought and symbolic construction. Critical for the discussion in this chapter is the fourth characteristic of SESs as complex and adaptive systems, with properties of self-organization and emergence.

Understanding cities as complex adaptive systems

Cities are complex: they are diverse, with multiple interconnected elements, and adaptive, having the capacity to change and learn from experience. Within complex, adaptive systems (CASs), micro-level agents interact to create the system's global properties, which feed back into micro-level interactions. For example, the influx of immigrants into inner-city Johannesburg in the 1980s and 1990s led to a cascade of transformations that irrevocably changed the character and functionality of the entire city (Bremner 2000).

Lucas (2004) explains the essence of CASs as self-organization to optimize the system's functions, creating new niches as necessary, and changing their composition to fit changing patterns and external shocks. Adaptive responses and interactions allow the whole system to undergo spontaneous self-organization into collective structures with properties that cannot be predicted from the properties of the parts and which the individual agents may not have possessed (Waldrop 1992), a concept referred to as 'emergence'. In Johannesburg this propensity for self-organization and emergence was observed in citizen responses, such as the development of City Improvement Districts, which colonized the functional niche left open by weakened municipal service delivery (Peyroux 2006). New urban forms emerged, such as enclosed neighbourhoods and gated communities in response to the fear and reality of violent crime (Landman and Schönteich 2002; Harrison and Mabin 2006).

The view of the city as a complex adaptive social-ecological system changes the perception of the city as an artefact to that of the city as an ever-changing socio-spatial-temporal meta-process, comprising innumerable interacting and nested processes resulting from self-organization and adaptation and resulting in the emergence of unpredictable patterns and events. This perspective also shifts the interpretation of how (urban) sustainability should be defined.

George Cowan (quoted in Waldrop 1992: 356) maintains that uncertainty and complexity question the very basis of a sustainability agenda, which 'has been put into the form of talking about a set of transformations from state A, the present, to a state B that's sustainable', a state, he says, that does not exist in 'systems that remain continuously dynamic, and that are embedded in environments that themselves are continuously dynamic'. Holling *et al.* (2002: 76) suggest that, instead, 'sustainability is the capacity to create, test and maintain adaptive capability, while development is the process of creating, testing and maintaining opportunity', implying that sustainability requires change and persistence. Thus Murray Gell-Mann (quoted in Waldrop 1992: 351) suggests that a sustainable human society is one that 'isn't static, but allows for growth, [and is] adaptable, robust, and resilient to lesser disasters'. This insight has led an increasing number of scientists to suggest that resilience is the key to determining sustainability in social-ecological systems (Walker and Salt 2006: 11).

Resilience as a new metaphor for sustainability

Walker and Salt (2006: 11) and Gotts (2007: 2) suggest that resilience thinking, as a conceptual framework, is constructed on the following system characteristics: multiple stability regimes separated by critical thresholds and episodic change (leading to the adaptive cycle metaphor); multiple distinctive scales with cross-scale interactions (the panarchy); and resilience (the ability of a system to absorb or recover from disturbances without losing its functional identity). From a resilience point of view, the objective of sustainability initiatives is not to resist or reverse change, but to accept that change is inevitable and manage the phase changes in adaptive cycles so that the system does not lose its fundamental identity and tip into another stability domain, or that such collapses do not cascade upwards into the larger system. (Holling and Gunderson (2002: 51) suggest the 'adaptive cycle' as a metaphor for the recurring cycles of rapid growth, conservation, release and reorganization found in nature.)

Walker and Salt (2006: 59) propose that the actors in a system can manage resilience by moving thresholds, removing a system from a threshold or making a threshold more difficult to reach. They suggest that this capacity is the adaptability (or adaptive capacity) of the system and propose three characteristics that determine adaptive capacity:

1   Degree of connectedness within system, both between internal controlling variables and referring to systems that consist of small groups strongly linked internally but only loosely connected to each other, e.g. distributed but grid-connected energy-generation systems.
2   Tightness of feedback: how fast and strong consequences of change spread through the system and how quickly proximity to a threshold is detectable.
3   Diversity within system, particularly response diversity achieved when each different organism forming part of the same functional group (e.g. predators) has different responses to a disturbance, or survival strategies (Elmqvist *et al.* 2003, cited in Walker and Salt 2006: 69).

Response diversity provides flexibility by optimizing possible response options available to a system. Thus while certain species become extinct, overall functioning is maintained. For example, the gated-community response to crime, through a chain of individual actions, led to an urban pattern of single houses on large individual stands being replaced by more compact housing models. This frees up potential in the form of well-located land without threatening the ability of the city to provide housing (although it may have created other problems).

However, not all responses are equal. For example, replacing functional building management agencies responsible for maintaining rental properties with slum lords with no interest in maintenance may have temporarily led to increased availability of affordable housing in the inner city. However, the combination of overcrowding and no maintenance of old buildings eventually results in the inner city's inability to provide housing. Depending on how the city responds to crossing this threshold, urban decay spreads or there is opportunity for urban regeneration. While the loss of landmark buildings is detrimental for heritage, it may be beneficial in tipping the system into another adaptive cycle phase that might result in the collapse of a dysfunctional stability regime.

Resilience thinking suggests that optimization of system behaviour is an inappropriate goal for managing dynamic systems, as optimizing around a single objective (i.e. growth, stability, change, variety) only sets up conditions for an opposite phase or next cycle (Holling and Gunderson 2002: 47), and that 'optimization (in the sense of maximizing efficiency through tight control) is a large part of the problem, not the solution' (Walker and Salt 2006: 141). This implies far-reaching changes in managing cities. However, crucially, this is not a simple direct feedback process. The effects of optimization in one part may only become visible in a different part. For example, after 1994, national policy required municipalities to optimize housing delivery in a very narrow band, namely producing essentially free low-cost state-subsidized houses. This led to a number of distortions in urban land markets (Napier 2007), for example, the so-called 'housing gap' between state-subsidized stock available only to households earning below a certain threshold and the minimum criteria of bank mortgagees (Banking Association of South Africa 2005: 16). Both the housing strategy and the resulting housing gap led to a number of survival strategies abusing the system, defeating the political objective and ultimately threatening the urban system's resilience (Cross 2006; Marx and Royston 2007; Urban Landmark 2007). An approach that understood cities as complex systems might have avoided this.

Conclusion

If we consider a reality of cities as complex adaptive SESs, it is clear that we need a different approach to urban sustainability that embraces the opportunities presented by complexity theory and resilience thinking. Complex systems theory explains that the best place for survival is at the edge of chaos, not in some utopian state of equilibrium and that the edge of chaos is where creativity flourishes, where evolution happens and where life is born. Perhaps, to fully understand sustainability, we should come to accept that the edge of chaos is the natural state of cities; that cities, by definition, are arenas of creativity and destruction; that cities ebb and flow between disaster and regeneration, and perhaps, that cities (if we are not careful) are also mortal. Urban sustainability is not necessarily about making 'correct' choices in technology or social and economic ideologies, or finding solutions to a range of pre-determined and often perennial problems, but about participating effectively in the natural evolution of the city, while keeping the urban and global SESs from crossing critical thresholds.

References

Alberti, M. (1996) 'Measuring urban sustainability', *Environmental Impact Assessment Review* 16: 381–424.

Anderies, J.M., Walker, B.H. and Kinzig, A.P. (2006) 'Fifteen weddings and a funeral: Case studies and resilience-based management', *Ecology and Society* 11, 1: 21ff. Online: www. ecologyandsociety.org/vol. 11/iss1/art21 (accessed 23 May 2007).

Banking Association of South Africa (2005) *Research into Housing Supply and Functioning Markets: Research, Findings and Conclusions*. Report prepared by Settlement Dynamics Project Shop and Matthew Nell and Associates for the Banking Association of South Africa, Johannesburg.

Beall, J., Crankshaw, O. and Parnell, S. (eds) (2002) *Uniting a Divided City: Governance and Social Exclusion in Johannesburg*, London and Sterling, VA: Earthscan.

Bond, P. (2000) *Cities of Gold, Townships of Coal: Essays on South Africa's New Urban Crisis*, Trenton, NJ and Asmara, Eritrea: Africa World Press.

Bonner, P. (1995) 'African urbanisation on the Rand between 1930 and 1960: Its social character and its political consequences', *Journal of Southern African Studies* 21: 115–130.

Bremner, L. (2000) 'Reinventing the Johannesburg inner city', *Cities* 17, 3: 185–193.

Cross, C. (2006) 'Attacking urban poverty with housing: Toward more effective land markets Urban LandMark', Position Paper 2, prepared for the Urban Land Seminar, November 2006, Muldersdrift, South Africa. Online: www.urbanlandmark.org.za/research/overview.php (accessed 12 October 2009).

Deakin, M., Huovila, P., Rao, S., Sunikka, M. and Vreeker, R. (2002) 'The assessment of sustainable urban development', *Building Research and Information* 30, 2: 108ff.

Du Plessis, C. (2008) 'A conceptual framework for understanding social-ecological systems', in M. Burns and A. Weaver (eds), *Exploring Sustainability Science: A Southern African Perspective*, Stellenbosch: Sun Press: 59–90.

Elmqvist, T., Folke, C., Nystrom, M., Peterson, G., Bengtsson, J., Walker, B. and Norberg, J. (2003) 'Response diversity and ecosystem resilience', *Frontiers in Ecology and the Environment* 1, 9: 488–494.

Finco, A. and Nijkamp, P. (2001) 'Pathways to urban sustainability', *Journal of Environmental Policy and Planning* 3: 289–302.

Gotts, N.M. (2007) 'Resilience, panarchy, and world-systems analysis', *Ecology and Society* 12, 1: 24ff Online: www.ecologyandsociety.org/vol.12/iss1/art24 (accessed 23 May 2007).

Harrison, P. and Mabin, A. (2006) 'Security and space: Managing the contradictions of access restriction in Johannesburg', *Environment and Planning B: Planning and Design* 33: 3–20.

Holling, C.S. and Gunderson, L.H. (2002) 'Resilience and adaptive cycles', in L.H. Gunderson and C.S. Holling (eds), *Panarchy: Understanding Transformations in Human and Natural Systems*, Washington, DC: Island Press: 25–62.

Holling, C.S., Gunderson, L.H. and Peterson, G.D. (2002) 'Sustainability and panarchies', in L.H. Gunderson and C.S. Holling (eds), *Panarchy: Understanding Transformations in Human and Natural Systems*, Washington, DC: Island Press: 63–102.

Jacobs, J. (1992) *The Death and Life of Great American Cities*, New York: Random House Inc. Vintage Books.

Kohler, N. (2002) 'The relevance of BEQUEST: An observer's perspective', *Building Research and Information* 30, 2: 130–138.

Landman, K. (2002) 'Gated communities in South Africa: Building bridges or barriers', paper presented to the International Conference on Private Urban Governance, Mainz, Germany, 6–9 June 2002.

Landman, K. and Schönteich, M. (2002) 'Urban fortresses: Gated communities as a reaction to crime', *The African Security Review* 11, 4: 71–84.

Lucas, C. (2004) *Complex Adaptive Systems: Webs of Delight*, version 4.83, May 2004. Online: www. calresco.org/lucas/cas.htm (accessed 9 February 2009).

Marx, C. and Royston, L. (2007) *Urban Land Markets: How the Poor Access, Hold and Trade Land*, Pretoria: Urban Landmark.

Maylam, P. (1995) 'Explaining the apartheid city: 20 years of South African historiography', *Journal of Southern African Studies* 21: 19–38.

Meadows, D. (1999) 'Indicators and information systems for sustainable development', in D. Satterthwaite (ed.), *The Earthscan Reader in Sustainable Cities*, London: Earthscan: 364–393.

Meadows, D. (2002) 'Dancing with systems', *The Systems Thinker* 13, 2: 2–6.

Napier, M. (2007) 'Making urban land markets work better in South African cities and towns: Arguing the basis for access by the poor', Fourth Urban Research Symposium, Washington, May. Online: www.urbanlandmark.org.za/research/functional_markets.php (accessed 12 October 2009).

Odell, J. (2003) 'Between order and chaos', *Journal of Object Technology* 2, 6: 45–50.

Parnell, S. (1997) 'South African cities: Perspectives from the ivory tower of urban studies', *Urban Studies* 34, 506: 891–906.

Peyroux, E. (2006) 'City Improvement Districts (CIDs) in Johannesburg: Assessing the political and socio-spatial implications of private-led urban regeneration', *Trialog* 89, 2: 9–14.

Rittel, H.W.J. and Webber, M.M. (1973) 'Dilemmas in a general theory of planning', *Policy Sciences* 4: 155–169.

Terreblanche, S. (2002) *A History of Inequality in South Africa 1652–2002*, Scottsville, South Africa: University of Natal Press.

UNCSD (1996) *CSD Working List of Indicators*, United Nations Division for Sustainable Development. Online: www.un.org/esa/dsd/dsd_aofw_ind/ind_csdindi.shtml (accessed 18 March 2009).

UN-Habitat (2004) *Urban Indicator Guidelines*, Nairobi: UN-Habitat.

Urban Landmark (2007) *Voices of the Poor: Community Perspectives on Access to Urban Land*, Pretoria: Urban Landmark.

Waldrop, M.M. (1992) *Complexity: The Emerging Science at the Edge of Order and Chaos*, New York: Simon & Schuster.

Walker, B.H. and Salt, D. (2006) *Resilience Thinking: Sustaining Ecosystems and People in a Changing World*, Washington, DC: Island Press.

Wilber, K. (2000) *Sex, Ecology, Spirituality*, Boston and London: Shambala.

Part II

Infrastructure and a Sustainable City

Overview

Ralph Horne

As places of competition, cities are centres of post-industrial production because of comparative advantages from the efficiency of their infrastructure, the connectedness of their economies and their ability to attract resources, knowledge and labour. Their 'pull' on skilled labour resources in turn creates growing pains in the form of pressure on existing infrastructure, indicating the tensions between urban infrastructure, growth and development (Seitz 2000; Munnell 1990). Cities also create most of the world's anthropogenic greenhouse gas emissions and there is growing consensus over the need to reduce these emissions radically, while at the same time to adapt city infrastructure to a changing climate (Newman and Kenworthy 1999; Low *et al.* 2005; Girardet 2004).

The physical fabric of the city shapes, and is in turn shaped by, human practices, including those of habitation and movement. Inevitably then, any attempt at sustainable cities must engage substantively with both this fabric and the 'soft' infrastructure – the institutions, socio-cultural contexts, natural environments and political-economic realities and possibilities (Anderson 1996). Giddens's (1984) theory of structuration and Latour's (2005) actor-network theory provide important insights into the 'two-way' nature of city people–city fabric relations in ways which recognize the effects both that infrastructures have on shaping the socio-economic city, and those of city inhabitants, designers and planners in reproducing and remaking their physical surroundings.

Both the history and the future of urbanization are ones of adaptation, replication and innovation in infrastructure for new purposes, to accommodate rapidly changing social practices and, invariably, expanding populations. Within these processes, three dimensions of city infrastructure can be conceptualized:

- the hidden city, where elements of city infrastructure are often hidden from view as the city 'innards', including reticulated systems, cabling, sewers, subways and foundations;
- the dynamic city, where, inevitably, the fabric is re-used, expropriated, exchanged and renewed, often such that elements are barely recognizable across generations;

- the imaginary city, where infrastructures don't just happen, but are planned purposefully, and their realization is a product of socio-technical and political-economic processes.

The four chapters in this section of the book are dedicated to infrastructure and a sustainable city, each highlighting different contexts in which the struggle to transform institutions, communities and technology arrangements is played out.

Sheela Nair's case studies of water and sanitation projects in India evocatively and powerfully illustrate the 'hidden city', illustrating in the process that our practices of disposing of bodily wastes are particular and personal – and change can be confronting. Peering under, into the sewers of Chennai, the twin spectres of population growth and more frequent harsher droughts led to an infamous and acute scarcity of drinking water. Surface catchments were sucked dry to supply the water and wastewater system of the rapidly growing metropolis, while aquifers were drawn down unsustainably, leading to salinity. Classic short-term fixes in the form of water transportation by tankers became common. By the 1980s it was clear that a major change in the water system was needed and, while water was still being sought elsewhere, the crisis had also prompted radical new visions for more sustainable solutions. Wastewater and rainwater harvesting, along with collection of storm water for aquifer recharging, moved up the agenda as local legislation and initiatives were developed.

Rainwater harvesting gave Chennai an alternative to desalination, providing a low-carbon, low-energy option for working within the obdurate limits of the urban water infrastructure, yet adding to it using more sustainable technologies. These more decentralized solutions have knock-on effects. They require less energy than equivalent centralized, reticulated systems. They also encourage or 'script' community co-management of water, with associated stewardship benefits. Flood-control systems now have local buy-in, with civil society groups and community members helping to ensure they are maintained, thereby protecting the community from flood events.

In the town of Musiri, low-lying land, a high water-table and frequent problems with the network of local latrines leaking into rivers together created a chronic problem of water resource contamination, with impacts on environmental and community health. Following extensive community consultation, a project with a civil society aid organization led to the installation of dry composting toilets. These addressed river contamination risks while also providing valuable composted faeces and urine for use by farmers on fields, so valuable in fact that it led to the world's first 'Use and Get Paid Toilet' instead of 'Pay and Use Toilet', where toilet visitors receive a small payment for their deposits!

Through these accounts of social innovation, Nair illustrates that water systems need not follow the nineteenth-century model of centralized, gravity-fed infrastructures where large quantities of water are used to carry waste one way (to the sea), out of sight and mind. In showing that a whole town can do without a sewer at all, she illustrates important sustainable models that may be relevant to many contexts, particularly drought-prone Australia. In developing visions as models of possibility and engaging stakeholders and user groups in the entire journey of transition, the Musiri experience indicates that even deeply personal toilet habits can be changed in radical, sustainable ways. The result is bold experimentation, innovation and, ultimately, a successful sustainable pathway being forged out of purposeful linking of appropriate technology with community capacity-building and engagement, involving both government and non-government organizations as key actors.

Crossing continents and contexts, Scott Boylston engages head-on with the obduracy of city infrastructure by way of oil-dependent, private-transport urban North America. Specifically, Boylston is concerned with the under-used post-industrial areas of the city, and its buildings and infrastructure. Instead of seeing derelict buildings as detritus of a bygone era, and solutions as high-capital demolition and wholesale physical renewal, in Savannah, Georgia, sustainable solutions to urban renewal challenges are being developed within the existing industrial fabric.

The benefits of re-using structurally sound buildings for alternative uses are significant and diverse, ranging from the embodied energy benefits of extending building material life to the retention of city skylines, character and urban heritage. Bold visions are derived from reflective development of possible models for sustainable refurbishment. In this activist-led series of initiatives, a closed-loop symbiotic redevelopment path is pursued. Local political-economic realities are confronted and redrawn alongside the plans for building repair and adaptation. The case studies illustrate the co-evolution of organizations, users and ideas of urban infrastructure, in a negotiated vision to remould the city by adapting the existing urban fabric.

Paul Downton confronts us with a paradox when he states that our problems with climate change derive directly from urbanization, yet appropriate responses also lie within urbanization. He advocates a more reflexive architecture, recasting urban development in line with the principles of urban ecology. Charting a century of urban ecology research, he points out that ecological architecture is not simply about solar panels and low-energy construction, and eco-cities are not constituted solely of technologies of renewable energy and storm-water recycling.

Drawing on the seminal works of Gehl and Mumford, he argues that it is the act of inhabiting which defines the urban, and so urban design must engage with the everyday and with the urban spaces in which the practices of habitation take place. The idea of a designed physical city infrastructure existing without people in it is nonsensical, even if it is cleverly dressed with 'green' technologies. It is the social and institutional context that gives meaning to the urban, and it is therefore the 'fit' of the technical and social realms that ultimately determines sustainability outcomes.

Downton's case study is Christie Walk, a community-driven project in Adelaide, South Australia, providing new, affordable housing primarily for low-income households. The development adopts a medium-density approach and the sustainability intent is reflected in the process as well as the design, involving extensive community engagement. The project extends over an eight-year design-build period, illustrating that successful sustainable communities can take time to form.

Giving the appropriate time to city infrastructure planning is a particular challenge in China, where, as urbanization continues apace, so the demands on infrastructure are continually being added to, and rights and access renegotiated. A combination of rapid economic growth and demographic and social forces are driving what Neville Mars terms hyper-urbanization, noting, 'China underscores the need to imagine an ideal green living environment for our future.' The speed, scale and literally awesome roll-out of the urban landscape across China is juxtaposed against the challenges of community involvement and the importance of getting it 'right' in sustainability terms.

The difference between sustainable urban futures and unsustainable sprawl hinges on critical infrastructure, such as the geographic limit of mass-transit systems. For designers, the choice dilemma lies between following established conventions and breaking these rules to try for higher environmental performance. Mars's examples amply demonstrate the latter, with bold mass-transit systems and 'E-trees' where you plug your car in under a solar shade and leave it charging while you are at work or play. Such eco-innovations are important in an era of rising living standards and consumption levels across China. However, he also points out that ecological modernization agendas limited to a vision for new green technology are not likely to deliver sustainable outcomes. With this insight, parallels can be drawn with the other case studies across this collection.

Conclusion

Comparing the contrasting examples of sustainability across the developed and developing worlds, five apparent tensions facing urban infrastructure in an era of climate change can be identified:

- City infrastructures are dynamic yet obdurate. Despite constant change, the physical and institutional arrangements of the city often appear to resist purposive transformation and instead exhibit a reproductive function.
- Imagined futures are important even if they remain unrealized. Articulated visions of low-carbon city infrastructures help orient change, even though the course of this change is less predictable in the long term.
- Sustainable does not mean steady state. Future infrastructures will be dynamic and diverse, where it is not the activity of remaking that must stop, it is the way of remaking that needs to change.
- Time is short, yet sustainable infrastructures need time. There is an urgency to act to minimize dangerous global warming, yet it is implicit that socio-technical infrastructure transitions take time.
- Sustainable built infrastructures need new social infrastructures. Sustainable transitions imply social and cultural co-evolution with physical infrastructure and this in turn implies a role for community actors.

The first three tensions taken together introduce a caution in the way we collectively might go about designing and building sustainable city infrastructures. Any normative notion that there is some 'fixed' or realizable and predictable outcome ('sustainable city infrastructure') appears to be misguided and doomed to failure. Human ingenuity and resourcefulness is such that infrastructures are 'misused' or, rather, used for purposes other than what their originators designed them for. These ways may involve more or fewer greenhouse emissions than 'assumed' by the designers. Moreover, the future course of events is inherently unpredictable, and so long-term investments designed to set in train (or enable) particular patterns of habitation or movement are likely to prove risky. Such risks are reduced only when social, political and economic structures are maintained in such a way as to 'set' the future demand for particular infrastructures in particular ways.

The rethinking of the structure of suburbia (O'Connor and Healy 2004) necessitates the rethinking of the relations between changing social 'needs' and the provision of infrastructure to meet those needs. Shove *et al.* (2007) talk of the 'design of everyday life' and in the process draw on social practice theory to explain the divide between conventional design being focused on 'things' and responsibility for greenhouse gas emissions being typically attributed to people. The gap is social practices, which are complex, dynamic, under-studied and hence poorly understood. They tend to be unpredictable and dynamic, yet they are reproduced regularly. A better understanding of the ways assemblages of materials, artefacts and practices co-evolve and how they relate to 'cycles of production, consumption and innovation' (Shove *et al.* 2007: 14) helps us to resolve the tensions inherent in imagining sustainable infrastructure while recognizing that the future use of it is uncertain.

Tensions 4 and 5 are about the roles of time and agency. Cycles of city fabric, urban change, social change and climate change are interrelated, yet also follow different trajectories and wavelengths. The idea of socio-technical transitions as envisaged by Geels (2002), building on the multi-layer perspective of Rip and Kemp (1998), consists of changing interrelations between three levels: niche innovations, socio-technical regimes and socio-technical landscapes. The regime is the dominant set of arrangements, consisting of rules, roles, relations, values, norms, beliefs and shared innovation agendas and guiding principles. Niches, on the other hand, are smaller, less stable communities and organizational fields where there is less in the way of consensus at the broad scale, and more risk-taking and open experimentation, both entrepreneurially and within social innovation groups. The socio-technical landscape (Rip and Kemp 1998) is both the physical form and the social context of the framing conditions for the system, and includes the things that the actors in the system cannot influence in the short term as part of a niche or regime activity.

In city infrastructures, landscape factors might include climate change, global financial crises and post-industrial economic restructuring. The 'sustainable infrastructure niche' includes the policy entrepreneurs promoting alternative 'low-carbon' transport systems and building forms, the construction industry innovators designing and (re)building experimental low-carbon structures, and the inhabitants and users of such infrastructures. According to Geels and Schot (2007), changes in the socio-technical regime – the dominant system of carbon-intensive infrastructure – can occur when the landscape conditions challenge the regime and, at the same time, niches emerge as social networks grow, resulting in a regime change either by replacement or by accommodation of the niche within the changed regime.

Geels and Schot (2010) propose that transitions exhibit the following characteristics:

- evidence of co-evolution processes that require multiple changes in socio-technical configurations;
- multi-actor, coordinated processes and radical change from one system of configuration to another;
- long-term (40–50 year) time spans (noting that 'breakthroughs' may take as little as ten years, with 20–30 year lead-ins);
- macroscopic, recognizable at the organizational field level (e.g. rather than the firm level).

The reference to timescales here is informative, since it draws on historical socio-technical shifts studied by Geels and others, and implies that any shift towards sustainable infrastructure is unlikely to happen without a set of linked processes over a period of decades. Clearly, from the case studies in this section new infrastructures need considerable time to emerge; time that many feel is somewhat short, given the predictions of emissions and climate change by the IPCC (2007). Invariably they also involve social stakeholders in various ways, invoking the idea of *co-management* of infrastructures and their planning and design – a term that has increasingly been applied in the arena of natural resource management (Olsson *et al.* 2004).

There is a wide variety of challenges to be overcome before any cities can be considered as having 'sustainable' infrastructure. Even where this term is constrained to 'low-carbon' infrastructure, the places, ways and opportunities for greenhouse gas emissions in the future cannot be known, since they will arise out of complex relations between fabric, resources, social practices of inhabitants and patterns of movement. A more constructive vision of sustainable infrastructure is one where the future is uncertain, ongoing change and experimentation is accepted as good and inevitable and the inhabitants and users of the new or reconfigured urban fabric are involved as important actors. The value of the case studies reported in the following pages lies in their illustrations of positive models of possibility and engagement towards such a vision.

References

Anderson, W. (1996) 'Urban form, energy and the environment: A review of issues, evidence and policy', *Urban Studies 33*, 1: 7–36.

Geels, F.W. (2002) 'Technological transitions as evolutionary reconfiguration processes: A multi-level perspective and a case-study', *Research Policy 31*, 1257–1274.

Geels, F.W. and Schot, J. (2007) 'Typology of sociotechnical transition pathways', *Research Policy 36*, 3: 399–417.

Geels, F.W. and Schot, J. (2010) 'The dynamics of socio-technical transitions: A socio-technical perspective', in J. Grin, J. Rotmans and J. Schot (eds), *Transitions to Sustainable Development: New Directions in the Study of Long Term Transformative Change*, Abingdon: Routledge.

Giddens, A. (1984) *The Constitution of Society: Outline of the Theory of Structuration*, Cambridge: Polity Press.

Girardet, H. (2004) *Cities People Planet*, Chichester: Wiley-Academy.

IPCC (2007) *Mitigation of Climate Change*, Intergovernmental Panel on Climate Change.

Latour, B. (2005) *Reassembling the Social: An Introduction to Actor-Network-Theory*. Oxford: Oxford University Press.

Low, N., Gleeson, B., Green, R. and Radovic, D. (2005) *The Green City: Sustainable Homes, Sustainable Suburbs*, London: Routledge.

Munnell, A.H. (1990) 'How does public infrastructure affect regional economic performance?' *New England Economic Review* September/October: 11–32.

Newman, P. and Kenworthy, J. (1999) *Sustainability and Cities: Overcoming Automobile Dependence*, Washington, DC: Island Press.

O'Connor, K. and Healy, E. (2004) 'Rethinking suburban development in Australia: A Melbourne case study', *European Planning Studies* 12 1: 27–40.

Olsson, P., Folke, C. and Berkes, F. (2004) 'Adaptive co-management for building resilience in social-ecological systems', *Environmental Management* 34, 1: 75–90.

Rip, A. and Kemp, R. (1998) 'Technological change', in S. Rayner and E.L. Malone (eds), *Human Choice and Climate Change*, vol. 2, Columbus, Ohio: Battelle Press: 327–399.

Seitz, H. (2000) 'Infrastructure, industrial development and employment in cities: Theoretical aspects and empirical evidence', *International Regional Science Review* 23, 3: 259–280.

Shove, E., Watson, M., Hand, M. and Ingram, J. (2007) *The Design of Everyday Life*, Oxford: Berg.

Sustainable Drinking Water and Sanitation

Two Indian Cases

Shantha Sheela Nair

This chapter considers two cases of urban water management. The first is Chennai, the capital of the Indian state of Tamil Nadu, one of the country's four big metropolises. It has a population of over 5.6 million and has been infamous for its acute scarcity of drinking water and huge unsustainable systems, which relied on tankers and pipelines to transport drinking water long distances. The city exploited the groundwater under it, and its neighbours' groundwater too. The other case is Musiri Town Panchayat, which had no town sanitation system, just a plethora of informal, inadequate and unhealthy ways of dispensing with human waste. Besides lacking funds, the town faced environmental difficulties in integrating conventional sanitation systems.

The need for *in situ* solutions at affordable costs, and more importantly sustainable solutions, led Chennai to harvest rainwater from rooftops and recharge rainwater into groundwater aquifers. This proved more lasting, wholesome, sustainable and environment-friendly. Thus this chapter explores a potable water-supply model for large urban cities to consider. It shows the significance of active citizens' participation in a wholly green-centric paradigm moving from water scarcity to water security. The case of Musiri Town Panchayat involved convincing householders to accept using waterless toilets and teaching the community how to use them appropriately.

Many waste management systems – especially waterborne sewerage systems, which were hailed as the public-health miracle of the industrial revolution – are no longer sustainable either ecologically or economically in burgeoning cities, especially of the developing world. With greater knowledge of ecological principles and the understanding that urban waste should not follow 'put out of sight' or 'flush and forget' systems, human waste management has assumed a strong significance in urban planning. This chapter discusses two Indian cases of meeting basic human waste needs in the face of distinct ecological challenges, Chennai and Musiri. Note that the Chennai City and Metrowater (Chennai) websites referred to at the end are the sources for all the statistical and other material.

Chennai: harvesting rainwater and groundwater recharge

All over the world metropolitan water supply system managers have valued using more water per capita from increasingly distant sources, leading to crises. Ironically, the inefficient design of such systems without regard to urban resources and constraints has aggravated drought–flood cycles. Harnessing rainwater and floodwater using urban space as a catchment is a striking example of environmentally sustainable service provision. A unitary drought-proofing flood-mitigation plan is a dream given current urban nightmares; the first tale, of Chennai, is one of water scarcity to water security.

Chennai, a small fishing hamlet on the Bay of Bengal in the seventeenth century, was developed by the British East India Company into a trading post known as Madras. Recently restored its original name, Chennai is the fourth largest metropolis and capital of Tamil Nadu, the southernmost state of India. It spreads over 76 km² of extremely flat coastal plains. The Kosathalaiyar, Cooum and Adyar rivers criss-cross the city and empty into the Bay of Bengal. Buckingham Canal, a large waterway, runs north–south. The population was estimated to be over 5.6 million in 2009. Chennai has an average annual rainfall of around 1250 mm, with more than 75 per cent falling during October–December.

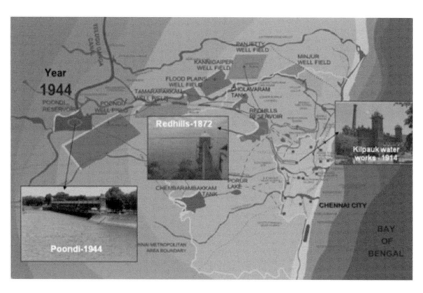

9.1
Sources of drinking water for Chennai city

Until about 1870, the people of Madras had depended on shallow household wells and on public wells and neighbourhood tanks. An organized system began in 1872 and formed the nucleus of Chennai's civic surface water supply system to this day. The civic authorities followed the principle of developed world countries by maintaining water supply at per capita levels. More than a century later, with several augmentation measures combining both surface and groundwater, in 2000 the supply was around 350 megalitres per day for a population of nearly five million.

However, in a bad monsoon year, even 200 megalitres per day proved difficult to supply. Averaged out, drinking-water sources consisted half of surface water and half of groundwater. However, in normal monsoon years, 80 per cent came from surface-water reservoirs and 20 per cent from groundwater reserves. In bad monsoon years, all drinking water came from groundwater as lakes went dry and surface water could not be used.

The increasing drinking-water crisis in the growing city led to master plans to access water from rivers, which required interstate negotiations and agreements, and obtaining water through canals or pipes running up to 200–300 km. A rising demand for water and ever-decreasing per capita availability led to excessive dependence on groundwater by private enterprises, individuals, and households and the civic authorities.

As mining and selling water increased alarmingly, groundwater aquifers became saline and fresh-water aquifers became depleted. Overdependence on groundwater and its excessive withdrawal led to the intrusion of sea water in the north-eastern coastal belt: an ingress only 3 km inshore in 1969 increased to 7 km in 1983 and up to 9 km in 1987. With diminishing water quality, private water vendors started 'mining' water from the southern coastal aquifer. Groundwater levels under the city fell and brackish water appeared in some localities that had had good quality groundwater. The seriousness of the problem was obvious when Chennai witnessed acute droughts in 1983, 1987, 1993 and again from 2001 through to mid-2004. Recurring droughts, almost every alternate year, meant considering the draconian measure of evacuating urban areas due to water scarcity.

The gravity of the water crisis prompted the Chennai Metropolitan Water Supply and Sewerage Board to revise its master plan to manage its water supply systems more sustainably. Besides augmenting drinking water by identifying distant surface sources, unique features of the plan involved regulating groundwater and conserving water through decentralized, *in situ*, affordable and sustainable solutions. The state and city legislated to prevent uncontrolled commercial mining and over-extraction of groundwater. The Government of Tamil Nadu introduced the Chennai Metropolitan Area Ground Water Regulation Act in 1987, amending it in 2002.

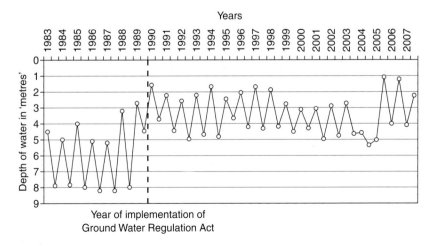

9.2
Changes in groundwater levels for Chennai (1983–2007)

Source: Sheela Nair

The city started wastewater recycling for individual and non-potable uses. The legislative and water-diversion measures contributed to improvements in normal years. However, in droughts both individual citizens and the civic body still depended on groundwater. As droughts were widespread, even water supplies from distant sources became unreliable, had to be shared and, in crises, were invariably retained by upper riparian populations. Persistent conflict forced the authorities to find better, internal, solutions.

The answer was tapping the potential of the almost 1250 mm rainfall which the city received in normal years but which fell in a short period of four months, invariably leading to inundation and floods, disrupting regular water supplies and sewerage systems. Due to its flat topography, floods took days to recede. Drainage was impeded further throughout monsoons by rising tides and high sea levels. Tapping this rainfall could augment drinking-water supplies and be used to charge the groundwater aquifer.

Small efforts were made to make rooftop rainwater harvesting mandatory in building rules in the metropolitan development authority's town planning requirements. In 1994 rainwater harvesting systems were mandated for permission to build multi-storey and special buildings. In 2000, such systems became mandatory in all buildings applying for new water and sewerage connections. But they received a very lukewarm response and were limited to large, newly constructed buildings. In 2003 systems to harvest rainwater were made compulsory in all buildings. The state legislature amended municipal and local laws giving owners one year from the date of notification to provide a system in every building.

The rainwater harvesting systems so promoted had three aims: to collect water from urban roofs; to filter water so harvested for consumption through pre-existing sumps; and to encourage appropriate filtering of excess water and run-off (e.g. from streets) for charging into the ground and the prolific urban wells, both open and deep-bore.

With the decentralized availability of drinking water, the paradigm shifted from a system wholly controlled by engineers and the Chennai Metropolitan Water Supply and Sewerage Board to a level of co-management. Households' accessing simple water supply systems was an innovative intervention in drinking-water management, while authorities maintained large professionally controlled and formal water supply systems.

The success of these measures depended on unrelated but concerted actions implementing the process 'in letter, spirit and functionality of the law'. A major step involved citizens' groups and print and electronic media, in an intense awareness programme to demystify the harvesting of rainwater and argue for its water quality and sustainability. Technical data were provided to residents' associations, civic groups and decentralized civic units. Rainwater harvesting models and rain collection centres were developed in various localities.

Further awareness and information were promoted through government and civic bodies undertaking the harvesting of rainwater from their buildings. Politically important persons, including the governor and chief minister of the state, went public on the benefits they received from adopting rainwater harvesting systems, which had an instant appeal to the common person. Celebrities, including cricketers, musicians and film stars, were actively involved in the campaign too. The campaign was strengthened by a discreet but effective message that non-adoption was punishable.

Rainwater harvesting enhanced the availability of safe and hygienic drinking water and became an important, novel urban feature. Besides meeting the gap in demand and supply, the city saves 300–400 million rupees annually. Households save on water charges to the water agency during monsoons and to private suppliers at other times.

Rainwater harvesting in thatched roof

Rainwater harvesting in sloped roof

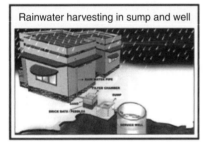

Rainwater harvesting in sump and well

Rainwater harvesting in multi-storied building

9.3
Four examples of rainwater harvesting systems

Source: Sheela Nair

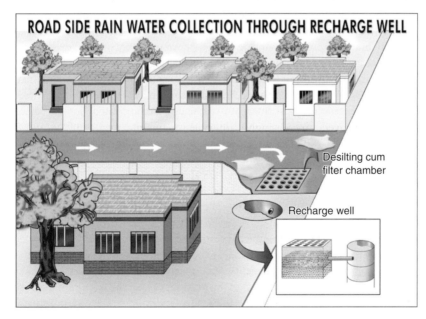

ROAD SIDE RAIN WATER COLLECTION THROUGH RECHARGE WELL

Desilting cum filter chamber

Recharge well

9.4
Collecting street rainwater to recharge wells

Source: Sheela Nair

Shantha Sheela Nair

The low-lying flood-prone areas became a source of water instead of the usual scourge after a downpour. Floodwaters were guided into aquifers through simple filters. The entire programme had drought-proofing and flood-mitigation features. There has been a perceptible decrease in sea-water ingress. Environmentalists and green groups ensure that these 2003 reforms are retained and functional for every monsoon.

The design paradigm adopted by Chennai – decentralized water supply systems for more conservative, more personalized water supply management systems to suit the household and the community – has led not only to less wastage of water but also in yet to be calculated savings in energy otherwise needed for water and sewage treatment. Decentralized water collection and usage is more democratic as well as more ecologically sustainable than conventional centralized water supply systems.

Rainwater harvesting gave Chennai an alternative to establishing desalination plants. Providing such services with people's participation is a model for all large urban cities to consider in the planning and managing of their drinking water. Chennai serves as a precedent and model for other similarly challenged cities. The experiences of Chennai and the measures taken are typical of responses to a crisis. A city that was infamous for its acute scarcity of drinking water and exploitation of groundwater is moving towards water security achieved by application of affordable and environmentally sustainable solutions created *in situ* and with social benefits.

Case of Musiri Town Panchayat: *in situ* waste management

Unlike Chennai, the small municipality of Musri Town Panchayat, in Tamil Nadu, had plentiful water but no sewerage system because of problems selecting an appropriate one. However, revolution in a small town was more feasible. It involved accepting waterless toilets. Thus a decentralized urban waste disposal system was introduced and proved less costly and more environmentally friendly than conventional models.

Traditionally, urban sanitation models depended on large volumes of water. A typical city sewerage system pumped solid and liquid human waste into massive slurries, which were transported miles into rural hinterlands for treatment and disposal. This was costly and risked ecological disaster as untreated and partially treated sewage polluted water bodies and rivers. River cleaning proved increasingly unviable economically and untenable ecologically. Meanwhile urban toilet users literally flush and forget.

The Musiri population of 35 000 spreads over 15.6 km^2. Of 6200-odd households, around 3500 have septic tank latrines, 1200 leach pit latrines and the rest use community latrines or the surrounding countryside. Situated on the banks of the river Cauvery, the town has a unique topography of criss-crossing natural drains, irrigation channels and a high water-table due to its proximity to the river. Open drains fed into various irrigation channels, groundwater was close to the surface and faecal matter leached from pit toilets, overflowing and polluting groundwater and well water.

Musiri had enough water but could not afford a conventional sewerage system so willingly entered a partnership to implement an ecologically safe sanitation system. *In situ* treatment of waste had found favour in neighbouring rural areas when the elected town body, supported by a local non-government organization, SCOPE, and the state government, decided to pilot models of urine diversion and *in situ* drying of human faecal matter.

To translate this vision into action, the Musiri Town Panchayat (supported by the state government) together with SCOPE conducted a baseline survey to assess the current sanitation infrastructure facilities and people's level of awareness of health and hygiene. The survey showed that most had leach pit toilets and septic tanks, which polluted the groundwater and river Cauvery. As most land was agriculturally fertile, there was no wasteland available for large sewage disposal systems. The existing community toilets were dilapidated and many people defecated in the open.

The underlying pressure was fear that any 'acceptable' system that used water would contaminate the town's sources, including drinking water, hence general acceptance of the concept of a waterless system. The first challenge was to convince townsfolk to adopt a waterless system for faecal disposal while using water for after-defecation washing. The second challenge was to show the potential for re-use of urine and faeces in an ecologically safe and economically wise manner. The third challenge was to upscale from household to community models by designing and setting up public latrines and urinals with their many inherent hygiene and maintenance issues.

The consortium decided to construct household and community toilets based on the EcoSan model. To address the problems of disposal of solid and liquid waste, an integrated decentralized wastewater treatment system and solid and liquid waste management plans were also undertaken. Ecological sanitation ('EcoSan') is an approach that contains, sanitizes and recovers human excreta for use in soil systems to enhance agricultural production. EcoSan involves soil-based composting toilets in shallow reinforced pits for the faecal matter and urine diversion with or without storage vaults. Some designs also mix the wash water with urine. 'Closing the loop' on sanitation and water is shortened and waste re-used through monetary incentives. EcoSan models protect water resources through reducing consumption and contamination. Recovery of nutrients for use to improve agricultural yields also minimizes water-based infections.

The first household-centred EcoSan toilet model designed in Musiri was based on the original developed in Thanneerpandal village training centre in 2002. In the two-in-one model, urine and washing water were collected in a mud pot outside the toilet. Faeces were collected in a chamber for composting. The successful demonstration model motivated Mrs Mangalathammal of Kaliyapalayam village to construct the first EcoSan private household toilet and, in turn, some 170 families from the nearby villages of Kaliyapalayam and Seventhilingapuram constructed similar household toilets.

Based on feedback from the local community, the EcoSan was redesigned into a three-in-one model in tune with the prevalent Indian practice of a drop hole in the middle, washbowl in the rear and urine bowl in the front. The washing water, urine and faeces do not mix and are collected separately. Nutrients recovered from urine and washing water collected in the toilet are used for irrigating vegetables and flowers in household kitchen gardens and community farms.

9.5
A newly built EcoSan toilet in Musiri

Source: Sheela Nair

As the EcoSan model and its usage and maintenance practices were novel and unfamiliar, an intensive awareness programme was organized for users and elected representatives. The purposes of the different pipes, twin chambers and features of the squatting slab were laboriously explained to ensure ease and comfort of use. Dos and don'ts were painted on the toilet's inner walls in the local language. All members of the community, especially women's self-help groups, were actively involved in planning, designing, constructing, operating and maintenance of the EcoSan toilets.

Intensive training for masons was undertaken. A training module and manual on EcoSan community compost toilets (ECCT) was developed and their operation and maintenance learned by self-help-group members and town sanitary workers. To ensure sustainability in the post-construction phase, SCOPE undertook regular monitoring and following up with the community. Families were approached to assess problems of use, availability of biomass/ash/sand to cover the faecal matter, the correct uncontaminated diversion of urine for best results and the filtering of washing water through simple systems before use for growing flowers or vegetables. Solutions were meticulously followed up. SCOPE even organized a beauty contest for EcoSan toilets to promote their use, maintenance and awareness.

The baseline survey had found that two community toilets were dilapidated, leading a large number of people to defecate in the open and on the riverbed. It was decided to construct an ECCT in Saliyar Street, perhaps

9.6
An EcoSan toilet under
construction in Musiri

Source: Sheela Nair

India's first. Again there was meticulous designing of the size and number of chambers, pipes conveying water and urine to the filter bed and urine collection tank, the pans and notices on use practices, along with the concept of EcoSan. The project had tremendous support from the highest district officials, with the foundations laid by the District Collector of Tiruchi in the presence of the potential users and residents of Saliyar Street.

The ECCT was built with bricks, with a 90-square-foot compost chamber. The redesigned three-in-one pan was used, faeces being collected and dehydrated in the chamber and urine collected in a tank outside. The washing water directly drained into a filter bed with banana trees. The attractive toilet had walls and floors of glazed and ceramic tiles for easy maintenance. There was no water tap or connection inside the toilet. A common water tap had provision for a small 4-litre bucket and a mug for body washing. The ash for sprinkling on faecal matter was stored in a bucket within the cubicle. This first ECCT had a block for men and another for women, each with seven cubicles, and mounted EcoSan pans for the physically challenged and senior citizens.

Learning from these experiences, a second ECCT with additional facilities and features was built at Parislathuri Road. A system for disposing of sanitary napkins and an incinerator was added in the women's block. A glass slit was added in the compost chamber for demonstration purposes, to observe dehydration. To prevent direct exposure to sunlight and crystal formation, the washing water and urine diversion pipes were given a higher gradient and concealed. Handles were added to the lid of the drop hole.

Both ECCTs provided clean, environmentally friendly and cheap community toilet facilities with the bonus of composted faeces and urine for use by farmers on fields. In 2009 it is estimated that around 1000 people use the toilet daily (70 per cent women). The facility also provided opportunities for research on using recycled human waste as organic nutrient for agriculture. Excellent agricultural returns from the fresh urine and the dried faecal matter after six to twelve months prompted civic authorities to consider offering a payment to users of EcoSan public toilets. SCOPE, duly supported by state officials, introduced the first incentive of its kind in the world at the Saliyar Street ECCT, aptly calling it the 'Use and Get Paid Toilet' instead of 'Pay and Use Toilet'. This New Year gift to the community was inaugurated on 15 January 2008 and meant paying toilet users 0.1 rupee per visit. This demonstrated the waste's economic value if properly recovered and used as a nutrient. Many users were a little embarrassed initially but everybody loved the idea!

Subsequently, a memorandum of understanding was signed with the Tamil Nadu Agricultural University of Coimbatore to scientifically study the effects of using liquid urine and dehydrated, composted human faeces on crops. Laboratory tests on dehydrated faeces have shown that pathogen and E. coli presence was nil, but more studies are being done to establish credible standards for safe agricultural practices. This approach can be broadened to cover all organic material generated by households, such as kitchen and food wastes, which can be sorted and composted into recyclable material rather than mixing with solid waste and dumping.

The Musiri town model has inspired several such efforts in India, mostly in peri-urban and rural areas. Adoption in the tsunami-affected eastern coastal area is very significant. High saline water-tables in such areas have rendered conventional systems ecologically unsafe. In both public and private urban domains the Musiri waterless loo offers a totally new concept in designs for urban sewerage.

9.7
Saliyar Street ECCT, Musiri Town Panchayat, the 'Use and Get Paid Toilet...'

Source: Sheela Nair

The challenge for urban social planners

There is a significant challenge for urban local planners, architects and builders to consider more economic and ecologically safe urban sanitation alternatives, such as introducing low-water or no-water human waste disposal systems, including vacuum flush toilets and separate piping systems for human waste collection. The most important beneficiary would be water. More uncontaminated fresh water would be available and the untold miseries of waterborne diseases caused by excessive use of water for transporting and disposing human waste could be put safely to rest.

Urban designers must take account of the spatial planning and engineering design implications of implementing innovative water supply and sanitation systems that will remain sustainable despite climate change and irrespective of both cost and whether the cities or towns are in the developed or developing worlds. Environmental costs and benefits must be incorporated into design. The time has come for urban planners, architects and engineers to create and share new designs that are cost and resource effective, ecologically safe and environmentally sustainable into the next millennium.

References

Chennai City website. Online: www.chennai.tn.nic.in.
Metrowater (Chennai) website. Online: www.chennaimetowater.tn.nic.in.

Sustainable Savannah

Scott Boylston

While the city of Savannah, Georgia, cannot presently be considered sustainable in any true sense of the word, a complex interplay of geography, history, industry and human proclivity has placed the city at an intriguing crossroads that promises to lead to a very different attitude towards nature, social relations and economic prosperity. This chapter discusses familiar and urgent challenges facing the city and examples of ways that the difficulties associated with water supply, overuse of cars and unaffordable housing are being addressed.

Challenges: water, transport and housing

With a population of around 130 000, Savannah still struggles with some historical, social and industrial ills. It is in Chatham County, which is the most industrialized county in the State of Georgia due to the presence of America's fastest growing and fourth largest container port. While the city sits atop one of the country's largest fresh-water aquifers, high water use throughout the south-east, combined with an historic drought, has threatened this source of fresh water with contamination from encroaching sea water. A proposed and controversial deepening of the Savannah River to accommodate larger commercial vessels threatens to reduce oxygen to dangerous levels in the river and exacerbate the saltwater intrusion. Meanwhile, a recent proposal to increase water intake at an upriver nuclear power plant and federal nuclear weapons site by twelve million gallons a day threatens similar encroachment of fresh water available from the Savannah River. Legal discharges from this same site have made the lower Savannah River the most tritium-contaminated environment in the United States (Kronquest 2008).

In the tri-county metropolitan area, home to 320 000 residents, 73 per cent of commuters drive cars alone, being commensurate with the national average, which speaks volumes about America's major hurdle to moving towards sustainability. Despite steadily increasing advocacy from pedestrian and bicycle activists, only 5 per cent use public transportation, while 4 per cent cycle or walk, and 3 per cent work at home. The average commute time, twenty-four minutes, is lower than the national average. Population density, at approximately 1700 per square mile, has recently begun increasing after a slight decline through the 1980s and 1990s.

The rising cost of housing in downtown Savannah over the last decade has threatened to force lower-income households into more remote locations where mass-transit systems are not equipped to match their needs. While the unemployment rate is lower than the national average, the poverty level within the city limits is 22 per cent. Subsidized inner-city housing provides about 13 000 units for low-income families.

Many low-income, minority neighbourhoods have had to contend with lead-poisoning problems within the older, non-renovated homes in Savannah, which is especially ironic since it is the historic nature of Savannah's city-wide architecture that has garnered so much tourist attention. Thanks to the efforts of local non-profit organizations like Harambee House, federal grant money has been made available beginning in 2008 to test over 12 000 children who live in these older homes, and to devise strategies to eliminate lead exposures, once and for all.

The emergent structures project

Since 2005, several affordable housing developments have been completed that are within reach of downtown via mass transit, and slated for completion in 2011 is a 300-unit neighbourhood that will be built to Southface Institutes' Earthcraft standards of sustainability, which is similar to the green building rating system, Leadership in Energy and Environmental Design (LEED). News of the amount of building materials scheduled for landfill as a result of this redevelopment was the impetus for a large-scale reclamation initiative being executed by a diverse array of designers, artisans, architects and regular citizens. The Emergent Structures Project was conceived as a means not only of harvesting materials resulting from the deconstruction of 210 Second World War-era houses, but also of nurturing community relations in the process. While the project's principal objective was to save and renovate all of the buildings rather than tear them down, the city was already set to erect new housing.

Through a broad collaboration of non-profit organizations, government agencies, local corporations and social activists, along with historic preservation, industrial design, design management, design for sustainability and architecture students from Savannah College of Art and Design (SCAD), the building materials will be harvested over the course of 2010 and early 2011, and given away to people who can make use of them. As the salvage and distribution of the materials proceeds, site visits, interviews and photographic documentation of individual projects will be conducted to record the creation of new objects from old materials. A gallery show and photographic exhibition of objects and structures that have been created with the salvaged materials will be held in conjunction with a symposium focusing on this community-wide endeavour to reduce material waste, to reinvent the meaning of material adaptation and to develop best practices and inspiring case studies.

Other larger-scale projects that involve the hauling and renovation of entire buildings have also developed, including the creation of an eco-village to mark the centennial celebration of the Girl Scouts of America, and a campus for a Montessori charter school. While much of what is presented in this chapter represents relatively standard fare in way of sustainable measures for cities, the Emergent Structures Project perhaps best exemplifies the innovative collaborative energy that is increasingly present in Savannah. The city continues to attract creative problem solvers interested in transforming the social environs through grassroots innovative collaborations.

Starland Design District

The Starland Design District is situated due south of the Historic District. For half a century this area was a no man's land that the well-heeled of Savannah closed their eyes to as they passed through on their way between work and the car-centric suburbs. By the late 1990s, 50 per cent of the houses were

10.1
Starland Lofts

Photo: Scott Boylston

abandoned, condemned or demolished. Greg Jacobs and John Deaderick, graduates of SCAD's Historic Preservation Department, set out to save the buildings that constituted the original Starland Dairy complex in 1999, hoping to turn the vacant industrial structures into studios for local artists. They have since renovated countless dilapidated houses with an on-site material recycling rate of over 85 per cent. In their construction of the Starland Lofts (Figure 10.1), a thirty-two-unit Gold LEED condominium in the neighbourhood, they pioneered a post-industrial, high-density cement mixture in partnership with a bridge girder company just seven miles away that eliminated the need for any other wall material, including moisture wraps, interior treatments and insulation. The ongoing rebirth of this area has attracted a diverse population back into the neighbourhood, and jump-started many small and minority-owned businesses.

A mixed-use development project under way just east of the Historic District will significantly expand the human-scaled ambitions of Savannah's original master plan that has played such an important part in saving the city from the autocentric debacle of mid-twentieth-century America. This development, residing on fifty-four riverfront acres of what had long been industrial lots will reserve 40 per cent of its land for public space, including a 2000-foot extension of the River Street walk, and six new public squares.

In 2007, approximately 450 000 cubic feet of soil was transported to the site to level the land. The soil was made available through another project less than a mile away that reintroduced one of the six original city squares into the city fabric, undoing a less visionary decision in the 1950s to sacrifice the open public space for the sake of a three-storey parking garage. Ellis Square, the newly reborn city square, sits atop an underground parking garage, and it was the excavation of that space that provided the earth for the new development's foundation.

LEED projects

Due west of the Historic District, Sustainable Fellwood broke ground in the summer of 2008, and phase one was completed in early 2009 (Figure 10.2). The 27-acre site will contain 220 public housing units, 100 senior housing units and ten single-family homes. Sustainable Fellwood is a part of the LEED Neighborhood Development pilot programme, as well as an Earthcraft Community. This venture, located on the site of Georgia's first public housing project, is guided by the Smart Growth Networks' principles for 'diverse, walkable, distinctive communities'.

Other sustainable development projects of note include the LEED-certified Frogtown condominiums (Figure 10.3) and the country's first LEED-certified retail centre (mall). Some of the more notable LEED-certified buildings built in Chatham County include the world's first LEED-certified McDonald's, a 50 000-square-foot public library, a 52 000-square-foot private elementary school, and the 11 000-square-foot Marine and Coastal Science Research and Instructional Center. In the last two years alone, the city has doubled the number of LEED-certified accredited professionals, and tripled its number of LEED-certified buildings.

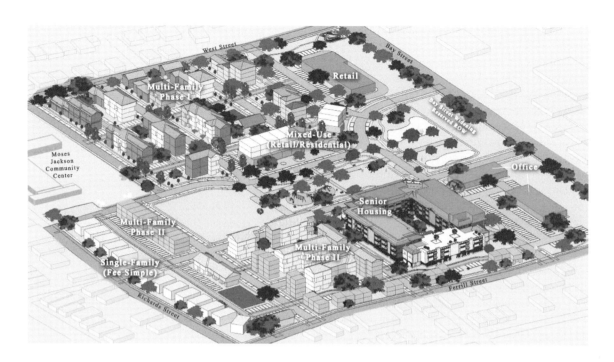

10.2
Fellwood rendering

Source: Developer Melaver, Inc.,
Architects Lott Barber

10.3
Frogtown

Photo: Scott Boylston

One of the most impressive contributions to the city's sustainable re-use of historic buildings, however, has been made by a single institution. In 1979, SCAD's first classes were held in the *c.*1892 Savannah Volunteer Guard Armory (Figure 10.4). The building's extensive renovation received a preservation award from the Savannah Historic Foundation the same year the school opened. Since this first encounter with historic preservation, SCAD has engaged in an unprecedented journey of adaptive re-use of eighteenth- and nineteenth-century buildings in the Historic District of Savannah, resulting in awards from the National Trust for Historic Preservation, the International Art Deco Society, the American Institute of Architects, the International Downtown Association, the Victorian Society of America and many other organizations (Pinkerton and Burke 2004: 8). Most recently, the college was awarded the 2009 Sustainability Award from Fashion Group International for its continued urban renewal and adaptive re-use of historic properties.

From the initial restoration of the armoury in 1979 to the two million square feet of integrated campus building space around the city today (Figure 10.5), SCAD has been engaged in a respectful re-adaptation of historic buildings throughout the city. This preservation-minded adaptive re-use, coupled with over $120 million a year in annual labour income (at all income levels) and a steady output of creative young minds, has made an indelible mark on Savannah's trend towards that of a sustainable city of the twenty-first century. A train storage shed built in 1856 will soon house the college's art museum, an institution that possesses one of the country's most expansive collections of African American art as well as the Walter O. Evans Center for African American Studies, and LEED certification will be sought. The renovation of a previously derelict public school built in 1922 is situated at the centre of the recently reinvigorated Starland Design District, and is registered

10.4
Poetter Hall

Photo: Scott Boylston

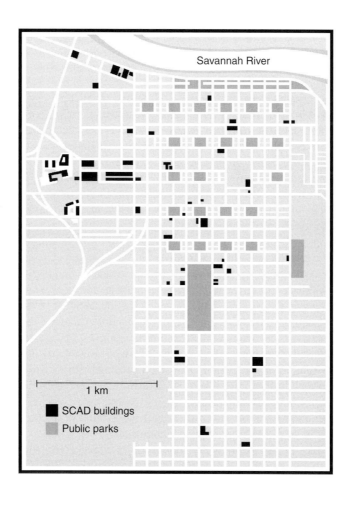

10.5
SCAD buildings in Savannah

Source: Scott Boylston

for LEED accreditation. Along with restoring so many historical buildings for its own use, SCAD purchased Savannah's first public black school, the Beach Institute, in 1986 and, after renovating the building, donated it to the King-Tisdell Cottage Foundation, a non-profit organization committed to preserving African American history.

The City of Savannah is a member of the International Council for Local Environmental Initiatives, and completed an all-encompassing emissions inventory in early 2009. The city has also become the first municipality in Georgia to receive designation as a Bronze Level Partner by the Partnership for a Sustainable Georgia, a state-sponsored voluntary environmental leadership initiative. It has committed to meeting or exceeding LEED standards for any new civic building, is well on its way to a goal of providing 50 per cent tree canopy throughout the city, is presently in the process of a city-wide footpath and bicycle route redevelopment programme, has converted over 7000 traffic lights to LED signals and has installed a new, ultra-efficient information technology data centre. Leaks in its water conveyance system have been reduced from an average of seven per mile to less than one per mile over the last few years, and another ongoing initiative has distributed over

3500 free low-flow toilets to low-income residents. Other initiatives include the creation of a zero-waste zone, a solar-powered recycling and education centre and several Recovery Act programmes for green-jobs training and transportation using green energy.

Along with purchasing eleven hybrid buses, Chatham Area Transit has retrofitted a 1925 trolley (tram) from Melbourne, Australia, with a hybrid electric–biodiesel engine that runs on waste vegetable oil from local restaurants. This trolley, which eliminates the need for vehicle use in this high-density tourist area, runs along the same stretch that a titanium tetrachloride freight train ran along only thirty years earlier. And plans are in motion to extend the trolley system to the intermodal public transportation centre in development, and then further along the western flank of the city so that it can better serve the local workforce.

This extension will coincide with the revitalization of Savannah's primary western corridor, Martin Luther King Jr Drive. The first paved street in Savannah, and once the thriving centre of the African American and Jewish communities in Savannah, this street was decimated during the 1960s by an ill-planned urban renewal programme that destroyed the urban fabric of the city for the sake of 'superblock' housing projects. Various projects along this corridor are already under way with the aforementioned Frogtown condominiums, developed by the same individuals who revitalized the Starland District, already complete. Walter O. Evans, a Savannah-born African American and the philanthropist after whom SCAD's aforementioned Center for African American Studies is named, recently purchased three blocks of dilapidated buildings and vacant lots along MLK Boulevard, and is developing a mixed-used, mixed-income, LEED-certified neighbourhood.

Chatham County is also committed to substantial engagement with sustainability initiatives, passing a resolution that charged the Chatham Environmental Forum (CEF) with devising a comprehensive plan to make Chatham County the 'greenest county in Georgia'. The resulting CEF Green Plan was complete by the end of 2008 and includes clear action points in seven categories: greenspace/land use, solid waste, water management, climate change, energy, creative infrastructure and transportation. Not only has the county government initiated the plan, but the City of Savannah has officially recognized the plan as their own, resulting in a rare collaboration between local government entities.

Other initiatives worth mention include the state-owned, non-profit Herty Foundation and its Advanced Materials Development Center, which has been developing commercial applications for pine tree by-products for seventy years. With a $76 million US Department of Energy grant, and historical access to the plentiful by-products of the region's pine forest harvesting operations, Herty aims to produce 100 million gallons of cellulosic ethanol a year once the plant – the first of its kind in America – is running at full capacity. Because the raw material for this biofuel is agricultural waste, its production has none of the negative impacts that first-generation biofuels like corn ethanol have had on global food sources.

Conclusion

The foundations of Savannah's sustainable promise can be said to lie in its original pattern of organization: General Oglethorpe's original urban plan that situated public squares evenly through the city grid, which is still in use today. Its natural beauty, human scale and historic integrity have built on this foundation, and act as magnetic invitations to those who think progressively and act creatively. A holistic, environmentally, culturally and socially equitable mind-set has emerged as the city's operating framework, and the growing signs of this trend attract more individuals who embrace such a philosophical stance. In an era where positive role models for sustainable living are badly needed, it just might be that this small town in the American South has some lessons to offer.

References

Kronquest, S. (2008) 'Drink or Swim?' *The South Magazine* 13 (February/March): 130–134.

Pinkerton, C.C. and Burke, M. (2004) *The Savannah College of Art and Design: Restoration of an Architectural Heritage*, Chicago: Arcadia Books.

Ecopolis

Small Steps towards Urbanism as a Living System

Paul Downton

The term 'sustainable' is on everyone's lips and features in almost every design proposal that wants to lay claim to contemporary relevance. The latest architecture and city plans are now almost invariably described as 'green'. Yet the disciplines of architecture and planning lack an epistemological framework to define exactly how their practitioners are supposed to deliver sustainability and 'green-ness'. There are plenty of articles, manuals and design courses that describe techniques and technologies for achieving sustainable solutions, but there appears to be no overarching theory that offers a rigorous means of assessing whether those solutions really work. We lack a generally agreed-upon understanding of what that 'work' really means. Too often, the organization of knowledge that is typical of architecture and planning offers superficial analyses and syntheses when addressing the issue of sustainability, while the natural world is regarded as an inanimate backdrop to design rather than a living system that encompasses it. Efforts to understand the built environment in properly ecological terms is muddled by the kind of revisionism that sees an architectural culture hero like Le Corbusier, who celebrated the city as 'an assault on nature', as a prototypical 'green' architect (Farmer and Richardson 1996).

A particularly impressive effort to get to grips with this is provided by Birkeland (2008), who talks about 'positive development' and going beyond the sustainability paradigm to create net positive ecological and social gains. To some extent this approach is paralleled in my own work in developing the concept of 'ecopolis', in which the ultimate purpose of architecture and city-making is to enhance the functioning of ecological processes in order to better sustain life in a way that enables human society and culture to thrive and survive.

Fundamental to this approach is the view of urbanism as an ecological system and the idea that the built environment has to be conceived and consciously created as a living system.

I have proposed that a cybernetic approach offers the basis of an epistemology that might make a coherent relationship between architecture,

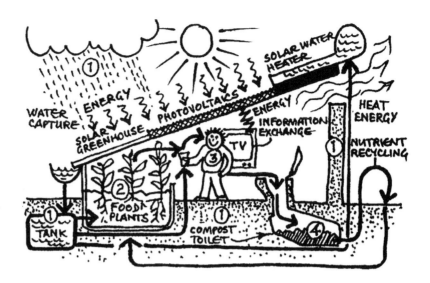

11.1

Ecological building. Key: (1) Abiotic substances: basic elements and compounds of the environment; (2) Producers: autotrophic (food-making) organisms; (3) Consumers/ macroconsumers: heterotrophic (food-eating) organisms; (4) Scomposters/microconsumers: heterotrophic organisms, chiefly bacteria and fungi, that reduce 'waste' to simple substances useable by producers

Source: Paul Downton

city-making, ecology and the life sciences, and is built around ideas of adaptive response and connectivity across and through traditional disciplines of knowledge and the fluid forms of popular culture. Architectural and planning ideas need to be embedded in an ecological framework to provide the basis for integrating cumulative knowledge that is presently dispersed. An example of that dispersed knowledge is the critical approach to regionalism, which offers a way to consciously integrate the making of buildings with the ecology of their cultural and physical landscape (Downton 2009: 15).

The literature and research devoted to what we might recognize as 'urban ecology' is diverse and distributed across time and the planet, from Geddes (1915) in the United Kingdom in the early twentieth century to Boyden *et al.* (1981) and Boyden (2004) in Australia, Douglas (1983) in the United Kingdom and Hough (1995) in the United States in more recent years. Powerful ideas about city-making, ecosystems, regionalism and architecture have been extant for decades. Nevertheless, even the later works have been pioneering and there is still very little quantified research into the performance of the built environment in ecological terms, i.e. in terms of its function as integral to the operation of living systems. To understand the world as a living system and be able to practise design in that context requires a system of knowledge that links design to the needs of individual humans, society and nature. Whether we look at individual buildings, social dynamics or the demands on environmental space, we find that urbanization is at the core of contemporary concerns.

Urbanization is the effective replacement of natural ecosystems by an artificial system (Dansereau 1957: 263). Humans have evolved to need shelter to the point that, unless specifically trained otherwise, modern humans cannot survive without it. The most so-called primitive human cultures construct environmental adjuncts to their bodies that modify the climate to make the function of their own bodies more efficient. Humans are essentially incapable of raising their young without constructing shelter for the purpose. Human settlement – that is, settling in place – is a precondition for the development of civilization. Yet we have a very poor record of assessing whether our building and city-making really works, although we know that most buildings perform poorly in terms of energy, water and resource use and that their manufacture damages natural ecosystems.

Our built environment is a manifestation of social behaviour. As social creatures who have always needed to live in groups to survive, our earliest makings of shelter were almost certainly done in a communal way, and from this we gained more control of the territory that supported us and provided food, water and the resources to make tools. In this lies the basis of the city. All of this is not only a consequence of consciousness. As Mumford reminds us, 'Even the technological complexity of the human town does not lack animal precedent', and, along with beavers and termites, from the beginning our efforts at colonizing territory brought about 'a deliberate re-moulding of the environment' (Mumford 1961: 6).

The purpose of cities has always been to control territory so that their populations could be fed, watered, clothed and protected from the elements and enemies. The culture of cities has developed in response to biophysical limits. Societies built with stone and featured it in their mythologies if it was plentiful and accessible, forest-bound cultures built with timber and venerated trees, maritime cultures developed in coastal regions. Control of territory involves managing resources for the long-term benefit of the city, but the ultimate response to resource shortages has invariably been to try to extend

11.2
Paper-wasps' nest: the wasps cannot procreate and survive without building these extensions of their physiology

Photo: Paul Downton

Paul Downton

the city's reach and expand its territory, and thus colonization began. The extent of collective control by our cities now extends over the whole Earth. Our problems with the ozone layer and climate change derive directly from urbanization, exacerbated by industrialization.

All living things have a life cycle. The assertion that cities behave as living systems, even organisms, can be substantiated by reference to definitions of life adopted in current life sciences, and particularly by the 'Gaian' hypotheses of James Lovelock and Lynn Margulis (1975) and Lovelock (1991). Cities possess discernible boundaries in space and time and have a life cycle. Employing organic analogies, Magnaghi (2005: 3) discusses human settlement in terms of living systems and organisms and identifies what he calls the *neo-ecosystem* as 'a living system apart from the two agents that generated it: human society and nature'. Cities are not merely simulacra of life, they exhibit enough of the characteristics of living organisms to be reasonably considered 'alive'. An inhabited city is a living system that possesses the characteristics of living organisms.

The 'city as organism' is a useful metaphor, but the 'city as ecosystem' is not a metaphor. It is an appropriate and scientifically defensible description. A city is a constructed device that integrates living and non-living components into a total living system that is a physiological extension of our species. It only lives when it is occupied, and it can die. Dead cities are studied by archaeologists, who can discern much about their once-living state from the condition and disposition of their carcasses. An analysis of their surrounding landscape tells much about the way cities lived and the impacts on their hinterlands.

A city is a system of living matter in which the most active component is people. 'Living matter embraces and reconstructs all the chemical processes of the biosphere ... Living matter is the greatest geological force, growing with time' (Vernadsky, quoted in Lapo 1982: 113). The processes of life capture, transport, refine and transform the minerals that make up the planet's substance, cycling matter from the lithosphere and atmosphere into and around the biosphere. Through biological activity, living organisms continually mine the planet for the substances essential to their existence. The scale of this activity is astonishing: 'the vegetational cover of our planet annually concentrates mineral matter in amounts comparable to most of the elements with their reserves in the lithosphere, accumulated there during millions of years of geological history' (Lapo 1982: 99). Human activity is a special case of biogeochemical activity, directed by organisms with some awareness of their impacts. Cities present concentrated examples of the transformative power of life and are our most advanced tools for terra-forming the world. As the current dominant drivers of biogeochemical action on the planet, we have greatly accelerated the movement of matter, particularly carbon, through the biosphere. And it is not only through what we might regard as conventional mining that we have extracted chemicals and cycled material through the biosphere but also through management and manipulation of organisms and organic processes, such as farming billions of head of cattle. As an integral part of the biosphere's operations, our species has increased the speed at which life reworks the world's geology. This accelerated rate of transformation of matter has been a direct consequence of our ability to think about what we do and to invent and create the means to do things that were not otherwise happening 'naturally'. Our ability to transform the world increased as a consequence of being able to think and put our thoughts into action, and the rate of transformation of the planet has risen in proportion to the growth of sentience in the biosphere.

In short, a city is not *like* a living system, it *is* a living system. Human culture is not *like* a force of nature, it *is* a force of nature. Working in a social and cultural framework, we have amplified our capacities as individual creatures and evolved the collective means to move mountains, dam rivers, level forests and reshape the planet. We have speeded up the processes of climate change and have accelerated environmental changes to the extent that other species have not been able to keep up. As Stephen Boyden (2004) reminds us, we are a force in nature, but we are also *of* nature. Our challenge, right now, is to understand how to use that force constructively rather than destructively. This is the role of the built environment. This is what being 'sustainable' or 'green' must be about.

Rees has argued that our highly consumptive cities now represent 'a new ecological reality' (Rees 1998: 3) in the context of an environmental crisis that results from deeply rooted cultural values (Rees 1998: 6). It is worth reflecting that those cultural values have allowed some responsiveness to the global environmental context (e.g. the Montreal Protocol 1987, the 1992 UN 'Earth Summit' and the Kyoto Protocol 1997). In the built environment manifestations of cultural responsiveness can be seen as climate-responsive, energy-efficient design has become more sophisticated (Szokolay 1987) and architects and urban professionals have realized the imperative to look beyond the impact of individual buildings (Szokolay 1989: 90).

Lovelock (1991: 50) describes an ecosystem as 'a stable self-perpetuating system, composed of living organisms and their non-living environment' and, in his view, 'a Gaian ecosystem sees the two components of the system, the living and the non-living, as two tightly coupled interactive forces, each one shaping and affecting the other'. There is a difference between the inhabited and uninhabited states of buildings and cities. While uninhabited, the abiotic components are 'at rest' in the form of art; when inhabited, the active state of the system presents the coming into being of the thing we call a 'building', or a 'city'. This distinction can clarify differences between conventional architecture, urban design and planning and their ecological counterparts. Ecological architecture is not simply solar panels, low-energy construction, etc., but only comes into existence when the architecture is occupied and 'alive'. Likewise, ecological cities are not made solely by storm-water recycling, renewable energy systems and so forth. Even more than architecture or buildings, cities depend on people to inhabit them to have a coherent existence. Buildings can be empty of people (as they typically are in magazine and promotional images) and still attract interest as art objects, but the 'dead' cities studied by archaeologists lack meaning without some knowledge of who lived in them.

The best writing about urbanism reflects this distinction. With its focus 'on ordinary days and the multitude of spaces that surround us', Gehl's influential *Life Between Buildings* (1987) is a good example, and Mumford's works are seminal in this regard. The idea that an occupied urban environment is different from an unoccupied urban environment reflects the difference between the *civitas* (the functional, cultural entity) and the *urbs* (the physical entity). Douglas (1983: 2) said, 'No biophysical study of the city can … be divorced from the ancient view of the city (*polis*) as a political conception.' Reducing the view of urban life to the single dimension of consumerism is a denial of its political reality, yet this is exactly what happens when buildings are seen only as isolated products and city planning processes neglect consideration of the realm of the *civitas*. Environmental concerns and urban management have long been inseparable. Douglas (1983: 2) demonstrates that 'political change or reorganization in cities is often prompted by the need for better management of such apparently mundane matters as water or transport'. Theorists like Bookchin (1995) maintain that social change can best be initiated and articulated through direct action in citizenship, rather than through centralized institutions. The reshaping of the *urbs* demanded by ecological concerns may be both a catalyst and a consequence of social change.

Just like termite mounds, buildings and cities are living systems only when they are occupied and populated. The conceptualization, design and operation of the built environment as a living system require that its occupants, users and citizens are understood as integral to it as the biotic components that literally enliven the system. The implications of this are profound. At the very least, it means that the design of 'communities' has to *involve* the community. The following case study outlines a South Australian experiment that used this approach to urban development.

11.3
Roof garden at Christie Walk: an artificial living system depending on, and supporting, its inhabitants and users

Photo: Paul Downton

Christie Walk: a small step

An adventurous spirit and willingness to experiment has paid off for the creators of Christie Walk, who have produced a rare community-driven project with applicability to sustainable urban developments worldwide (Farr 2008: 229).

Every demonstration project of urban and social change is a social experiment. Such projects are often conceived as microcosms of the larger whole that they seek to encourage. They are what I have termed 'urban fractals'. The 'ecopolis' proposition is that urban fractals are 'demonstration projects that provide a means to catalyse change' and further:

- Changes in the process of city-making can be catalysed by 'pieces of Ecopolis' developed as demonstration projects.
- A living system of human relationships that displays the essential characteristics of the larger culture of which it is a part can be thought of as a 'cultural fractal'.
- Cultural change can be catalysed by the creation of cultural fractals that display essential characteristics of the preferred cultural condition.
- An 'urban fractal' is a network that contains the essential characteristics of the larger network of the city. Each fractal will possess nodes, or centres, and patterns of connectivity that define its structure and organization, and it will exhibit characteristics of community associated with living processes. It is a particular type of cultural fractal (Downton 2009: 27).

Community energy

An attempt to create a partial fractal of this type, consciously working with the idea of creating a built environment that was conceived and operated as a living system, was made with the development of 'Christie Walk', in the middle of Adelaide, South Australia. 'Christie Walk has incorporated a variety of energy saving techniques, sustainable design principles, waste minimisation strategies accompanied by an emphasis on social cohesion and interaction, to make it a truly unique and innovative sustainable project' (Burke 2004: 24).

Christie Walk was started in 1999, completed and occupied by 2007. Situated on a 2000-m^2 site, it is designed to accommodate up to eighty people (400 per hectare) and on completion had a population of forty-two (210 per hectare). The site is close to Whitmore Square at the centre of the most mixed-use, least wealthy, least culturally self-conscious and perhaps most culturally rich part of the City of Adelaide. This medium-density project sought to fulfil a brief that not only demanded energy efficiency, healthy environments and high ecological performance but also insisted on user participation, ethical investment funding and engagement with its context – assisted by Urban Ecology Australia, the non-profit organization that initiated the Centre for Urban Ecology, having been based in the neighbourhood since 1993.

'Activist-driven from its inception, Christie Walk is pioneering sustainable urbanism in South Australia on the strength of a small team committed to realizing their vision of an "EcoCity"' (Farr 2008: 226). Christie Walk is a co-housing development, with extensive common facilities organized and managed by its residents (McCamant and Durrett 1988: 16). As a microcosm of the processes, plans and propositions contained in the ecopolis vision, it represents perhaps the smallest viable size for an urban fractal with sufficient mix of accommodation, community and commercial facilities to demonstrate social and economic dynamics as well as built form and technological features of city-making for living systems.

Research and education

> Christie Walk was always designed to be an educational experience, and it has fulfilled that promise.
>
> (Farr 2008: 229)

Christie Walk is a research and development project. It contains a small interpretive Centre for Urban Ecology run by UEA as a focus for ongoing educational activities and as an interpretive centre for the project. Thousands of people have visited here to learn about sustainable development and the importance of living systems in urban environments and how community processes are integral to overall goals of sustainability.

Organization and design strategy

> Christie Walk's creators – a cooperative essentially comprised of concerned citizens moonlighting as developers – imagined it as a small-scale template for larger urban projects, and so were careful to include all the important elements of good sustainable design.
>
> (Farr 2008: 226)

Organizational arrangements for the making of the Christie Walk project were unusual compared with conventional developments with participation by the wider community, a cooperative management structure, use of non-profit structures and engagement of volunteers in the design, development and construction process.

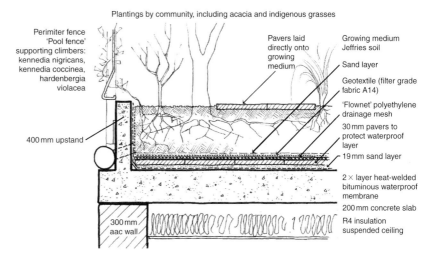

11.4
Section through the intensive roof garden

Source: Paul Downton

The overall design strategy was to work with the flux of natural energy, as living systems do, using passive design principles throughout. Living landscape threads through the project, linking built form to community and natural systems, with the intensive roof garden being productive and providing important amenity. Urban environments build up a patina of pattern and texture from a continuous history of intimate human engagement with place-making. A key design idea in Christie Walk was to accelerate this process. Residents were encouraged to make their mark and occupy the place with evidence of their presence and provide 'instant patina'. Working bees,

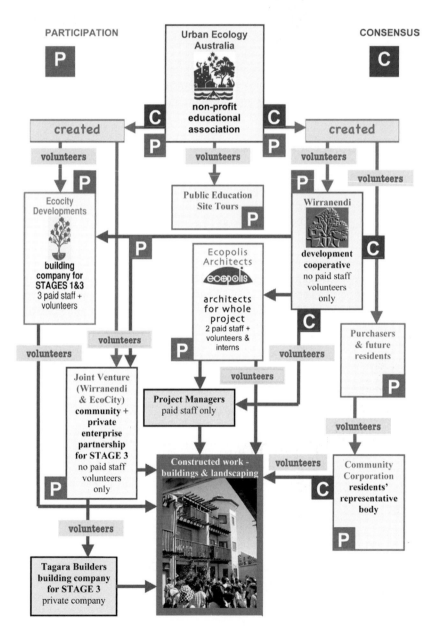

11.5
Christie Walk organizational chart

Source: Paul Downton

essential to the practical completion of the landscape, have been de facto planning and design exercises at the micro level and have created an important social focus to the process that has, in turn, amplified the experience of participation and built the reality of the place as a living system.

'One of the founding principles of Christie Walk is that a true sustainable development engages with the community rather than existing as a separate, privileged enclave' (Farr 2007: 226). The client was the development cooperative Wirranendi Inc., created by UEA. This community-based development was heavily reliant on voluntary effort in its early stages. Overall, the development structure enabled the project to proceed and to withstand delays and personal tragedies and survive where a conventional development approach would probably have resulted in the project being abandoned or changed beyond recognition. This is another strength of the 'living systems' approach, where substantial reliance is placed on a community's capacity to be responsive rather than work solely around brittle, legalistic contracts.

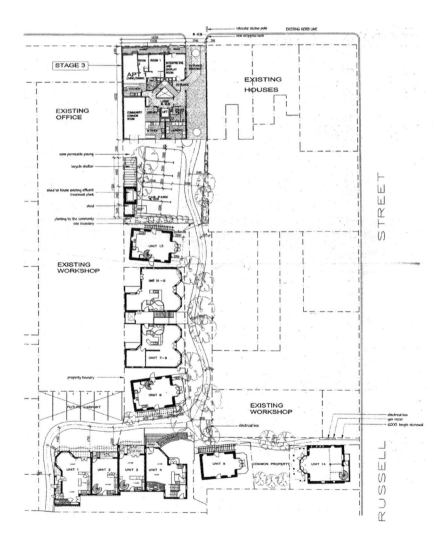

11.6
Site plan of Christie Walk

Source: Paul Downton

The project demonstrates that it is possible to substantially address most key environmental issues through the manner in which the built environment is planned and developed, and that social sustainability, the support of community processes and the making of convivial places is integral to achieving this possibility. Discovering the pragmatics of making 'community' work with 'commercial' has been a defining experience for the project protagonists, some of whom are keen to see their hard-won knowledge put to use, while others never want to be involved in development again!

Awareness

By having a project located in an inner-city neighbourhood within five minutes' walk of the central business district it was hoped that its impact as a small exemplar of 'eco-city' principles would be enhanced both in terms of visual presence and through the presence of an active, eco-city community living, working and playing within the local social networks. This has happened, and the project has been instrumental in raising awareness from the local level to the international level, featuring in international textbooks on sustainable urbanism. It is used in consumer-awareness programmes and educational establishments, from schools to universities.

Monitoring and evaluation have borne out the high performance of the project in terms of energy use. There are some researched data, which at least partially substantiates the view that the integrated nature of the place and its community has led to improvement of environmental quality, energy efficiency, resource efficiency including recycling rate and levels of awareness.

Monica Oliphant, Adjunct Professor of Research at the University of South Australia, reported on Adelaide's Christie Walk housing development and 'confirmed what residents and regular visitors had already noticed. These comfortable, beautiful homes really are energy efficient, preventing tonnes of greenhouse gases from damaging our planet and saving their owners hundreds of dollars each year in electricity costs' (Oliphant 2004).

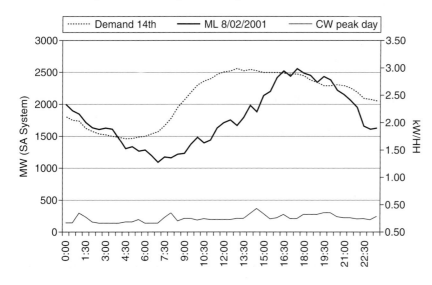

11.7
Peak day power consumption: Christie Walk compared with Mawson Lakes and average South Australian consumption

Source: Monica Oliphant (2004)

Daniell's (2005) researches concluded that the buildings and infrastructure assist good performance in much the same way that you can drive a fuel-efficient car badly and still return better fuel economy than a gas guzzler: '[T]hese results show that even with the worst recycling behaviour, the infrastructure at the Christie Walk development, including composting and recycling services, helps to reduce the effect of behaviour to below the 50th percentile of the greater Adelaide population.'

The Christie Walk Urban Fractal

Christie Walk was a breakthrough development which we've all learnt from.

(Lou de Leeuw, reported by Stott 2007)

Sustainability specialist Danielle McCartney cited Christie Walk as a mixed-density community housing project that demonstrates that sustainable living can be achieved in the inner city and praised the project 'for what it gives back to the community' (McLeod 2004: 36).

Even where there is a poverty of financial resources there are still people. Mobilizing the human power of the community through volunteerism can provide a wealth of resources not available through monetary exchange. In the eco-city context, volunteerism can also be seen as using somatic energy in the production of the built environment in a way that, because it uses human energy that is already, in effect, 'latent', doesn't add energy costs to that production process.

Table 11.1 Comparison between Christie Walk and conventional development (based on an actual example) (source: Paul Downton)

	Conventional development	Christie Walk
Site area	2000 m²	2000 m²
Number of dwellings	24	27
Productive landscape	200 m²	700 m²
Productive roof area	None	170 m²
Resource conservation, including recycling/re-use of materials	No	Yes
Energy efficiency	No	Yes
Non-toxic construction	No	Yes
Community space	No	Yes
Storm-water capture	No	Yes
Effluent treatment	No	Yes
Renewable energy	No	Yes
Community engagement	No	Yes
Educational programmes	No	Yes
Diversity of dwelling types	No	Yes

The challenge of dealing with accelerated climate change demands tremendous levels of organization and social mobilization, as well as applying military urgency to put solutions in place. The South Australian experience has demonstrated that by treating urbanism as a living system, inspired, grassroots community action is able to get uncompromising ecological development projects up and running despite a lack of resources and funding and when government and mainstream industry are languishing.

References

Birkeland, J. (2008) *Positive Development: From Vicious Circles to Virtuous Cycles through Built Environment Design*, London, UK and Sterling, VA: Earthscan.

Bookchin, M. (1995) *From Urbanization to Cities: Toward a New Politics of Citizenship*, London: Cassell.

Boyden, S. (2004) *The Biology of Civilisation: Understanding Human Culture as a Force in Nature*, Sydney: University of New South Wales Press.

Boyden, S., Millar, S. and O'Neal, B. (1981) *The Ecology of a City and Its People: The Case of Hong Kong*, Canberra: Australian National University Press.

Burke, S. (ed.) (2004) 'Sustainable snapshots: Six Australian projects of best practice in action', *Australian Planner* 4, 41: 22–26.

Daniell, K.A. (2005) 'Sustainability assessment of housing developments: A new methodology', in *CABM-HEMA-SMAGET*, Montpellier, France.

Dansereau, P. (1957) *Biogeography: An Ecological Perspective*, New York: Ronald Press Company.

Douglas, I. (1983) *The Urban Environment*, London: Edward Arnold.

Downton, P.F. (2009) *Ecopolis: Architecture and Cities for a Changing Climate*, Dordrecht: Springer Science+Business Media B.V.

Farmer, J. and Richardson, K. (ed.) (1996) *Green Shift: Towards a Green Sensibility in Architecture*, Oxford: Architectural Press/WWF-UK.

Farr, D. (2007) *Sustainable Urbanism: Urban Design with Nature*, Hoboken, NJ: John Wiley and Sons Inc.

Geddes, P. (1968 [1915]) *Cities in Evolution*, London: Ernest Benn.

Gehl, J. (1987) *Life between Buildings: Using Public Space*, New York: Van Nostrand Reinhold.

Hough, M. (1995) *Cities and Natural Process*, London and New York: Routledge.

Lapo, A.V. (1982 [1979]) *Traces of Bygone Biospheres*, trans. V. Purto, Moscow: Mir Publishers.

Lovelock, J. (1991) *Gaia: The Practical Science of Planetary Medicine*, Sydney: Allen & Unwin.

Lovelock, J. and Margulis, L. (1975) 'The atmosphere as circulatory system of the biosphere: The Gaia hypothesis', in *The CoEvolution Quarterly*, POINT, Sausalito, Summer, pp. 31–40.

McCamant, K. and Durrett, C. (1988) *CoHousing: A Contemporary Approach to Housing Ourselves*, Berkeley, CA: Habitat Press/Ten Speed Press.

McLeod, C. (2004) 'Sustainment in a shrinking world', *Architecture Australia* 5, 93, September–October: 36.

Magnaghi, A. (2005 [2000]) *The Urban Village: A charter for democracy and local self-sustainable development*, trans. D. Kerr, London and New York: Zed Books.

Mumford, L. (1961) *The City in History*, London: Secker & Warburg.

Oliphant, M. (2004) *Inner City Residential Energy Performance Final Report*, Urban Ecology Australia/SENRAC, June. Online: www.urbanecology.org.au/publications/residentialenergy.

Rees, W.E. (1998) 'The built environment and the ecosphere: A global perspective', in *Green Building Challenge '98 Conference Proceedings Volume 1*, Minister of Supply and Services, Vancouver, pp. 3–14.

Stott, J. (2007) 'Echoes of success', *Adelaide Review*, 10 February–1 March.

Szokolay, S.V. (1987) *Thermal Design of Buildings*, Red Hill: RAIA Education Division.

Szokolay, S.V. (1989) 'PLEA principles beyond the individual building', in *PLEA 1989 Nara: Proceedings of International Conference*, PLEA, Nara.

The Green Edge

China between Hope and Hazard

Neville Mars

Nobel Laureate Al Gore reminded us that the United States and China are the two major causes of global climate change in his Nobel Peace Prize acceptance speech (10 December 2007, Oslo). The United States warns us China will be the biggest polluter of the twenty-first century, but China argues it has to catch up with the West and is, in absolute terms, decades behind in polluting. So we have a political deadlock. The real difference is that the United States has become a nation dependent on fossil fuel while China still has an opportunity to redirect its development.

Embedded in urbanization patterns are behaviours that will shape energy usage for many decades. Green ambitions include adding vegetation or employing basic technical 'greenification'. In reality, a collection of well-designed low-emission buildings can still amount to a poorly operating and unsustainable city. Pressured market-driven development simply leaves no time to conceive of a holistic approach, so China's window of opportunity is rapidly closing.

China is facing all the problems of modern industrialization at once. Yet sustainability as a discipline is very young in China. The problems are enormous but the level of ambition is awe-inspiring. Going green is often passionately embraced and high on the agenda of policy makers and concerned citizens. Still, beyond basic non-toxicity, the meaning of a sustainable environment remains unclear. China will need to use its breakneck pace to leapfrog the patchwork solutions of traditional urban development. It must conceive a comprehensive vision of a future green environment and apply flexible development frameworks that steer towards this goal.

Rise and shine

China's rise over the last three decades involved lifting millions of people out of extreme poverty. According to the World Bank (2009), between 1981 and 2004 those consuming less than US$1 each day dropped from 65 per cent to 10 per cent of the population. If current growth rates continue, China will outstrip the United States in the next twenty to thirty years. This remarkable economic and urban growth, the 'Chinese Dream', has established a confidence that the country is in full control of national development. Environmental problems are countered by stated goals in terms of solutions in the distant future. The reality is profoundly pragmatic.

The world observes this Chinese boom with anxiety and anticipation. Set against a backdrop of diminishing resources and bleak forecasts for capital markets, emerging economies can make big gains. Suddenly the absence of a mature power grid, lower levels of urbanization, lack of cars and so on offer hope. 'Leapfrog development', so often vaunted in China yet seldom observed, is demanded by the West in order to align China's course of progress with global sustainability goals. Big solutions are required to move beyond fuel-dependent landscapes such as the American Dream produced. Indeed, for China to leapfrog effectively, solutions must be found and implemented nationwide, and immediately.

Yet, neither ambitions to leapfrog nor big schemes and outstanding objectives acknowledge the reality that 2008 marks the thirtieth anniversary of China's open-door policy and subsequent economic rise: a shift in employment from primary to tertiary industry, and the movement from predominantly rural to predominantly urban settlement. The popular belief is that China is essentially a clean slate. Often developers and 'green dreamers' approach China with similar ambitions to supply this young market with trendy ideas: not guiding visions of a new economy but rather stylistic features that can be used to satisfy existing market-oriented development. China, along with the rest of the world, is in dire need of a systematic model that implements green development through an evolutionary and flexible process. Only then can a half-built China redirect its course of development and create future-proofed solutions. Current pragmatism hinders any conceptual leapfrog.

As well as introducing some solutions, in this chapter the complexities of China's challenges are analysed by outlining three contradictions:

- A collection of well-designed sustainable buildings can still amount to a poorly operating, unsustainable city.
- While Western suburbia produces concerns for fuel-dependent urbanization, Chinese suburbs offer hope by accommodating in a compact way the mass rural migrations from smaller inefficient settlements.
- Boom economies like China's are geared towards consumption and force us to direct efforts away from reducing consumption towards stimulating 'green consumption' and 'green consumers'.

How can China make a conceptual leapfrog?

There is no convincing model for China to follow when it comes to green cities. The strategy of copy and paste that has so effectively expedited China's building process cannot be applied. Historic Western cities are only slowly greening existing urban systems and infrastructure. Initial proposals for entire green cities suggest leapfrogging to sustainable planning. However out of touch with the society they aim to serve, and barely connected to the surroundings they are part of, such cities are only green in limited ways.

Unable to understand the local end-user, large-scale foreign plans by renowned companies (such as Ove Arup and William McDonough + Partners) were ill-received and consequently cancelled. Especially in China, sustainability should be understood as the balance of the all-encompassing system of economy, society and environment and the constraints the environmental limits impose. Growing under its own pressure, only a holistic approach to planning that can unfold over time and adapt to local conditions will suffice.

China's goal, as articulated by the central government's Agenda 21 plans, is to live in a way that is more ecologically sound than it does currently. This objective, now formalized, arises out of a variety of complex interactions between the state, provincial and local constituents, and international governance regimes such as the United Nations' development and environment programmes. While it is difficult to predict the outcome, a mélange of ideological and political forces have real ecological consequences in the near future (Schienke 2008). Making choices about China's environment relies mainly on the future it envisages for its people and environment, including recognizing the sacrifices implied to achieve sustainability. The task is overwhelming.

Not surprisingly, so far China's green ambitions have mostly meant topping green features onto existing development. Most importantly, government ambitions, market forces and cultural heritage continue to pressure building and planning projects to be realized all but instantly. Ironically, the inability to address the most immediate urban issues, such as congestion and air quality, seems to provide a starting point for a more future-oriented debate.

Green imaginaries

In anthropology and political ecology the concept of an 'imaginary' (Lacan 1949/1977) refers to ideological, ethical and rhetorical forces that scientists, planners, decision makers and citizen activists (i.e. 'environmental subjects') engage with to accomplish goals. Imaginaries are higher-order discursive systems that allow local environmental subjects to work through double-binds. An example is creatively turning a 'no-win' situation (e.g. traditionally paradoxically presented by greening versus development) into a 'win-win' situation.

Environmental imaginaries provide environmental subjects with ways of expressing problems and solutions in new terms, concepts, metaphors and symbols. Local environmental subjects tap into systems sustained at a higher order of magnitude or larger scale than apparent if reading only the local context – a mode of thinking particularly important to sustainability (Schienke 2008). The Dynamic City Foundation has introduced a number of new imaginaries. The heart is the concept of the 'dynamic city', a strategically evolving green metropolis, which consists of other new sustainability concepts, such as 'green edge', 'dynamic density' and 'D-rail' (all described later).

Beyond environmental indicators and emission standards our imaginary questions what Chinese ultimately want from our living environments. It forces us to think of where we want to be in two decades and to construct a path to get there. A daunting challenge involves the rapid and fragmented urbanization of the Chinese countryside, half a billion dispersed rural villagers increasingly inefficiently dependent on urban economies and motorized transport. Now, more than ever, 'to be green, is to dream'.

Dynamic density

Imaginaries offer a common goal to achieve cohesion between long-term plans. China, already half-built, needs a model that adheres to its accelerated market-driven urbanization. In the midst of a building frenzy, Chinese planners, policy makers and designers feel few limitations. Yet such notions will be inadequate as urbanization occurs faster than planners can map, driven by macro-planned and micro-organic constructions.

On the ground designers juggle pursuing the clean modernity of an economic miracle or stimulating the human vibrancy of Chinese entrepreneurialism. While designers deliberate, there is more market-driven unintentional development (MUD). At street level new urban realms look perfectly micro-planned, while the same polished island developments at the scale of the metropolis merge together to reveal macro-organic systems. The building blocks of China's cities are designed in days but ensuing MUD configurations are fixed for decades, flouting any efforts towards sustainability. It is not just energy intensive – farmland is permanently lost, while the configurations that define China's future energy needs consolidate.

Dynamic density (DD) aims to work with the natural tendencies of cities to differ over their life cycle in ways that can be monitored and responded to in terms of optimal compactness (based on a dynamic relationship between footprint and population). Analysis of prevalent urban distribution patterns suggests a normative density curve with two essential components:

- high performance density composed of a contextual matrix of densities, including people, programmatic mix and functionality;
- density within a temporal continuum of urban expansion and shifting densities.

Planning density must incorporate an understanding of the fluid interactions within space and time, DD, rather than static achievements. With population and building densities among the world's highest and amid MUD-defined interactions, China produces naturally compact typologies. Applying dynamic planning logic, MUD offers opportunities to set China's predilection for high-rise high-speed development towards producing compact efficient configurations. In stark opposition to the multi-generational evolution of European towns, Chinese cities are built rapidly and become outdated equally fast. DD offers a Chinese planner a tool to produce environments that anticipate future developments.

Green edge

Modernism exhibited a density fetish that cultural consciousness grants a metropolitan aura. The iconography of an advanced society, leaning towards science fiction, invariably assumes ultra-dense structures. In reality the average residential consumer despises density; those who can afford to do so move to a detached home in suburbia. High-density urban peripheries and satellite towns have proved notoriously unsuccessful in the West. While boosting population density, they have failed to increase services and diversity commensurately.

Yet in China a Le Corbusian tower block has great marketability. More importantly, grey Chinese suburbs that Western planners would label 'sprawl' exhibit vitality. At hyper-speed, Chinese suburbs mature, with appropriate planning and connections to urban cores, evolving into healthy tissue. Suburbs that steer growth away from inefficient settlements, to accommodate hundreds of millions of people more compactly, are potentially invaluable for China to nurture, to enhance its loose-fit urban periphery.

If Chinese sprawl is often temporary, how can we define the city's limits? As shown by Tokyo, bigness does not imply efficiency. Any urban expansion beyond the reaches of high-end public transportation should be considered unsustainable. We have coined the zone outside the urban core but within the mass-transit system, the 'green edge', a transitional zone between city and countryside. It is highly sought after by residents, delivering lush suburban living and fast access to the centre. The mayor of Beijing, Wang Qishan (2004), acknowledges that a schism between real estate and infrastructural development is the city's main concern. Yet it could expand its green edge if public–private partnerships akin to Hong Kong's could be forged through close collaboration between rail and real estate developers.

Aiming for flexibility, it is crucial to avoid the all-too-popular model of a fortified residential island. Through more connections, alternative routes and a greater spread of vehicles, grids facilitate a much more efficient road system less hampered by congestion.

Green consumers

China is caught up in a delicate economic and social equilibrium, ostensibly only sustained by fast widespread growth. Thus we need to help people out of poverty to become green consumers. Laws and planning do not produce a green society; the individual consumer will realize (or not) most green ambitions. Top-down government interventions and bottom-up incentives combine to generate profound transitions. Yet, arguably, China's double-digit economic growth is at a standstill when environmental squalor costs an estimated 10 per cent of gross domestic product annually and air pollution directly affects millions of individuals' health. This is poignant considering that the average Chinese consumes only a fraction of what a Westerner does. Increasingly China splits into rural and urban divides. The imminent danger is excluding most Chinese citizens from progress and making the poorest pay for rampant environmental degradation.

Though propagating massive schemes at the periphery, the Chinese Communist Party (CCP) trusts the growing middle class with its future. This trust seems to be paying off today as the future 'harmonious society' is supposed to be steadily carved out by every producer-cum-consumer. However, as economic reforms unfold, the tendency to produce MUD accelerates and dreams of designing the city or society slip away. Ultimately the Chinese Dream is at odds with the CCP's grip on power. Widespread urbanization jars against centralized control. Exclusivity clashes with the harmonious society. The design of a society contradicts empowerment of individuals.

To retain its marketability, consumers will need to be offered more than personal space and commodities: a city that performs. The urban dream can only take shape along with growing urban expectations. Counterintuitively, this requires more coordinated planning and increasing the status of being a homeowner. Micro-planned projects will need to be integrated into coherent macro-level structures. Urbanization will need to be streamlined for quality (efficiency and comfort) rather than speed.

Breaking the rules

There is a feeling that if only Chinese developers abided by the rules, if only buildings were not so haphazard, things would be better. After publishing our book (Mars and Hornsby 2008) we learned some important lessons through our urban planning practice. Some illustrative case studies follow.

Tianjin CBD

Most policies and planning regulations are significant barriers to sustainable development, as revealed by a recent project for a new city business district (CBD) in Tianjin (Tangu). Building setbacks, road widths and other rules are restrictive and marginalize sustainability concerns. Streamlining the building boom has produced regulations that intuitively make China's cities more human, spacious and green but actually result in low sustainability performance. Large omnipresent urban spaces and obligatory building setbacks lower the potential density of China's new cities and make them increasingly inaccessible to pedestrians. The potential to forge connections between buildings and public spaces is all but lost.

A first analysis for Tianjin (see Figure 12.1) showed it was crucial to ignore regulations and systematically design a new urban system from the bottom up. Wedged between industry and a booming smog-covered harbour, our usual first step for a master plan – mapping the ecological surroundings – was impossible.

Starting with emergency systems, such as run-off and floodwater prevention, we reintroduced natural water and vegetation networks. In addition to basic green technologies and mixed-use urban typologies, we encouraged the CBD to expand along an urban backbone and discouraged regional and local car use, thus allowing three-dimensional neighbourhoods to develop, providing pedestrians with stacked commercial networks in low-rise yet dense living areas. With China's fast pace of development, ignoring the rules is a risk for the designer and for the client. Yet the rules must be altered to effect real change at block and neighbourhood level.

Seen from space, the north-east triangle is a wedge created between the major urban centres of Beijing, Shanghai and Xian and forms a rapidly developing megalopolis. The small communities and villages in this area are developing faster than anywhere else in China. We call this area the People's

12.1

Tianjin CBD: a compact grid
system around a green ring,
natural water filtering system
and subway connections lay the
infrastructural foundations of a
green CBD

Source: Neville Mars/DCF

Urbanity of China (PUC), the world's largest urban region and scheduled to
grow into the world's first megalopolis (see Figure 12.2). Soon it will become a
massive urban field with an average density of a mid-sized American city. This
forces us to think again about levels of urban and population densities.

Within the PUC the combination of demographic, social and economic
forces gives rise to hitherto unseen hyper-urbanization. Policies to avoid
hyper-urbanization in large cities promote scattered low-level developments
('policy sprawl'). Migration to larger cities is often temporary 'rollover'
migration, mainly contributing to peripheral urbanization. New forms of
village and township urbanization have emerged, such as 'doorstep
urbanization' and 'brickification'. The intensity of such recent growth suggests
village mushrooming will dictate expansion patterns for decades to come.
They are the most space-extensive settlement types. In addition, both
grassroots industrialization and officially planned economic and industrial
development zones pull investments and migrants away from the urban core.

China's urban landscape is concentrated on one-third of its surface. The
projected growth of population and built environment for 2020 reveals layered
areas with the density, but not coherence, of a continuous urban region. The
distinction between urban and rural conditions has been steadily lost as China
has moved towards a hyper-suburban road-dependent landscape. The space
available will not allow for suburban solutions such as in the United States. Thus,
stimulating compact urban growth of larger settlements through job incentives
and policies aimed at concentrating development will allow a more sustainable
layout and allow China to become a prosperous and advanced nation.

Beijing,
Population: 23 m.
Tangshan
Tianjin

Baoding
Population: 1.5 m

Population: 1.5 m

Jinan
Population: 2.5 m

Qingdao
Population: 2 m

Handan
Population: 1.6 m

Anyang
Population: 1 m

Jining
Population: 0.7 m

Jiaozuo
Population: 0.9 m

Zhangzhou
Population: 1 m

Xuzhou
Population: 1.5 m

Changzhou
Population: 28 m

Suzhou
Shanghai

12.2
The People's Urbanity of China

Source: Neville Mars/DCF

The L-building: social sustainability block by block

The L-building attempts to address the many problems and opportunities of the green edge and draws its inspiration from the traditional Beijing *hutong* (see Figure 12.3). It introduces planning concerns with the individual rather than the community. This approach is integrated into larger-scale developments, such as proposals for an area of East Beijing (near the fifth ring-road), which attempts to bring coherence into the city via transportation routes, public services and recycling waste. In short, by imagining greening on levels relevant to the consumer, the green edge is realized. The letter 'L' in L-building embodies these qualities. L is the primary shape of the apartment and stands for 'loft'. We designed the units as lofts, the epitome of the architect's dream apartment and as a flexible space for different owners (see Figure 12.4). The apartments can be either compartmentalized or left open and thus suitable for couples, small families or sole tenants born out of the one-child policy.

The L-building introduces social sustainability. Nothing is more desirable than an apartment with amenities, such as hot and cold running water, a toilet and a view. But moving from a *ping fang* (a derivative of the famous *hutong*) to the modern tower block is often less rewarding in the long term. The traditional Chinese neighbourhood, including the *danwei*, had exceptional social coherence. Taken-for-granted qualities of the *ping fang*, particularly a sense of community, are disappearing. Thus the L-building mediates between China's traditional

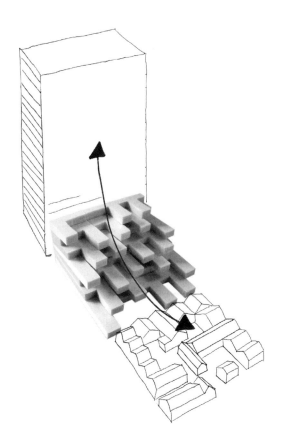

12.3
The L-building (hybrid *hutong*)
concept

Source: Neville Mars/DCF

12.4
L-building sketch

Source: Neville Mars/DCF

urban environment and a contemporary trend of up-scaling from low-rise to the modern tower block. The L-building complies with rudimentary suburban desires: a large private garden and a car at the door. But, as a medium-size and collectively developed, owned and operated form, the L-building (Figure 12.4) resonates with more traditional Chinese principles.

D-rail

Trying to overcome existing voids created by the cities' status quo monosprawl and immense ring-road system is a daunting challenge in a city so geographically large and fragmented as Beijing, which is fast becoming laden with transport systems yet impossible for pedestrians. So we designed the D-rail (Figure 12.5), an innovative mass-transit system that combines the speed of the maglev train with the efficiency of a travelator (flat escalator). In a 64 km ring, the D-rail stretches all around Beijing's third and fourth ring-roads. People get on and off without the system ever stopping. The commuter is transported around the city in minutes. Existing ring-roads, currently dividing the city and inhibiting pedestrian movement, will be bridged with the elevated D-rail network. The ring-roads will become not only a transport platform for cars, but for a much more efficient platform of concentrated pedestrian traffic. The D-rail grows Beijing a new circular centre.

E_Tree

Our ambition has been to work on every scale on which the city operates and to interrelate various insights into our proposals. The E_Tree is a product design that tries to learn from nature (see Figure 12.6). Today's large hot and unattractive parking lots call out for innovation. They produce severe heat islands in downtown areas, augment cooling loads and heat cars in summer to scorching temperatures. To cover cars on the Shanghai World Expo assembly, we designed the E_Tree panel structure. Aimed at casting the maximum shade, the project increasingly looked like a forest of trees. The logical next step was to make the leaves out of solar panels and to have them rotate and follow the sun. Under the E_Tree, electric cars can park and connect to a tree to recharge their batteries.

12.5
D-rail: a major transportation project designed to bridge Beijing's ring-road network and promote interactive mobility over existing walls of congestion

Source: Neville Mars/DCF

Neville Mars

12.6
The E_Tree offers shadow, uses sunlight and hides parking lots

Source: Neville Mars/DCF

Conclusion

China underscores the need to imagine an ideal green living environment for our future. The technological approach dominating green efforts today will be of limited impact if it is not embraced by society and supported by local cultural and economic realities. Moreover, we need to imagine a green future in order to give coherence to efforts made in many different fields and on different scales. The green city is at the centre of this overarching imaginary. That is the first step to address the challenge of accommodating hundreds of millions of first-generation urbanites in a sustainable fashion. Then we must come to terms with the aggressive ongoing change China represents. Planning solutions must be future-proof and allow urban expansion while in effect increasing efficiency. Ultimately aiming for sustainability at this scale, the learning process itself must be able to evolve and mature organically.

References

Lacan, J.-M.-E. (1949/1977) *Mirror Stage as Formative of the I as Revealed in Psychoanalytic Experience*. Trans. by Alan Sheridan from 1936 French original delivered to the Fourteenth International Psychoanalytical Congress. Reprinted in 1977 as *Écrits: A Selection*, New York: W.W. Norton & Co.

Mars, N. and Hornsby, A. (eds) (2008) *The Chinese Dream: A Society under Construction*, Rotterdam: 010 Publishers.

Schienke, E. (2008) 'Pondering the green edge', in N. Mars and A. Hornsby (eds), *The Chinese Dream: A Society under Construction*, Rotterdam: 010 Publishers.

Wang, Q. (2004) *China State Congress*, Beijing.

World Bank (2009) *From Poor Areas to Poor People: China's Evolving Poverty Reduction Agenda*. Online. Available at the World Bank site (Home > Countries > East Asia and Pacific > China webpage) at: http://web.worldbank.org.

Part III

Architecture and a Sustainable City

13.1
Overview

Drawing: Leon van Schaik

Overview

Leon van Schaik

Javier Marias (1995) is famous for his page-long sentences consisting of strings of subjunctive clauses. A character will make an observation, step back and consider on what grounds he is able to make such an observation, then step back and reflect on the human condition that allows for reflection, and then step back again and wonder whether his reflection merits comparison with the reflections of others … 'Architecture and a Sustainable City' as a title begs so many questions that it occasions several back-flips. And the book section that it introduces contains five theatres of architectural endeavour, each of which generates ripples of contemplation oscillating between professional pride and despair.

Let's begin with a bite of humble pie. Observers have often attempted to measure how much impact architects have on the constructed environment: landscapes and buildings. Mostly our influence is in the '20' zone of the ubiquitous 80:20 ratio that crops up in so many analyses. In the anglophone world it seems that architects are directly responsible for around 3 per cent of custom-built houses and around 8 per cent of housing. Looking deeply into the staffing of developers and construction companies, some sociologists push the direct influence to as high as 20 per cent (Gutman 1988).

In her chapter Andresen points out that 50 per cent of the Australian rainforest has been cleared for agriculture. This has happened without recourse to architects or landscape architects. In fact, in settler societies the professions that are called on are, first, surveyors, who map terrain and enable people to stake claims on it; second, lawyers who enable them to register title and trade the land; and third, engineers, who provide the infrastructure that enables exploitation. Designers are last on the scene, late in the day, when the wealth that has been mined from the landscape has flowed into the cities. They are called on to embellish, make sense of or camouflage what has gone before. Some archaeologists even argue that cities come about purely to secure the wealth that has been extracted from the environment, and some sociologists see these walled cities as engines allowing new forms of exploitation of humans by humans – forms that eluded nomadic power seekers. It is pleasing to note that archaeologists are also challenging these bleak views. They have uncovered what is thought to be the oldest city ever found. It is devoid of any defensive feature, littered with clay flutes and the largest structure seems to have served as an amphitheatre. Now that it appears that there was a form of writing 40000 years ago (Ravilious 2010), the arguments will wash about us for years to come.

It seems fair to say that the biggest gains in sustainability will come from the design and implementation of regimes of care that will have an impact on our landscapes – urban and rural – and our built form. We need these spurs to reform, for example understanding that an area of rainforest in the Amazon equal to the size of France was once a managed landscape (Day 2008) could help us to cohabit in the land in new ways. Architecture will respond to these new conditions with as much creative joy as flowed through the music of that ancient city. I step back and fear those who argue that circumstances are so dire that we cannot wait for the political processes of democracy, and that those who know what must be done will have to take command if we are to avert disaster. We build on the efforts of our mentors, peers and challengers, and I look at the efforts displayed in this book through lenses first worn by others, as we all do. Here are some of these lenses: Colin Rowe, now excoriated for being an uncritical supporter of the New York Five and their 'white', socially autistic aesthetic, studied cities through their grain. He looked at them through the eyes of intellectuals like Karl Popper, who had thought and argued their way to a vision of micro-democracy (as Chantal Mouffe (1992) later termed this) that would thwart the emergence of totalitarian governments. Rowe's idea of a 'good' city, as adumbrated by his students Fred Koetter and Grahame Shane among others, was one in which various utopian ideas were being trialled and sustained *at the same time*. Michael Sorkin (1993) took this up in his 'local codes': visioning cities with radically different granulation of built form and open space, governed by vastly different regulations and each intensifying the possibility of living in a distinctive way. As this book shows, there are so many different ways of responding to situations: we should not specify these. What we must fight for is the political will to create policy frameworks that harness our creativity and our difference. Anyone who has worked where self-help is the only readily available help can tell stories about how well people do in limited circumstances and how badly experts serve them.

So my first mental space – the one influenced by Rowe and his love of the difference between cities and city districts – lights up when I see the *jeu d'esprit* of Stuhlmacher's parasites; of Andresen's timberland city so reminiscent of Yeang's (1987) dream of a Tropical Verandah City, itself looking like drawings of an idealized Chinese peasant village from a history of traditional architecture; of Pieprz's tidal flow embracing city district with its clear boundary. That clear delineation of an edge is a thing Rowe approved of – a 'minitopia', specific to its own bend in the river and not what Rowe saw as totalitarian in effect if not in intention – a 'monotopia' sprawling endlessly across the delta (as SOM's earlier Saigon South urban design was). Of course, any thinking that begins with Collage City (Rowe and Koetter 1978), based on work commenced at Cornell in 1964, has to contend with the way it appears to ignore 'dirty realism' as theorized by Robert Venturi (1966) and Venturi *et al.* (1972). Koetter himself interpreted Rowe's position at the International

Leon van Schaik

Institute of Design in London in 1971 in the following way. Take two routes into New York: the Hudson Parkway and a road running 'surface' through car yards and commercial shopfronts, namely a 'strip'. What you do is create regimes of care that reinforce the Arcadian nature of the parkway, even to the extent of preventing developments that impinge on the skyline, and on the strip you create regimes of care that allow for and encourage more flamboyance, more vulgarity. Grahame Shane's PhD with Rowe proposed an analysis of London as a 'Collision City' in which classical figures – the boulevards, squares and terraces of Bloomsbury for example – occupied the high ground and waves of infrastructure created by new technologies came crashing into the city along the drainage channels, colliding with the classical figures. The thesis is that cities need to provide for the inevitability of catastrophic change. His best-selling book is titled aptly: *Recombinant Urbanism* (Shane 2005). What forms best suit this? There is a hint of this thinking in the plans for Saigon South. Lifschutz is firmly in this tradition, negotiating in spaces between figures colliding with the ever-pressing needs of the ever more populated river edge. However, I fear that the network plans for China envisage a perfected whole rather than something as open-ended as the epic of city development demands. (I very much like the way Mark Cousins (Fretton *et al.* 2008: 5) draws an analogy between the epic in literature and the city.) Venturi and Scott Brown bring us to the challenge of designing for '70 miles per hour', and here Rowe has been seen (wrongly, as proved above) to be silent. Someone who addresses this directly and as the core of his research is Mario Gandelsonas (1999). His studies of Boston, then Chicago and now Des Moines reveal something very important about urban planning that I do not think either of the schemes here shown deal with. Discontinuities in grids have dramatic impacts on the ways in which development happens. Large fractures divide districts and cement in place demographic differences. Syncopations, small deviations, 'T' junctions and the like encourage the clustering of neighbourhood services in unpredictable ways, first celebrated by Jane Jacobs. There is almost a case to be made for deliberately injecting random disturbances into large plans: first to allow for future infrastructure collision because we cannot predict what is coming, and second as a way of encouraging organically the emergence of distinctively different nodes of activity.

My second lens is also more political than as a designer, though the result is a design icon. I look carefully at designs for cities with Ildefonsa Cerda in mind (Soria y Puig 1999). His years of research and designing for a sustainable city (as we would say today) only came into play when a political solution was found that enabled the owners of myriad parcels of land on which his grid was to unfold were persuaded that they would get an equitable swap between their surface area and a proportional development volume in the new grid. This is why, in the Cerda-designed city, no block was ever completed by one architect; every block is a complex argument between architects vying to establish the best design for their slice. The new extension to the Diagonal, however, has none of this tension in it. Single architects have designed large parcels, and the result is bleak and unforgiving. So I look at the grids of Brearley and Fang and wonder what politic will enliven them, opening up opportunities for developers of every size, and fear that if they are built as rendered they will be as deadly as any other 'monotopic' development. As deadly as our own Docklands, where the parcels of development were uniform in size and all too large. Here the patient, opportunistic knitting together of space and river edge and filtering in of housing that Lifschutz has engaged in seems an exemplar.

Like Rowe, I do argue that intensely designed argumentative cities, where buildings and city grains say (Munday 1977) 'Listen to me! I am trying to tell you something!', capture our attention, engage our energies, make us citizens transacting the meaning of life in our daily rituals, and diminish our desire to escape into some impossible wilderness and contribute to the 50 per cent of emissions that the combustion engine is responsible for. Like Cerda, I do argue that our health and well-being depends on great design rooted in evidence about what affects us. Cerda used demographic data linked to spatial location, and proved beyond doubt the benefits of light, air and aspect. Architects could and did embroider every possible and wonderful concoction of meaning onto the armature, and overdeveloped it beyond his rules as evolving technology allowed...

The five architectural theatres you encounter in this section of the book are argumentative; they are filled with their own prioritizing of the relationship between delight, commodity and firmness. In this tri-polarity, architects have always served their communities as, generation after generation in city after city, communities seek to forge their own independent, idiosyncratic and inspired vision of what life is about for them in that particular place in their particular time.

References

Day, P. (2008) *Lost Cities of the Amazon*, 'National Geographic Explorer' documentary.

Fretton, T., Steinmann, M. and Cousins, M. (2008) *2G: Tony Fretton Architects*, Barcelona: Gustavo Gili.

Gandelsonas, M. (1999) *X-Urbanism: Architecture and the American City*, New York: Princeton Architectural Press.

Gutman, R. (1988) *Architectural Practice: A Critical Review*, New York: Princeton Architectural Press.

Marias, J. (1995) *A Heart So White*, London: Harvill Press.

Mouffe, C. (1992) *Dimensions of Radical Democracy*, London: Verso.

Munday, R. (1977) 'Passion in the suburbs', *Architecture Australia* February/March.

Ravilious, K. (2010) 'The writing on the cave wall', *New Scientist* 2748: 30–34.

Rowe, C. and Koetter, F. (1978) *Collage City*, Cambridge, Mass.: MIT Press.

Shane, D.G. (2005) *Recombinant Urbanism: Conceptual Modeling in Architecture, Urban Design and City Theory*, Chichester: Wiley-Academy.

Soria y Puig, A. (1999) *Cerda: The Five Bases of the General Theory of Urbanization*, Madrid: Electa.

Sorkin, M. (1993) *Local Code*, New York: Princeton Architectural Press.

Venturi, R. (1966) *Complexity and Contradiction in Architecture*, New York: Museum of Modern Art Press.

Venturi, R., Scott Brown, D. and Izenour, S. (1972) *Learning from Las Vegas*, Cambridge, Mass.: MIT Press.

Yeang, K. (1987) *The Tropical Verandah City*, Selangor: Longman.

A Landscape Framework for Urban Sustainability

Thu Thiem, Ho Chi Minh City

Dennis Pieprz

Ho Chi Minh City, the historic Vietnamese city formerly known as Saigon, has long been a dynamic centre of human habitation. The historic downtown area features grand public boulevards and narrow tree-lined streets, French-influenced architecture and throngs of citizens and tourists on motorbikes and on foot. Today, this character and the city's sustainability are threatened by over-sized office and commercial development and population growth that is expected to increase from six million in 2010 to ten million by 2020. Rapid urbanization is also placing significant development pressure on the city's historic core, which sits on the west bank of the great Saigon River.

Concerned that the city could not easily integrate the demands of these twenty-first-century developments, the city government initiated a planning process to envisage a new urban district on a peninsula of land along the east bank of the Saigon River. Almost totally surrounded by the sweep of the river, this peninsula is known as Thu Thiem. Its transformation has represented a momentous opportunity for Ho Chi Minh City to become more sustainable and it has been a major national initiative for the economic development of Vietnam. This chapter explores a development that follows in the great urban tradition that produced places such as Back Bay in Boston in the nineteenth century and, in the twentieth century, Canary Wharf in London and Pudong in Shanghai (see Figure 14.1).

Thu Thiem peninsula

Thu Thiem is 740 ha in area and located 200 m from the historic city centre of Ho Chi Minh City across the Saigon River. Development of the peninsula has been limited in the past. As early as 1900, attempts were made to develop it, although frequent flooding conditions on the peninsula, extensive canal network and unique soil composition made the land more suited to rice and fish farming. Consequently, there are few if any direct physical connections from the city across the river, and an absence of modernized infrastructure

14.1
The Thu Thiem urban design
plan

Source: Sasaki

improvements on the peninsula. In addition, three early-twentieth-century industrial port facilities currently exist on the west bank of the river to process large ship containers and other goods and materials from the South China Sea. These large ports further separate city and site.

A number of planning and development initiatives coalesced to focus the city's attention on this strategic peninsula (see Figure 14.2). The *Detailed Master Plan* and *Urban Design Guidelines for Thu Thiem New Urban Area* prepared by Sasaki established a comprehensive twenty-year vision for the waterfront peninsula as a dynamic and environmentally sensitive mixed-use urban district, reflecting a uniquely Vietnamese way of life. Composed of housing, commercial, office, cultural and institutional uses, the new district is set in an extensive framework of waterways and public spaces. Key destinations include a 50 000-m^2 convention centre, a regional outdoor stadium and indoor arena complex, a 300-metre-high television tower and visitors' centre, a new central plaza and central lake, and the new Museum of South Vietnam. On completion in 2025 Thu Thiem will accommodate over 130 000 new residents. Initiatives include: the construction of an east–west vehicular tunnel under the Saigon River that connects to a new international airport north-east of Thu Thiem; a new Thu Thiem bridge that connects the peninsula to existing residential areas in the north and employment centres in the south; municipal proposals for water, sewer and electrical power upgrades; and relocation of the river ports to points farther south along the River.

This chapter describes how these innovative solutions that centre on Thu Thiem have addressed sustainable urban development challenges facing Ho Chi Minh City. In the Vietnamese context, sustainable design must address the culture of the integrated city, multimodal transit, density and compact development, the response to climate, economic and social diversity and the

Dennis Pieprz

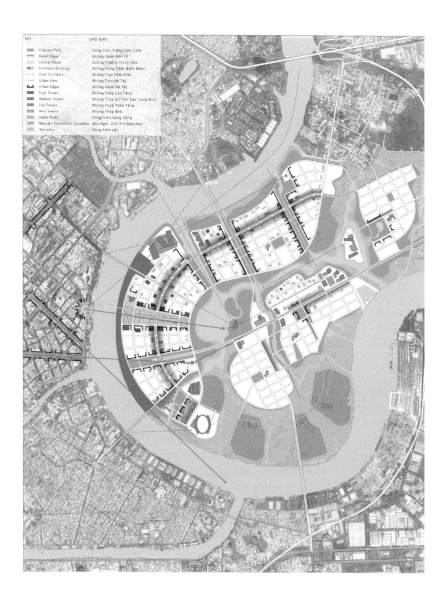

14.2
Urban design strategy

Source: Sasaki

ecology of the natural systems that so significantly affect life in subtropical South East Asia.

Planning process

The *Thu Thiem New Urban Area* project was completed between May and December 2004 on behalf of the Investment and Construction Authority (ICA) for the Thu Thiem New Urban Area of Ho Chi Minh City, in collaboration with the Urban Planning Institute (UPI) of Ho Chi Minh City. The primary objective of this planning process was to facilitate the update of master plans previously completed (in 1996 and 1998) and approved for Thu Thiem. These plans lacked public support and were not implemented.

In order to launch the idea of a new urban area project, Ho Chi Minh City and the ICA held an open International Urban Ideas Competition for the Thu Thiem peninsula. The Sasaki Associates design scheme was awarded first prize. Subsequently, ICA, UPI and Sasaki established a working process for the detailed master planning of Thu Thiem at 1:5000 and 1:2000 scales, including urban design guidelines. A detailed planning process and seven-month schedule were outlined. The process included four work sessions and three seminars in Ho Chi Minh City and Hanoi to discuss planning and design considerations related to infrastructure, transportation, environment, real estate and socio-economic issues for Thu Thiem.

The work sessions and seminars included representatives from ICA, UPI, the Ministry of Construction in Hanoi, over seventy local city agencies and

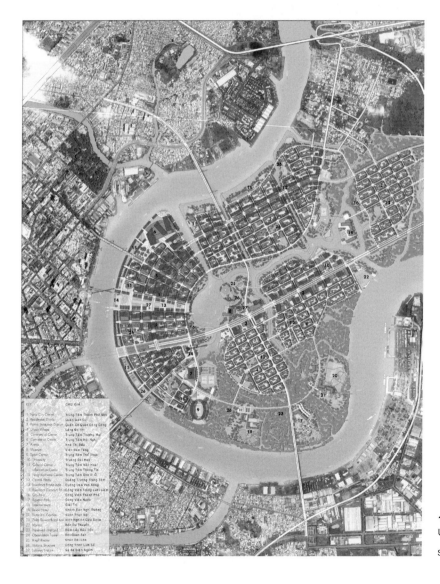

14.3
Urban design plan

Source: Sasaki

hundreds of individuals, as well as local and international experts. Furthermore, a bilingual project website – the first of its kind in Vietnam – was established to allow for the participation of numerous agencies, citizens and other interested parties in the process of developing the plan. The fact that many points of view (social, cultural, technical and economic) were taken into account strengthened the viability of and support for the plan (see Figure 14.3).

Elements of the plan

The urban morphology of the new urban district is tightly bound to the unique location of the site. This is key to establishing Thu Thiem as a place that is particular to Ho Chi Minh City.

An ecological strategy

The existing waterways and canals, low-lying lands, distinctive upland areas and opportunistic native vegetation on Thu Thiem form a unique ecological identity specific to South Vietnam, in particular to the Ho Chi Minh City area. The new urban district at Thu Thiem integrates this natural landscape system into an *urban delta* configuration, incorporating the wet conditions of the delta as part of the urban development rather than obliterating it. Certain land areas will be slightly raised (by 2.5 m) above flood level for development, while those areas below flood level will be kept 'green' as storm-water management assets. In particular, the southern (and lowest) part of the site will remain mostly undeveloped with slightly raised roadways and elevated pedestrian board-walks. A restored mangrove forest will purify the air and water, control erosion and protect the canal banks.

Within the urban district, new urban canals, lakes and reshaped natural canals will become ecological corridors able to absorb typical and extreme tidal changes, seasonal flooding and 50-year and 100-year floods. Thu Thiem is designed as an open system without locks or dams to control the flow of water through the peninsula. As water from the Saigon River infiltrates the peninsula, moving south through Thu Thiem's canals and lakes, the water will be filtered and cleansed by natural means before rejoining the river along the peninsula's southern edge. The city also proposes a new wastewater treatment facility at Thu Thiem to mitigate direct storm- and wastewater run-off into the canals and river.

As a designed ecological environment, the Thu Thiem peninsula will benefit the ecology of greater Ho Chi Minh City and encourage new and sustainable strategies for planning and developing other land areas within the city.

Public spaces and pedestrian orientation

A diverse network of public spaces extends throughout the new Thu Thiem district and includes neighbourhood parks, riverfront parks, urban and natural canals and an extensive boardwalk system through the existing delta landscape. Due to the humid South Vietnamese climate and the importance of being outdoors during the hot summer season, the concept of 'outdoor living rooms' is expressed throughout Thu Thiem.

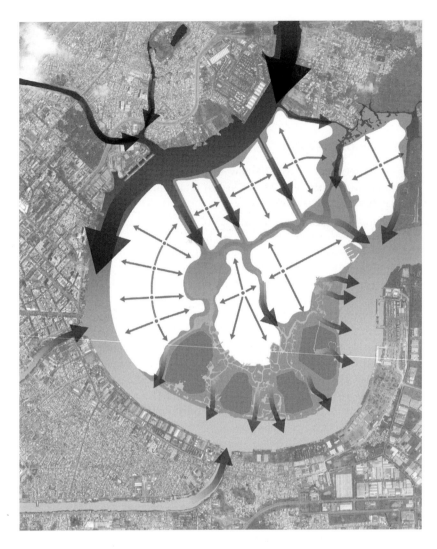

14.4
Integration of canals and
wetlands

Source: Sasaki

Stretching a distance of some 1600 m from the Saigon River to a new internal central lake is the central plaza, which is designed as a primary destination and gathering point within Ho Chi Minh City, accommodating tens of thousands of people during the many holiday celebrations and festivals that occur each year. It is located at the end of a new iconic pedestrian bridge over the Saigon River, directly connecting Thu Thiem to the historic city. It features a grand set of steps to the river, shaded paths, open lawns, paved promenades, concessions and fountains within an active and dynamic public space.

At 75 ha, the lake is designed as a central landscape element within Thu Thiem to add value to the interior lands. Able to accommodate fluctuations in water levels of the Saigon River, the central lake also provides a major public park and internal 'edge' at Thu Thiem on which urban development can occur. Parcels fronting onto the lake will be valuable areas for a variety of land uses

Dennis Pieprz

14.5
Canal district

Source: Sasaki

and experiences. A key public park with an amphitheatre is located behind the Museum of South Vietnam on the new lake.

Crescent Park is a spectacular new 5-km-long public park for all of Ho Chi Minh City along the east bank of the Saigon River. For the urban district of Thu Thiem, it offers a 'front door' onto the river, linking a convention centre in the north to a stadium and arena district to the south. In the centre of this great arc, Crescent Park intersects the central plaza at the pedestrian bridge. Both the convention centre and stadium district are ten-minute walks to the central plaza. Sports fields and tennis courts complement residential areas near the southern end of Crescent Park. The edges of the park are defined by multiple tree rows, while key street and pedestrian linkages tie back into the new urban district.

Neighbourhood and riverfront parks are distributed throughout the north, south and east residential districts at Thu Thiem. Located close to residents in the centre of each neighbourhood, the parks will provide passive areas for strolling and relaxing, and active areas for exercise and recreation. Water-based public spaces include three urban canals in the north district of the plan (see Figure 14.5). Tying in to the central lake, these canals also control and disperse flows of water from the river, while offering attractive tree-lined and lighted promenades along their edges.

Transportation linkages

A multi-lane east–west boulevard with median planting and on-street parking areas will promote Thu Thiem as a place for people and pedestrians, and not for through car and truck traffic, which will be rerouted around Thu Thiem on the regional highway system. The concept of the east–west boulevard modified a previous proposal by the city for an east–west highway connection across the peninsula, tying in to the new tunnel underneath the Saigon River. Now the east–west boulevard accommodates a mixed-use environment of cultural, civic, institutional and residential buildings with generous footpaths. A 300-metre-high television tower, proposed as an iconic element in the Thu Thiem skyline, terminates the west axis along the east–west boulevard.

Local and regional connections to nearby districts and developments will tie both banks of the river into a coherent area. A network of primary, secondary and tertiary streets at Thu Thiem tie in to the regional transportation system of Ho Chi Minh City and allow for the movement of the ubiquitous motorbikes and bicycles as local transport. A comprehensive public-transit system of subway, buses and water transportation will link Thu Thiem further to the historic core and all surrounding districts as well as to major nearby employment centres. Each sub-district within the Thu Thiem area is within a five-minute walk of the transit system.

The proposed underground subway system will have stations at the central plaza, Museum of South Vietnam, and a university institute along the east–west boulevard. An expanded ferry service on the Saigon River and new water-taxi service within the canal system will serve other key landmarks and neighbourhoods. A key challenge will be how to balance private development with the public investments that transit systems entail.

Connection to water and the existing city

The new district enjoys nearly 10 km of frontage along the Saigon River. For years the river has been the 'back door' and edge of the city, lined with industrial port facilities and used primarily to support commerce and transport. As the new district is developed, the design aims to change past perceptions of the river. The river will be transformed into an important visual and environmental asset to enhance the overall quality of life and urban environment. It is expected that Ho Chi Minh City will be perceived as a riverfront city, an enduring image of a world-class metropolis.

The overall form of the Thu Thiem urban design is influenced by the great bend of the Saigon River in this location. The crescent of the waterfront parks and interior Crescent Boulevard, which defines the core area, take the form of the river. The core area, with the highest density, is located directly opposite the historic centre of Ho Chi Minh City. Strong visual and physical linkages connect the historic city with Thu Thiem's residential areas and other key destination nodes such as the convention centre, stadium and arena and the central lake. The pedestrian bridge connects a plaza, known as Me Linh Square, on the historic west side with the central plaza. This linear composition in turn establishes a strong link between the existing city, the new urban district, the central lake and the proposed Museum of South Vietnam into one overall civic composition.

14.6
High density along Crescent
Boulevard

Source: Sasaki

Dense and compact urban form

During the planning of the peninsula, compact development was a major objective in order to limit the need for extensive earthworks and infrastructure extensions. Therefore the densest areas will be concentrated on the highest ground while the lower lands will be more selectively developed. Medium- to high-density development in the core area is placed along Crescent Boulevard, providing a 'high point' and setting for Thu Tiem's tallest buildings, which are approximately forty storeys high (see Figure 14.6). Lower floors will be reserved for commercial uses, such as shops and restaurants. The increased density and compact form in this area, with strong connections to public open space, will further encourage a pedestrian-oriented environment.

The north-east residential neighbourhoods and mixed-use development around the east–west boulevard will offer medium- to low-density opportunities as a counterpoint to the higher-density core area. Building heights will step down as one moves away from the core area and eastward to the interior of Thu Thiem. Conversely, the southern side of Thu Thiem is the lowest land area on the peninsula and therefore the least developed. Accessed by a curvilinear roadway that is raised above the natural canals and vegetation to allow the free flow of water from north to south, selective development zones are established to allow for sensitive construction of a botanical research centre and ecological resort. A public boardwalk system connects the various developments and includes viewing points at intervals along the banks of the river.

Throughout all areas, the orientation of development blocks in a primarily east–west direction respond to climatic conditions (such as wind and sun), further grounding the new urban district in its particular setting.

Land use program

Thu Thiem will support a diverse range of land uses to form a dynamic and vibrant urban area (see Table 14.1). Seventeen different land uses are accommodated within the plan, with primary uses including commercial, residential, public, cultural, educational and open space. The gross floor area ratio of the district is 4 : 1. The primary commercial and office uses are clustered along Crescent Boulevard and the Central Plaza within the core area at Thu Thiem. Residential and institutional uses will predominate away from the core area. The density of residential use will vary, but will be primarily multi-family buildings of six to twelve floors, often integrated with other uses such as ground-floor commercial in the form of convenience retail, small shops and restaurants.

Major public and institutional uses such as museum, government complex, library, research institute, post office and university are located along the east–west boulevard, which will serve as a major gateway to the new urban area. Educational uses, community centres and other civic uses are strategically distributed within the neighbourhoods. The largest programmatic elements will be the 50 000-m^2 convention centre and the 15 000–20 000-seat stadium, positioned north and south of the core area. The convention centre occupies a strategic point along the river edge, viewed from multiple angles from within and beyond Thu Thiem, whether on foot or by boat. A new Thu Thiem ferry station and a water taxi will service the convention centre. The stadium is the cornerstone element of a sports and entertainment district that includes the arena, indoor swimming facility, entertainment venues and unique residential loft-style buildings.

Implementation

Within a twenty-year planning horizon, dynamic social, political and economic forces will come to influence the pace and scale of development at

Table 14.1 Planned land uses for Thu Thiem (source: *Detailed Master Plan* and *Urban Design Guidelines for Thu Thiem New Urban Area.* Prepared by Sasaki)

Designation/purpose	Area
District area	740 ha
Parks	92 ha
Wetlands	137 ha
Residential	3 300 000 m^2
Office	1 700 000 m^2
Retail	800 000 m^2
Civic/institutional/educational	400 000 m^2
Total building area	6 200 000 m^2
Projected permanent population	140 000
Projected daily visitors	350 000

Thu Thiem. The plan anticipates these forces of growth and change by providing a framework of land use, circulation and open space within which development may be accommodated over time. The *Urban Design Guidelines* express this framework and will guide the character and expression of the new district through the definition of land-use zones, open spaces, road widths, setbacks, density and tower zones.

Development parcels will vary in size, location and uses such that both the public sector and the private sector may be engaged in development activities. Phasing of the master plan involves five-year increments, linked to off-site improvements such as the port relocations and bridge construction. A mix of uses in each five-year development phase allows for a flexible response to changing market-led demands.

International and domestic investment interest from high-quality groups with a long-term perspective has been stimulated by the comprehensive vision and by the considerable political and public support for the plan. Major multi-billion-dollar public investments in transport and infrastructure improvements were either significantly altered or positively affected by the process of developing the plan.

Over twenty years, plan implementation will be administered and monitored by development agencies of Ho Chi Minh City, the Urban Planning Institute of Ho Chi Minh City, local planners and experts, and the many local and foreign architects, planners, landscape architects and engineers who will be involved with the realization of this new urban district.

Significantly, the planning process used for Thu Thiem has become institutionalized within Vietnam's governmental framework and now serves as a model for the evolving collaborative relationships between urban design consultants in the West and public clients in Vietnam. National and city standards and processes in Vietnam will be modified to reflect the process that has been followed in the development of the plan and urban design guidelines for the district.

Conclusion

Ho Chi Minh City is fortunate to have a rich cultural history and an identifiable historic core on which to build. The historic centre, symbolized by the Hotel de Ville (Town Hall), Opera House, Le Loi Street and Nguyen Hue Avenue, represents the city's development in the nineteenth and twentieth centuries. Thu Thiem will represent the twenty-first-century evolution of the city, presenting a continuum of growth and scale.

For years, the Saigon River has been the edge of the city, supporting commerce and trade. In parts, the river is heavily polluted and edged by shipping facilities, warehouses and storage yards. The development pressures on the historic core have led to over-sized projects, which disrupt the existing city fabric of narrow tree-lined streets and active footpaths. A new urban district at Thu Thiem will alleviate development pressure on the historic core and will transform the river into an important visual and environmental asset for the city.

As a visionary plan for a growing South East Asian metropolis, the Thu Thiem plan is a historic milestone effort in the development of Ho Chi Minh

City. By providing a unique urban framework of land use, circulation and open space based on local influences and conditions, Thu Thiem is a unique development and model for future sustainable urban developments throughout the world. Thu Thiem will be realized at a scale that recognizes its city context and establishes links to both the past and the future of Ho Chi Minh City and its citizens.

Dennis Pieprz

Networks Cities in China

Sustaining Culture, Economics and the Environment

James Brearley and Qun Fang

Introduction

To achieve the current extraordinary pace of its urban development, China has one standard urban planning formula, which is very efficient in creating well-engineered expanses of urban space at low cost and high profit to the state but fails to provide a fertile foundation for social, economic and environmental sustainability. The default planning formula has large-scale, highly segregated land-use zones connected by sparse road grids. Housing zones are the bulk of China's new urbanity, characterized by arrays of residential enclaves, each occupying an entire super-size city block surrounded by large city streets lined with fences.

Although Chinese enclaves have a long tradition, today's gated communities have new characteristics. They are on a super-scale, socially isolating rather than community forming, exclude non-housing pro-grammes, and often incorporate buildings higher than ten floors. Oppor-tunities to balance these isolated enclaves with an active public realm, allowing business activities close to these large residential markets, are overlooked. Residents of high-density cities commute, which is clearly neither sustainable nor convenient. With thousands of Chinese cities applying the default planning formula, a reappraisal and range of new approaches is urgent and crucial if only because land-use zoning is difficult, if not impossible, to undo.

In 2001, BAU (Brearley Architects and Urbanists) and Steve Whitford developed an alternative planning strategy: 'networks cities', which utilizes networks of land-use zones to achieve integrated (not segregated) cities through adjacency (rather than mixed-zone assimilation) of land-use zones. This case study shows that the strategy reintroduces complexity without diminishing clarity and enhances flexibility for unknown futures through creating hybrid zones. Since 2001 five BAU network proposals have been awarded prizes and the construction of a 12-km^2 model addition to Chengdu city has started construction.

Networks cities

Conventional modern city planning segregates primary functions into large monofunctional land-use zones. These cities have a high degree of order and clarity but suffer from being inconvenient, monotonous, transport-dependent, isolating and inflexible. 'Networks cities' address these shortages using a framework of continuity, connectivity, adjacency, complexity and dispersion in order to maximize the potential for the city to sustain vigorous environmental, social, cultural and economic life.

Zoning bands

Organizing land-use zones into narrow bands, rather than broad swaths of blocks, gives each zone a greater boundary length along which to align with dissimilar activities. This allows for a high degree of unpredictable synergies between the different land uses. The idea was first enunciated in OMA's Parc La Villette competition entry in 1982 (Lucan 1991: 86) and later by Toyo Ito in 1992 in his urban design proposal for Liu Jia Zui, Shanghai (Ito 1994).

A city's programmes (residential, office, light industry, retail and green land programmes) gain freedom and potential when aligned with one another. The boundaries of zones are the places of highest potential for cross-fertilization between functions. These boundaries have a tendency to blur, where programmes can overstep their planning demarcations, and where non-conforming uses are most likely to be tolerated. This is where new, marginalized and less conventional programmes have the highest probability of emergence. It is where culture can emerge and evolve.

Zoning networks

By adding land-use bands perpendicular to the parallel bands described above, a network of land-use is formed. Each land-use can be spread more or less continuously across the city. A networks-zoning scheme has the characteristics of a banded organization but the added benefit of overlapping land-use classifications, where one network overlaps another. These overlaps provide arrays of hybrid land-use areas throughout the city. Each provides the city with flexibility to accommodate more of one or other of the overlapping land-use programmes, depending on the demands at any time.

To a greater extent than the banded structure, the networks organization provides continuities throughout the city providing a range of beneficial qualities: residential networks allow the city to be traversed in a relatively safe environment along residential streets; park networks can provide eco-corridors in many directions; and commercial networks allow the natural tendency of growth of retail activity along roads.

Dispersed and accessible programmes

The networks cities approach distributes primary land uses throughout the city. Each district contains work, living, recreation, services and green land. This diversity creates cities of convenience and reduces commuting. The complexity within each district enhances the potential for informal communities to emerge. Incremental growth of networks cities occurs without the phenomenon of highly diminished amenity that occurs when conventional cities grow.

Parkland networks

Organizing a city's parkland into a network, rather than a series of centralized and disconnected parks, brings numerous advantages. Parts of a network can provide eco-corridors to link natural wilds and enable flora and fauna to migrate through urban areas (Erickson 2006: part 2, ch. 3). A network park system provides a more equitable distribution of a city's green areas, bringing it within reach of all people. The strong legibility of networked park systems encourages exploration and use of a city's green resources. Circulation paths in green networks can encourage cycling and walking rather than motorized road transport. Compared to central parks the network park provides great potential for extensive treatment of storm-water run-off in local natural systems.

Ecological meta-networks

Networked open space strategies can be amplified to a scale that produces a balance between urban and rural environments within the metropolis, making the rural highly accessible while maintaining continuities essential to a thriving city. Large-scale green networks about 1.7 km wide can provide an escape from the intensity and summer heat of the high-density city. The scale allows for local food production to reduce a city's food carbon footprint as well as provide educational and leisure opportunities.

The green meta-network allows for localizing city infrastructures to maximize efficiency. Organic waste, grey water and black water can be treated locally and by-products used to benefit local agriculture. Energy resource in the form of methane can be extracted from organic waste and used locally. Sustainable urban water drainage systems can be highly efficient with the benefit of local countryside. Such a large green network allows each district to generate a portion of its power requirements utilizing renewable sources: primarily wind, but also geo-thermal, solar PV, solar thermal and biomass. Localizing and exposing such infrastructure can bring awareness of the eco-footprint of the local district and, by extension, the eco-footprint of the individual.

Networks cities framework

The networks framework provides a city with equal distribution of programmes, making them more accessible across the entire urban environment. It allows for the flexible and unpredictable emergence of programmes and their combinations by overlaying land-use bands and by situating dissimilar programmes adjacent to one another. Although the framework utilizes conventional statutory planning tools it remains open for creative interpretation according to physical, cultural and economic contexts. The networks framework can provide a robust and flexible city within which culture, social life, entrepreneurial business and environmental health can thrive.

Case study 1: Xin Yu Networks City

The first case study is Xin Yu Networks City, a 25-km² extension to Xin Yu City and winner of first prize of an invited competition in 2002. New Chinese cities separate primary city functions from one another; in particular working places are planned far away from dwellings. However, while heavy industry should be kept well downwind from residences, most workplaces, including most types of light industry, can be accommodated without conflict in the city proper. The Xin Yu design utilizes a networks strategy to integrate programmes throughout the city: living, working, services, education and recreation. By restricting truck movement to selected roads and by separating industrial sites from residential sites with either a green network or a commercial network, the city can attain complexity, convenience and flexibility. For instance, Figure 15.1 shows how networks zoning weaves city programmes of work, dwelling, education, entertainment, shopping and recreation throughout the entire city.

Figure 15.2 shows how a complex urbanity is created by the use of existing planning tools applied in a new scale and organization. Industrial buildings, indicated as big boxes, are required to situate their office components along certain street edges for scale, activity and character objectives, while other streets are allowed to take conventional industrial characteristics.

Figure 15.3 shows how diverse the green network is: eco-corridors following waterways link ecological parkland on either side of the city; recreation and community farming occur in distributed linear parks; local markets and plazas occur wherever the commercial network overlaps the green net; and major public-event spaces and sports can be found in the wide

15.1
General arrangement plan

Source: BAU

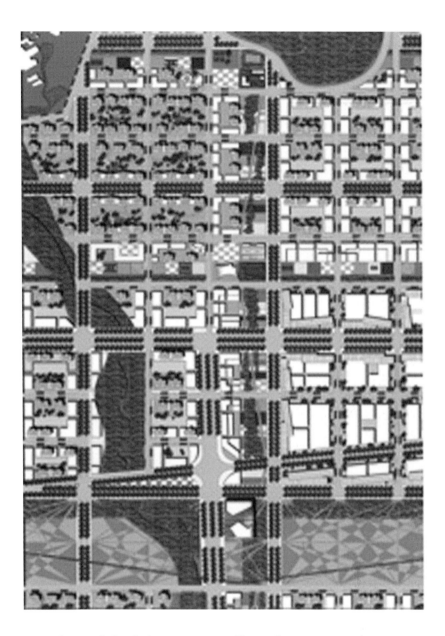

15.2
City detail plan

Source: BAU

network strand that links new city to old. Finally, Figure 15.4 demonstrates how overlaying four land-use networks creates areas of hybrid and pure programmes close to one another.

Case study 2: Chengdu East

The second case study is Chengdu East, a 12-km² city extension that won first prize in an invited competition in 2005. Infrastructure and roads are due for completion in 2010. The networks organization is utilized here to ensure that all residents are within walking distance (400 m) of both retail services and the

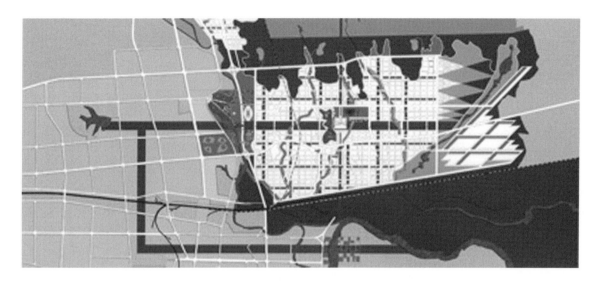

15.3
Green network plan

Source: BAU

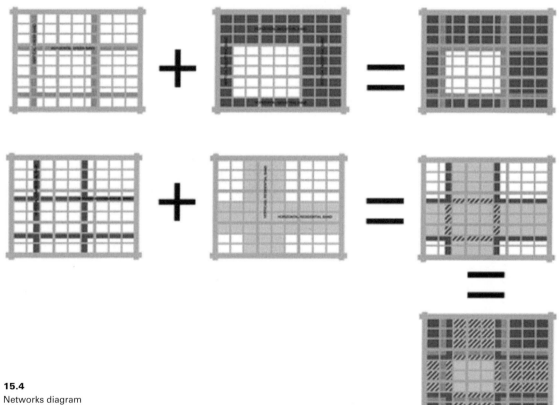

15.4
Networks diagram

Source: BAU

city green network. A network of commercial programmes is distributed along alternate streets throughout the 12 km², enabling local offices, retail and shop-top housing to emerge.

In the contemporary Chinese city, offices and retail premises are usually located in central business districts. Almost all housing is in residential zones and takes the form of medium- to high-density gated communities. These enclaves provide residents with an escape from the intensity of the city. However, when accompanied by inactive streets these gated residential districts lose many of the advantages that the high-density city usually brings: rich cultural, social and public life; opportunity for street-based entrepreneurial endeavours and places to work; and the convenience of being able to do most things locally.

The massive size of enclaves in China reduces the permeability and walkability of the city. The green network (Figure 15.5) is utilized here to reduce the scale of these enclaves and provide greater choice and more direct routes for walking and cycling. Organizing the allocated city green areas into networks rather than central parks enables the green parts to do more: to accommodate a green bike network; to support natural storm-water cleansing systems; and to provide a legible system for encouraging people to discover the city's entire park system. The network connects to railway green corridor to the west, ecological corridor to the east, farmland city green wedge to the south and future city extension to the north.

The green network traces and engulfs the existing network of country lanes, villages, tree stands, dams, waterways and other features. The green network is also used as a strategy for preserving places, communities and nature: a preservation network.

15.5
Green network

Source: BAU

Commercial network

A commercial network (Figure 15.6) is planned within walking distance of all residents. It provides places of work, entertainment and services. At network intersections it provides designated pure commercial sites for loud programmes, and otherwise provides hybrid zoning with options for alternative housing typologies.

Case study 3: Symbiotic City

The third case study is Symbiotic City, Hangzhou Xia Sha, a 178-km² city growth plan. Working with Steve Whitford, BAU proposed a networks strategy at a scale that radically changes the form of the metropolis.

By 2050 Hangzhou may have become one of China's mega-cities with a population of more than twelve million (McKinsey Global Institute 2008). This proposal seeks both a spatial shift from the unrelenting urbanity of the contemporary megapolis and an efficient organization for environmentally sustainable outcomes. By introducing a 1.7-km-wide network of rural land and a 1.7-km-wide network of urban land, a territory of both urbanity and countryside can be achieved.

Overlaying the two networks results in an array of three types of 1.7 × 1.7-km cells: urban, rural and hybrid (urban/rural) cells. Each group of

15.6
Commercial network

Source: BAU

城市网络
Urban network

乡村网络
Rural network

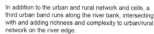

在城市与乡村网络单元的基础上，沿江地带设置了一
条城市带，增强了江边地带的丰富度与复杂度。

In addition to the urban and rural network and cells, a
third urban band runs along the river bank, intersecting
with and adding richness and complexity to urban/rural
network on the river edge.

网络城市
Network city

■ 城市区块 Urban cell
□ 乡村区块 Rural cell
□ 混合区块 Hybrid cell

15.7

Rural and urban networks

Source: BAU

four cells makes a module of one urban, one rural and two hybrid cells. The rural cell in each module is designed as an eco-cell: treating waste, managing water, harnessing renewable energy and producing a portion of the food needs of the module.

A public transport network of trams and metro follows the spatial configuration of the urban network. Within the green network an eco-corridor network is created to support bio-diversity and allow flora and fauna to remain on the transforming site. The 178-km^2 site is planned to accommodate approximately 1.8 million people (10 100 people per square kilometre). A meta-network of urban and rural programmes creates a metropolis in which all people are within reach (900 m) of countryside (Figure 15.7).

Figure 15.8 shows high-density urbanity with building envelopes designed to protect sunlight access to public spaces and footpaths. In Figure

15.8

3D urban

Source: BAU

15.9
Four cells

Source: BAU

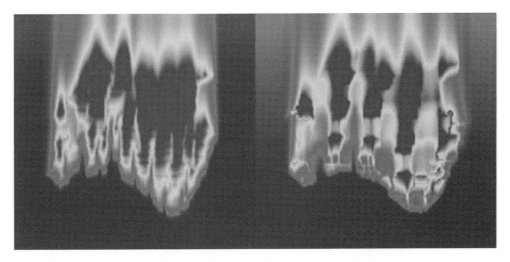

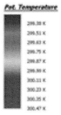

15.10
Urban heat island programme

Source: BAU

James Brearley and Qun Fang

15.9 each four-cell module is conceived as an entity, which manages most of its own waste, water and energy production and part of its food production. Figure 15.10 shows Arup consulting engineers' temperature modelling, comparing the heat source effects of a conventional planning proposal on the left with those of BAU's Symbiotic City proposal on the right. The rural network enables a significant respite from Hangzhou's oppressive summer heat. The rural network is aligned with the dominant southerly winds to create corridors of relatively cool air, and corridors of wind energy, which can be harnessed by turbines.

City of ghettos: the Chinese urban planning formula

BAU has run its practice in China since 2001, working on hundreds of architectural proposals and dozens of urban planning and designs proposals and public landscape projects. This has given the firm a good look at China's planning model.

Planning high-density cities within a couple of months is routine for Chinese planners. These instant cities are made possible by the national acceptance of one planning formula, a super-scale and super-zoned urbanity of enclaves: the new ghetto city. The high population density of the new Chinese cities gives them the potential to sustain diverse forms of culture, economics and environment. Ghetto-city planning guarantees that this potential will never be realized.

The Chinese planning formula, or model, is a reaction to the chaos of the existing cities. The formula delivers living environments that are clean, safe and green; business districts that are slick, predictable and clear; and industrial districts that are out of sight and out of mind. The planning model allows cities to be developed rapidly with a minimum of government investment, and a minimum of government responsibility for the ongoing maintenance of the city.

The model is based on mid-twentieth-century modernist planning practice, which has led to modern ghetto cities throughout the world. Theorists and practitioners in countries that previously embraced ghetto zoning began discrediting the formula in the 1950s (Risselada and van den Heuvel 2005: 84–85). It is now unanimously discredited in those countries and they are dealing with its ramifications. The formula's primary flaw is the scale of its land-use zones. The new cities are divided into super-scale zones of housing, industry, office, education, R+D and retail/entertainment. The results are areas of single usage, isolated from all other uses. Lengthy motorized travel between work, home, shopping and playing becomes a daily inconvenience and a toll on the environment. The cities struggle to sustain informal social and economic life.

Planners and governments throughout the developed world face an uphill battle of undoing ghetto zoning. If perceived to diminish land value or community value the re-zoning of land is an expensive, slow and virtually impossible task. Property owners exert their legal right to financial compensation and community groups utilize political power to thwart changes to the status quo.

New ghetto cities

China has 2862 prefectural cities, 333 regional cities and thirty-four capital-level cities, each experiencing explosive growth. All, except perhaps for a handful, are implementing new ghetto city planning.

All new housing in new Chinese residential zones takes the form of large gated communities. The vast income inequality found in Chinese cities breeds fear and a desire for living in gated communities – a culture of enclaves. The typical size of housing enclaves ranges from 6 ha (300 × 200 m) to 28 ha (400 × 700 m). Office developments are also frequently super-sized and take the form of gated office parks. Universities, government centres, factories and many other organizations are super-size enclaves, frequently larger than that of the housing. The enclaves create major barriers within the city, adding significant distance to each trip and discouraging walking. Long distances, from front door to enclave gate, further discourage inhabitants from leaving their apartments or offices to engage frequently with the city.

Street grids follow enclave dimensions and typically are 300 × 200 m to 400 × 700 m. Streets alongside enclaves of housing, office parks, universities and government centres are typically lined with endless fences, broken only by a guarded gate. With such a large street grid, all streets are destined to carry a large traffic load. There are few intimate-scale quiet streets and fewer intimate-scale local shopping streets.

There are few housing options. The only alternative to enclave living in the new ghetto city takes the form of SOHO (single occupant home office/small office home office). SOHO gives flexibility but no certainty with respect to neighbouring tenancy programmes. SOHO is situated in commercial zones. The buildings are not required to have direct solar access, balconies or green land.

In the roll-out of the new ghetto city it is assumed that most, if not all, existing settlements are to be erased. Farming populations are allocated apartments in medium- or high-density housing enclaves. Land parcels within the new ghetto cities are developed with primitive instruments and rudimentary controls: land use, FAR (floor area ratio), building setbacks, heights, footprint ratio, green area ratio, car parking ratio and car crossover locations.

The development process is characterized by fast-track design and fast-track approval. Vast projects of up to 1 km² of high-density housing, office or industry are frequently designed to concept design stage within weeks of their architect commencing work. Permission is as-of-right, based on the urban planning control plans of each site. The speed usually requires massive repetitions of site-planning typologies, building typologies and styles. After decades of Soviet-style mass-produced housing, repetition in buildings has become the acceptable, if not preferred, norm.

Although new Chinese districts have a high population density, few residents live within walking distance (less than 750 m) of employment, services, parkland or entertainment. Thus, cars are an attractive option. Each city seeks to create one or more slick new CBDs. Ideally, they are free of housing. The streets in these slick business ghettos are dull during the day, lifeless, and hostile at night. At the same time active parkland is new in most

Chinese cities. City parks in the new cities are usually large and central. They are frequently gated and therefore lack vitality. Cities are rarely willing to develop parkland in excess of the 8–12 per cent minimum national requirement.

The central government requires that city plans be initiated by competition. After competition there is no requirement whatsoever for the winning designers to complete the work, bid for the next stage of work or even act as advisers as the project develops. A brilliant competition design is usually (un)developed by the local design institute to a point where any unique ideas of the winning scheme cease to exist. The common belief, or excuse, for this lack of continuity is that a local design institute can combine all the best ideas from the various competitors. The local design institute's team is young and driven by time-related profit. As the team proceeds to develop the design they inevitably cut off all communication with the original designers. Without question they amend the urban plan to follow the whims and desires of politicians acting as entrepreneurial property developers.

The average time given for a city design competition (for 1–15 km^2) is eight weeks. Deliverables usually include physical models, computer fly-throughs, 3D renders, bound booklets and multi-media presentations. The designs require urban planning, urban design, several building designs (urban design level), landscape designs, control plans and guidelines. Control plans for each block of land include designation of FAR, height limit, set-backs, car crossover locations, green area ratio and footprint density. Competitors are given around forty minutes to present their city designs. Translation may reduce this to twenty minutes. Frequently projects are not presented in person but via multi-media, reducing time to less than twenty minutes. A five-minute question time may follow.

Most of the judging panel will arrive in the city on the evening before adjudication. They frequently have no time to visit the site, nor the opportunity to study the proposals before the presentations. The judges are often expected to summarize their findings immediately after the presentations in a speech to the group, after which lunch is served and the judging deemed complete. Most judging is finished within the day. Frequently a jury of politicians joins the experts or votes subsequently, which emphasizes the importance of accessible computer 3D imagery, especially fly-throughs.

Written competition briefs for large (1–15 km^2) urban design projects frequently consist of around five written A4 pages of background information. Another five pages will be devoted to the competition procedures and deliverables and another twenty will contain general information about national and local standards and about generic good design principles. Accompanying the sketchy written brief is a group briefing of around one hour, followed by a one- to two-hour drive around the vast site, with occasional stops for clarification and photo opportunities. The teams rarely come from the city in question. Many a design team never returns to the city until submission day. All unique settlement patterns existing on sites remain unexplored.

Competitors are expected to propose the number and type of most city institutions. Aerial photographs are not available due to national security.

Ideas previously developed for sites are rarely provided. Beyond a zoning plan or, at best, a master plan, no information is given regarding previous concepts. No transport strategies, economic planning information, regional planning information or socio-cultural data are provided. Some information may be available on request. Research starts from scratch and is rarely performed by the consultants in the short time available.

Planning projects frequently require a proposal of city density (FAR) and green land ratios. The parameters of these vary from city to city but fall within the national parameters. The market rules: economic growth is seen as the primary measure of progress in Chinese urbanization. Politicians are rewarded according to the quantity of urbanization, not its quality. Cities compete vigorously for property developers, effectively designing cities and sites to attract their investment.

The Cultural Revolution's university closures have created a gaping absence of professionals aged in their mid-forties to mid-sixties. Most new Chinese cities are designed by young planners whose university projects (even at Master's level) were not based on research, design or experimentation but were high-speed commercial production for their professor's planning firm. Few planners have the time, inclination or energy to broaden their planning education. Chinese planners are ruthlessly efficient at reproducing the one and only planning formula. They are motivated by financial bonuses relating to the speed and efficiency of each project.

Typically Chinese companies place only two people on a competition or commission for a 1–15-km^2 urban design. Additional staff are brought in at various stages to do production work. The planning departments of explosive cities of population between a half and one million typically have fewer than ten planners on their staff. Instead they rely heavily on the ex-government, profit-motivated, local design institute.

The planning process is opaque. In a culture where all manner of things are contextual, and where development is explosive, it is impossible to ascertain the motives behind many urban planning decisions. Few decisions, including changes to an urban design, are documented in a format accessible to even the urban planning consultants. Furthermore, professionals and academics receive little respect. They are only just regaining credibility nullified during the Cultural Revolution. Politicians' opinions outweigh all others in urban planning.

Conclusion

This chapter has outlined the failings and challenges that China's new ghetto city planning pose as well as describing viable alternatives. Constant warnings of the diabolical nature of new ghetto city planning have been delivered in China for more than fifteen years even though criticism of government planning is censored. China's leading universities host conferences, seminars, workshops and lectures involving international design practitioners, academics and even politicians. Still, most professors and design institutes continue to produce new ghetto cities ad infinitum. No argument can counteract a developing country's blind faith in modernity. Learning from Western urban planning mistakes seems impossible. Professionals and academics alike are too busy in private practice to find the time or the energy for research and criticism, and there is shockingly little exchange of ideas.

References

Erickson, D. (2006) *Metrogreen: Connecting Open Space In North American Cities*, Washington, DC: Island Press.

Ito, T. (1994) Shanghai Urban Project, *El Croquis* 71, 156–161.

Lucan, J. (1991) *Rem Koolhaas – OMA: Architecture, 1970–1990*, Zurich: Artemis and Winkler Verlag.

McKinsey Global Institute (2008) 'Preparing for China's urban billion', March. Online: www.mckinsey.com/mgi/publications/china_urban_summary_of_findings.asp (accessed 24 February 2010).

Risselada, M. and van den Heuvel, D. (2005) *Team 10: In Search of a Utopia of the Present 1953–1981*, Rotterdam: NAi Publishers.

The Responsive City

London South Bank Experiences

Alex Lifschutz

As a firm of architects and urban planners, Lifschutz Davidson Sandilands (LDS) has been closely involved in the renewal of London's South Bank. This area, in the metropolitan boroughs of Lambeth and Southwark, is now the main cultural hub of the capital and has a growing and dynamic resident community. However, when we started to work there twenty years ago, it was run down and lifeless – a twilight area in the heart of London.

The area bore the scars of damage inflicted in the Second World War, but even more from a legacy of disastrous post-war planning policies. Its long river frontage had been cleared of nineteenth-century warehouses and wharves, filled with major arts venues, such as the National Theatre, Hayward Gallery and the Royal Festival Hall, and even larger commercial headquarters for multinationals, such as Shell and IBM. But the spaces between these imposing structures had been neglected. Whatever was happening in the offices, concert halls and galleries, it was doing nothing to enliven the streets, which managed to be simultaneously dull and threatening. The large numbers of office workers and theatre audiences coming and going each day had no reason to stay.

The streets lacked animation as the new buildings were turned away from the public realm; the residential population was declining, schools and shops closing. This was bizarre given that the South Bank is in a central part of London, with excellent local, national and international transport links. It enjoys the unparalleled advantage of a long stretch of Thames River frontage with views of world-famous landmarks, such as St Paul's Cathedral, Somerset House and the Houses of Parliament. It had received massive investment for over three decades following the Second World War. This chapter explores the reasons why, despite all this investment, urban blight descended on the South Bank. It defines some of the factors that led to socially and economically sustainable renewal of the area and centres on enhancing social sustainability in urban environments.

Early development

Historic maps show a pattern of development on the South Bank quite distinct from the rest of London or even from other parts of the river frontage. The earliest modern development of the South Bank started in the late eighteenth century and consisted of industrial buildings, timber yards, boatyards, breweries, dye works and piers for transporting goods and people. Later in the nineteenth century the hinterland developed around narrow thoroughfares with pattern-book housing of narrow-fronted terraces enclosing strips of garden to the rear. Little remains of this densely built artisans' housing other than two rows of early-nineteenth-century speculative housing. The Oxo Tower Wharf, built in the late nineteenth century, is the only remnant of industrial buildings.

The railways came to the South Bank in the 1860s. They were driven through existing residential areas on brick viaducts to destinations on that side of the river and via a new bridge to Charing Cross station on the north bank. In the early part of the twentieth century there were two significant insertions: Waterloo station and County Hall, the headquarters of the London County Council, which were completed in the 1920s. Both structures were typical of future thinking about the area as a sort of marshalling yard for large-scale new development to serve the rest of the capital city rather than as a locality with its own needs and identity. Both buildings survived the Blitz, which affected other parts of Southwark and Lambeth greatly. In the post-war period, the clearance of bombsites and 'slums' combined to empty a swath of riverfront land.

1950s: 'big event blight'

The first big post-war intervention on the South Bank came in 1951. The Festival of Britain was a national celebration of emergence from years of suffering and austerity. It was an enormous fair, with the Royal Festival Hall at its heart, surrounded by smaller, temporary pavilions set in pleasure gardens along the riverbank. As a symbol of national resurrection the festival was a critical and popular success, but its legacy was more problematic. Festivals provide metropolitan crowds with an exciting day out mostly to the detriment of indigenous communities assailed by the tidal influxes of people attending events, parking their cars, dropping their litter and then departing. Once the festival closed, much of the land was cleared and the site became a ghost town.

The same pattern of 'big-event blight' occurred on other sites developed for large, one-off events. Other London examples include Alexandra Palace, Wembley and White City. A recent example is the Millennium Dome at Greenwich, which was to have been the catalyst for regeneration of the local area. The spectacular structure was to have been dismantled at the end of 2000 after a year-long exhibition and the site redeveloped according to the existing master plan for the Greenwich Peninsula. In 1998, however, the recently elected Labour government decided to retain it as an iconic building that would be a 'lasting legacy'. Unfortunately, although the dome has been converted into a successful entertainment venue, little progress has been made with the new residential quarter.

1960s and after: building for prestige

After the Festival of Britain departed from the South Bank several large, introspective, single-use buildings eventually arrived, apparently independent of one another and denying any coherent street pattern. More large cultural buildings were built adjacent to the Royal Festival Hall: the Queen Elizabeth Hall and Purcell Room, the Hayward Gallery and the National Theatre. These performance spaces were eventually bracketed between large office developments, starting in 1963 upriver, with the Shell Centre, then the tallest office tower in Britain.

These large, monocultural buildings were attractive to government departments and blue-chip companies, seduced by statement architecture with direct connections to the suburbs via the excellent transport system. But they had a disastrous effect on the urban grain and the local community of the South Bank. The new buildings were not only physically unconnected to their surroundings, turning their backs on the streets, but also their management-grade staff served remote corporate or national interests and they provided only unskilled jobs for local people. Employees were generally commuters who spent little in the local economy.

Monument and fabric

In the 1970s and 1980s the response to the depressed and disjointed condition of the South Bank was to consider monocultural development on an even larger scale. By 1970 Lambeth Council was considering plans for a self-contained office development to cover a broad largely derelict area behind the riverfront buildings. This would have confirmed the institutional character of the area, removed the last traces of the industrial and commercial activities, and placed a corporate-controlled barrier between the hinterland and the river.

The proposed development had intentions of renewal, but the monolithic scale of the buildings and dedication to specific uses would have had the opposite effect. An approach to regeneration that treats the city as a blank area into which highly specific, architecturally impressive buildings are placed is guaranteed to destroy the urban grain. Nevertheless it remains seductive, and can be seen in cities right across Britain since Frank Gehry's Guggenheim Museum brought remarkable benefits to Bilbao. It is worth noting that the Guggenheim attracts more than 80 per cent of its visitors from outside the city (Bailey 2002), which may have benefits for the wider local economy, but the cultural magnet still depends on outside funding and political commitment. The effect is similar to the big-event buildings described earlier.

Another paradox: the more extraordinary their collection of inter-nationally significant architectural set pieces, the more alike cities become. Like zoos, our cities are being filled with clusters of exotic imported creatures, each different from the other but often indistinguishable from other clusters in other cities; like zoos, the menagerie of spectacular but curiously unconnected buildings can engender a considerable ennui: seen one tiger in a cage, seen them all.

This is not to say that architectural set pieces are not magnificent. But they stand apart, literally and metaphorically, from the more workaday fabric of the city. We gawp at them and are impressed, but do we like their artificial environment or are we drawn to the old city or the red-light district where vernacular buildings burst with local culture and intriguing delights? Does not the search for the conceit that will make a building stand out among ever more intriguing structures reduce this kind of architecture to what Campbell (2004) has referred to as 'prestigious garnish' on the city, forcing architects to 'assume a duty, not just a licence, to challenge norms'?

The gradual evolution of an old European city, such as Parma (Italy), shows a different way to evolve cities where curiously all buildings are alike in form but can be adapted to different uses (Rowe and Koetter 1984). Successful, liveable cities consist mostly of apparently homogeneous fabric with no identified author – buildings that accommodate all forms of activity, from living quarters to local businesses, bars and cafés, linked by the network of streets and open spaces that make up the public realm. In this kind of city it is impossible to view buildings as isolated objects, only as a set of unfolding spaces.

Top-down vs. ground-up

'Top-down' urban design – the kind that produces 'big events' and specimen buildings – is well established, widely understood, highly valued and predictable because it is enshrined in the planning system. By its nature it leaves little scope for urban processes to bubble up from below. It is inimical to the 'street ballet' of many different kinds of people coexisting and pursuing diverse and overlapping activities, which Jane Jacobs (1961) identified as a principal indicator of a healthy, diverse and vigorous neighbourhood.

More recently, Stephen Johnson (2001: 18) suggested an explanation for the development of Jacobs' city, that of 'a common thread running through recent research in biology, zoology, software development and urbanism: "emergence", or the spontaneous development by apparently disorganized groups of unintelligent individuals, of solutions'. The key is that groups are large and active enough to generate sufficient exchanges of information between individuals – the very essence of the city. These encounters cause individuals to modify their behaviour, which in turn kick-starts the process of developing change. The distinguishing feature of these systems is that they are not imposed but appear to arise spontaneously out of an infinite number of small exchanges. Such 'self-organized', 'emergent' or 'ground-up behaviour' systems 'solve problems by drawing on masses of relatively simple elements rather than a single, intelligent "executive branch"'.

Instead of thinking about the city as a collection of fixed, set-piece buildings, initiated from the top down, we might encourage ground-up design and low-key incremental changes at street level. The planning and development process could abandon its reliance on zoning and instead promote imaginative design that is capable of responding to changing economic and social conditions without the need continually to demolish and redevelop. In this scenario new projects should be assessed not for their conformity with the current 'land use' plan or for their exterior expression, but for their adaptability and the contribution they make to a flexible urban grain.

Planning and profit: Coin Street Community Builders

South Bank residents were alarmed by the office and retail development proposed on a key site on the river frontage in the late 1970s and early 1980s. The lack of housing and community facilities in the proposals galvanized them to a well-organized and high-profile protest. In 1984, after a decade of campaigning, Coin Street Community Builders (CSCB) acquired the freehold of the 5.26-ha (13-acre) riverfront site that had been slated for office development (Figure 16.1). Persuading the Greater London Council to save the land for the community was, in the words of one Broadwall resident, Tom Keller, 'an amazing political feat' (personal communication, 25 April 2008).

CSCB's goals were simple: to bring ordinary people back to living and working in the area, and to provide the necessary support (schools, nurseries community centres and sports facilities) for them. Far from conflicting with the area's arts and cultural tourism or corporate employment, these objectives acknowledged that a fully supported residential population was an essential basis for the South Bank to function as a self-sustaining part of the city (see Figure 16.2).

The Greater London Council (later in 1986 abolished by the government of Margaret Thatcher) was willing to forgo the potential profit to be made from redeveloping the site along purely commercial lines in order to encourage a new way of approaching development of the area. This not-for-profit principle underpinned the activities of the CSCB. As a social enterprise its opportunity and desire to raise a surplus in the pursuit of its social or charitable goals was not restricted, just reinvested rather than being distributed

16.1
The cleared Coin Street sites

Photo: Iain Tuckett/CSCB

Alex Lifschutz

16.2
Coin Street housing

Photo: Iain Tuckett/CSCB

to investors. This model of urban development that CSCB commissioned LDS to pursue was based on the growing residential community's needs. Jane Jacobs' thinking about the formation of urban neighbourhoods underpinned our approach.

Mixed use and adaptability

We sought opportunities to create a more permeable, connected architecture that had some relationship to its physical, social and historical context. The site contained a strong candidate for re-use in a redundant warehouse, known as 'Oxo Tower Wharf', which became a focal point for the redevelopment of the area. It is a relatively undistinguished industrial building, typical of the buildings and wharves that once lined this stretch of the Thames, except that it had a ninety-foot tower incorporating large windows that spell out 'OXO' (Figure 16.3). This was a blatant attempt to use architecture as advertising, not permitted on the Thames, for a meat-cube product. Although the building lacked charisma it harked back to the industrial past of the South Bank; the fondness of local people for this last relic of a bygone age added emotional texture to efforts to preserve it.

We converted the warehouse into a mix of affordable apartments, small studio/workshops and retail outlets, with a 400-seat restaurant and a public viewing platform on the top floor. Because of its simple frame it was, and will continue to be, very adaptable. We saw the conversion as merely a stage in the evolution of a structure that had initially been an electricity generating station, then converted into a meat warehouse and finally, before we arrived on the scene, was a factory making 'endless eggs' for pork pies.

Providing space for small-scale activity by independent traders created interest and variety at street level and began to address local demand for more job opportunities and a better mix of shops and services, including small

16.3
Thames Riverside Walk looking
towards the Oxo Tower

Photo: Marcus Robinson

businesses that are the modern equivalent of those that employed the artisans that once populated this area. The public viewing platform brought into the building people who would otherwise have been excluded from the 'private' zone of the restaurant. The latter was an essential feature in bringing revenue to the area and over 300 jobs. Did the residents on affordable rents living in the same building mind having an internationally famous restaurant above their heads? Not at all; they recognized the income stream helped subsidize local services and rents.

Architects raised on the orthodoxy that form follows function may struggle to accept that buildings no longer need to reflect their initial uses, but that new forms have to be devised that will lend themselves to multiple functions or activities that change over time. In the light of our South Bank experience, we find it difficult to justify highly specific, single-use structures in any urban renewal programme; rather we believe that buildings have to be capable of being reconfigured again and again in order to meet changing needs.

Pattern-book housing

The flats in the middle floors of the Oxo building were followed by new housing along Broadwall immediately behind it. A terrace of eleven houses with a small tower of twenty-six flats was designed in close consultation with prospective tenants. As architects we were challenged and stimulated by their demands. The result was a streetscape uncannily close in texture to that characterizing the area before the Blitz, yet realized in a contemporary design.

Stewart Brand (1997) suggests ways in which the life of buildings may be extended by designing-in flexibility from the start, after which incremental, low-cost, low-tech interventions can be made, based on the changing needs of the occupants. The Broadwall housing incorporates a central service core, so that kitchens or bathrooms can be sited on different or multiple floors, to create a granny flat or accommodate teenage lifestyles. A staircase can be inserted into the double-height space on the third floor, to make a sleeping platform, study or storage area.

This housing for South Bank has taught us the importance of a more responsive form, composed of modest and adaptable structures that will nurture a large number of different, overlapping and successive uses. The buildings make a positive, low-key contribution to the local character and visual richness of the area. The architecture does not need to assert itself, merely provide an inhabitable structure for the inexhaustible variety of people who use it and for their activities.

An inviting public realm

Public realm improvements were the first tangible results to follow the CSCB takeover of the South Bank site. Local people desperately needed routes and spaces that were inviting, safe and comfortable to use. CSCB's first project was the creation of a new park and river walk, which they maintain to this day, partly funded by income from the Oxo building.

Later CSCB combined with other interest groups in the area, including key employers and arts institutions, to create the South Bank Employers Group, a major force for improvement to the area. Understanding that their buildings stood magnificent in a rather squalid public realm, the South Bank Employers Group commissioned a large master plan to set out possible improvements to the urban environment and community facilities.

Pollster MORI conducted an opinion poll of all local residents and small businesses in 1999 and local residents were invited to give their views at a series of planning workshops. They called for an improved public realm with better streets and connections, better shops and better services (including a swimming pool and indoor and outdoor sports pitches). The resultant master plan, based on initial concepts by Llewellyn Davis, contained a menu of projects that would work in an integrated manner to revitalize the area but which could be tackled separately, in order of priority and as funding emerged. By the end of 2009 about half of the projects had been, or were being, built.

In one scheme, existing traffic routes through and into the heavily congested site, which was being used as a 'rat run', were upgraded and enhanced. Traffic was calmed, and a new 'spine' route created through the heart of the area, making the city fabric more porous and multiplying the connections between its different parts.

Another scheme designed by LDS provided an important new link between the South Bank and central London, replacing a dank and dirty footway, which for half a century had been the only direct pedestrian access. The design of the pair of new footbridges, one on each side of the Hungerford railway bridge that carries the track from Charing Cross on the north bank of

16.4
Hungerford Bridge

Photo: Ian Lambot

the Thames into Waterloo station on the south, pays tribute to sundecks suspended over the Thames that were a popular feature of the 1951 Festival of Britain (see Figure 16.4). Later we re-landscaped the river walk along the only stretch of the Thames in central London not blighted by a vehicle road.

These new public open spaces, the park originally laid out by CSCB, the enhanced river walk and footbridges provided focal points and meeting places that brought activity into previously 'dead' areas. Residents, workers and visitors quickly colonized these spaces. Clarity and connectivity were reinforced by better street furniture and signage making it easier to use and navigate the area; a public art programme brought colour and movement to the spine road behind the river frontage. These changes did more than simply erase the degradation caused by decades of neglect: they restored local pride, sustainability and a sense of ownership in the local population, and were a highly visible statement of intent.

The responsive city

The South Bank experience encourages us to re-examine our ingrained habits of overprovision and overspecification. The modernist insistence on dividing the city into zones for different activities lives on in local plans, which prescribe percentages and places of the city that can be allocated to living, shopping, restaurants and other uses. 'The future is no more controllable than it is predictable,' Brand (1997: 181) writes, describing the pointlessness of trying to anticipate urban development requirements, and continues, 'The only reliable attitude to take towards the future is that it is profoundly, structurally, unavoidably perverse.'

On the South Bank, CSCB recognizes that modern city-dwellers pursue multiple activities (living, working, shopping and eating) on overlapping timetables, requiring an environment in which all can be pursued in the same space, simultaneously and sequentially. The success of the Oxo redevelopment suggests that building-in the potential for changes of use might take some of the risk out of the development process. It takes several years to develop a site, but the economy moves much more quickly than that. This leaves developers in a weak position, making decisions on the state of the market two or three years hence in an increasingly volatile economic environment. Six floors of specific office space cannot be let out if the commercial market slows down, whereas if those six floors could just as easily be offices, flats, shops, studios, restaurants or a mix of such uses, they will always find tenants.

Conclusion

A combination of approaches has unlocked the potential of the South Bank and could do the same for inner-city regeneration elsewhere, with:

- planning systems that encourage developers to avoid demographic and economic forecasting and, instead, create flexible urban fabrics;
- economic models that balance commercial interests with social benefits;
- enhanced and interlinked public realms;
- permeable city fabrics of converted buildings and new pattern-book architecture that can be easily colonized and adapted by their users.

All these create a model for a lively and stimulating urban environment that has a mix of amenities for residents, workers and visitors to use and enjoy over many generations, in their own way, at their own pace and on their own terms.

References

Bailey, M. (2002) 'The Bilbao effect', *The Art Newspaper*. Online: www.forbes.com/2002/02/20/0220conn.html (accessed 20 November 2009).

Brand, S. (1997) *How Buildings Learn: What Happens after They're Built* (rev. edn), London: Phoenix Illustrated.

Campbell, P. (2004) 'At Somerset House', *London Review of Books* 26, 24.

Jacobs, J. (1961) *The Death and Life of Great American Cities*, New York: Random House.

Johnson, S. (2001) *Emergence: The Connected Lives of Ants, Brains, Cities and Software*, New York: Scribner.

Rowe, C. and Koetter, F. (1984) *Collage City*, Cambridge, Mass.: MIT Press.

Small-scale Sustainability

Parasite Las Palmas and Beyond

Mechthild Stuhlmacher

This chapter explains a small-scale approach to sustainability. It opens with a discussion of the approach of French architect Anne Lacaton, followed by a description of the ongoing exhibition, the 'Parasite project', which has dealt with city densification, temporality and small-scale architecture. Environmentally sound structural systems and their architectural implications are then dealt with. Finally, a small 'cultural house' in the Netherlands summarizes our practice's ideas about material and cultural sustainability.

The architect

In a lecture in Rotterdam in April 2004, French architect Anne Lacaton described her daily practice, showing pleasantly unpretentious images of private houses that the practice had built over the years. Most photographs were taken after years of habitation. The houses were made of unassuming materials, such as glasshouse components, corrugated sheeting and cheap timber panels. Still, they appeared remarkably 'local' and comfortable.

According to Lacaton, the twenty-first century is 'the age of the user'. Contemporary architecture, she submits, is subject to demands that go beyond the image, beyond the statement, beyond the narrative concept. For Lacaton, architecture is a service, eco-friendly building is an obligation and spacious living is a right. To achieve these ideals both technically and financially it is necessary to accept the building industry as a partner and to master industrial and other production processes. The work on display was a perfect illustration of her thesis. The houses built by her practice are spectacularly big and spectacularly cheap, thanks to the use of sophisticated building systems developed for utilitarian applications. They have their own aesthetic: sometimes light and poetic, sometimes provocatively blunt, even ugly, and usually both.

The role of the architect here is that of someone who is technically competent, socially engaged and prepared to serve. Someone whose specific expertise enables him or her to evaluate and balance the priorities of all the other factors and parties involved in a building process and to combine them into an aesthetic whole; in short, the architect as master builder.

The attitude to the discipline of architecture seems to be compellingly independent of style or ideology. In fact, what Anne Lacaton is saying (or, at any rate, what I like to think she is saying) is about the same as many of her European colleagues try to express, often with very different and literally much heavier means: let us rediscover architecture as a discipline. Let us concentrate on our particular expertise and use it in an intelligent manner. Let us focus on new possibilities and tasks, but from within the discipline and not from outside. And let's embrace the issue of sustainability as a central concern. That is the only way to continue to play a significant role in the present day and age.

I still fully identify with the way Anne Lacaton defines her profession, or my interpretation of it. For us too 'sustainable thinking' deals with the way we look at architecture in general, the city as a whole, at the issue of time, durability and temporality, and at cultural, social, aesthetic and functional issues. In the work we do in our practice in Rotterdam, mainly relatively small-scale architectural buildings, these different kinds of sustainability are underlying concerns that determine the development of our projects in general (see Figure 17.1).

The 'Parasites' exhibition project (1999–2006)

As a result of a success in a competition involving Swedish housing, we were asked to develop a proposal for an exhibition alongside the larger event. The result of the commission was an exhibition scenario with the name: 'Parasites: prototypes for advanced, ready-made, amphibious, small-scale, individual,

17.1
Parasite Las Palmas, Rotterdam

Photo: Anne Bousema

temporary ecological houses.' The subject of our exhibition proposal was the design and realization of small structures for unconventional sites involving some thirty architects and student teams from all over Europe. The 'Parasites' were to be prefabricated by the architects in their own country and according to their own specific manner, and reassembled on the exhibition site, and were meant to occupy temporarily available sites, unused roofs, water-surfaces, and hang or cling onto existing buildings. The way we planned them to spread out over the neighbourhood stressed their slightly subversive character.

The concept of the Parasites project was partly inspired by a Glenn Murcutt house for an Indigenous family. The prototype airy, poetically simple building had made a lasting impression on us, showing us the architect's deep appreciation for his clients' close relationship to nature. Murcutt had designed a sturdy yet ephemeral building that would not leave any permanent trace in the landscape. To achieve the material quality he aimed for, he organized the building work close to himself. The complete house was prefabricated in large elements in a workshop in Sydney and assembled in a short time on site by very few people. Starting to develop ideas about the Parasites, we aimed to adapt similar ideas to our own urbanized European environment, adopting the principle of prefabrication to much smaller buildings and budgets, trying to work as responsibly and carefully as Murcutt had shown us.

When we thought about temporary buildings we thought about experiments, about the enjoyable feeling of not being forced to make decisions for the long term, to be able to try out things, look for extremes, escape rigid building rules and take risks. And we thought about our own cities as multi-layered organisms that stay liveable and lively only as long as they absorb and accommodate the planned and unplanned, the old and new, the established and the experimental.

Initially our exhibition proposal was received with great enthusiasm. As a prelude to possible realization at a later stage, we asked the participants to make a 1:20 model of their Parasite object, and used these to put together an exhibition that travelled from Scandinavia to Great Britain before arriving at its final location, Las Palmas (Rotterdam).

After the sudden bankruptcy of our first Swedish host, however, the project changed and the Parasites exhibition was transferred to the Netherlands. The organizers of another large-scale cultural event, the programme for the year 2001, when Rotterdam was selected as the 'cultural capital of Europe', embraced its idealistic aims alongside making it accessible to the general public.

In Hoogvliet, a Rotterdam post-war suburb, a gentle reanimation process had just been started, a rather complex process loosely linked to the programme of this cultural year, 2001. It provided our initiative with a harsh but challenging venue. With their varied and optimistic appearance, the Parasites were expected to contribute to the intended successful regeneration of Hoogvliet. The objects would gradually be built in full scale to be used for various purposes during several years of spatial restructuring.

Owing to the Dutch location, the project provided us with an unexpected opportunity to react against the superficial image of Dutch architecture of the time being generated by international magazines. Our exhibition was not about fancy objects and not about architectural virtuosity. While everyone else was talking about bigness, our concern was with smallness. We propagated 'acupuncture' instead of 'tabula rasa', the cherishing and augmenting of the existing. And, while many colleagues around us were working on impressive housing blocks, we were concerned about individual expression and discrete urban densification. Our reference for the desired 'sustainable impermanence' was not the impressive Dutch pavilion in Hanover at the World Expo 2000 that everyone admired at the time, but the rough, re-usable Swiss woodpiles a few streets away. In that remarkable *Klangkörper* (the 'Body of Sound', Swiss pavilion, designed by Peter Zumthor) we could hear, feel and smell real material, and therefore enjoy the astonishing power of a space in which it seemed that idea, form and construction were one and the same.

The final Parasite designs varied enormously, ranging in character from pragmatic, poetic, dreamy, naive and even clumsy proposals, to elegant and utopian constructions. It struck us that the ultimate quality of the designs depended almost exclusively on whether the material had determined the form rather than vice versa. In the end, for various reasons, only two of the projects designed for the exhibition were actually built: first, the Parasite on top of the lift-shaft of our exhibition venue, the Rotterdam workshop building in Las Palmas, designed by us and, second, a temporary community centre, designed by the Swiss firm, Meili Peter Architekten. In line with our exhibition concept, the two buildings were prefabricated in specialized workshops, in Germany and Switzerland respectively, and assembled in Rotterdam. Adding social relevance to the architectural and technical aspects of the project, three school Parasites – to be used as high-quality emergency classrooms – joined them in 2004 and there is every prospect that more will be built in the future.

Our own little building, with its conspicuous colour and shape, was in the first place intended to act as a highly visible three-dimensional logo for the Las Palmas architecture and exhibition site. It symbolized innovative urban densification, experimental housing construction, improvised town planning and a touch of anarchy. The Parasite was constructed of solid timber panels using a wood construction system imported from Germany and never previously used in the Netherlands. Walls, stairs, floors and roof were all of the same structural material. In the middle of this commercially successful development area there arose a rudimentary, completely wooden space that formed a remarkable contrast with its rapidly changing, watery-grey metropolitan surroundings. Here our primary concern was a simple solution to a structurally complex task and the consistent, almost brutal application of a sustainable construction system that we imagined capable of opening up new possibilities fitting well within the pragmatic Dutch construction culture.

Solid timber construction

Solid timber construction panels have been produced since the 1980s in countries that are large producers of indigenous softwood, such as Germany, Austria, Switzerland and the Scandinavian countries. Looking at the long history of timber construction, this development is revolutionary. For the first time a timber construction system is no longer based on the assembly of linear elements with an infill, but on the assembly of solid, more or less homogeneous, panels. Both the idea and the technique are simple. Comparable to the production of plywood, solid timber panels are produced by laminating different layers of timber sheets crosswise on top of each other. In recent years a number of manufacturers offering slightly different products and services have entered the growing and therefore highly competitive market. The panels vary in thickness, composition, layering, structural performance, aesthetic quality and price.

There are many arguments for the use of solid timber construction. It may be the need for sustainability in the literal, material sense: the desire to build exclusively with renewable resources and timber as a carbon-neutral material. Some projects express wood's structural performance, functioning as an undirected slab, enabling generously cantilevering constructions and corner windows. Other projects require an extremely short building time. Still other projects benefit from the material's texture, colour, smell and atmospheric qualities. For the projects worked on since the founding of our office in 2001, all aspects mentioned somehow played a role, with differing priorities each time. The really decisive arguments for us, however, had to do with the possibilities of the material offered for spatial and architectural expression (see Figures 17.2–17.5).

Starting with our first building experiments we were fascinated by the stunning simplicity of the panel building system and the freedom for designing it offered. We also were charmed by the lively characteristics of its natural surface. To us the material was convincing proof that industrial prefabrication does not necessarily limit spatial possibilities. The specific production technique of the solid timber elements does not require standardized

17.2
Private house under construction

Photo: Korteknie Stuhlmacher
Architecten

Mechthild Stuhlmacher

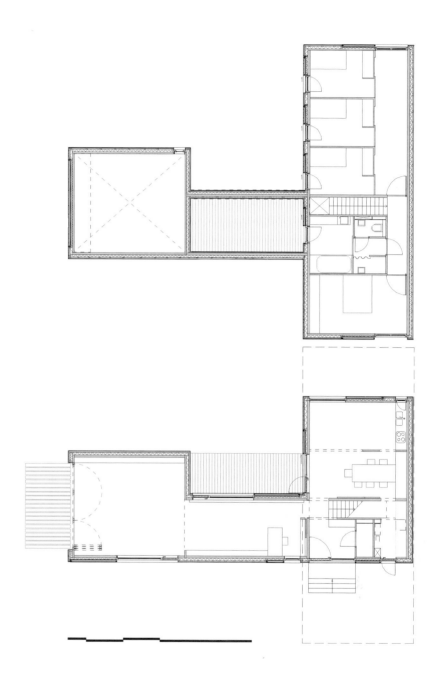

17.3
091 Plans of private house

Drawing: Mechthild Stuhlmacher

dimensions or large quantities of similar elements to be efficient. Therefore, the system easily combines the qualities of tailor-made design with the advantages of industrialized mass production.

Dutch professional culture is largely determined by trade rather than by production and craft, and this applies also to the building industry. Most projects are built by general contractors, who determine (and limit) the range of technical possibilities and standards. This contrasts with the practice of many other European countries. For many practical reasons involved with this

17.4
Private house, west façade,
during construction

17.5
Private house, west façade

Photos: Moritz Bernoully

specific way of organizing the building process, Dutch architecture is dominated by a strict distinction between raw construction and interior (and exterior!) finishes. Therefore, the raw construction itself plays the role of a load-bearing skeleton without any spatial or material qualities of its own. In this particular context there has developed over the years an architectural culture that is largely determined by conceptual and visual concerns rather than based on the experiential qualities of materials and a tectonic language.

The import of half-prefabricated building elements fits into this culture of trading, and local builders can execute the assemblage quickly and economically even without special skills. The import of these systems enables us to incorporate the material expression of its raw construction into our architecture without the requirement of traditional craftsmanship that has become unaffordable and therefore culturally superseded in the Netherlands.

Parasite Las Palmas

The very first project built by our office, the Parasite Las Palmas, would not have been built at all without solid timber technology simply because of its challenging site. At the time we embarked on the project we only knew the material from publications and fairs but happily decided to take the risk of the unknown. As our exhibition project had been set up mainly to communicate our ideas about sustainability in the city to a wide audience, the choice of building material played a decisive role. The project aimed to underline our conviction that environmental consciousness and healthy building can be translated into architecture with a clear, outspoken, contemporary, formal language and atmosphere.

The structure of the Parasite was designed to generously display the specific quality of the panels as two-directional slabs, resulting in its sculpturally cantilevered appearance. The material enabled us to cut holes for windows wherever we felt that the spectacular views of the surroundings would be most flatteringly framed. In the interior the surface of the untreated and exposed timber with its characteristic texture determined its architectural expression.

House No. 19 or 'nomads in residence'

Following on from this first project we took on a second commission for a similarly small-scale project, this time in collaboration with the Rotterdam-based artists BikvanderPol. It was our task to design and build a transportable studio for artists to serve as a temporary dwelling and exhibition space. Due to the uncertainty of site and context we designed a closed 'black box' with the maximum dimension that Dutch regulations allowed for transport on public roads: $4 \times 18 \times 3.6$ m.

Despite the temporary character of House No. 19 (Figure 17.6) we aimed to design a space that was pleasant all year round. The house should respect the privacy of its temporary inhabitants and at the same time facilitate different and much more collective uses. The compact plan was organized around a simple core containing all facilities, such as a shower, toilet, a small store, a kitchen and a large dining table. The building could be either used as one space or subdivided into smaller rooms. The skylights gave all spaces a reserved, gallery-like atmosphere. When the large shutters in the different façades were opened, the interior space changed completely to be used as a veranda or a podium.

These first small projects became important to us because of the freedom the kind of commission offered in supporting their experimental character.

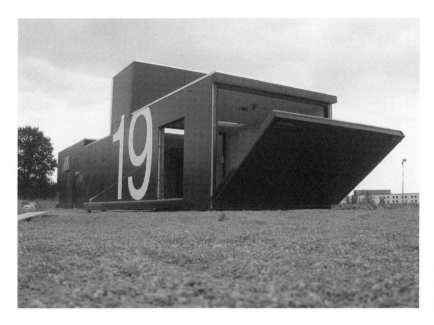

17.6
House No. 19, Utrecht

Photo: Christian Kahl

The experience we gained with the solid timber construction and the discovery of its spatial possibilities were elaborated further in later projects.

Cultural House: De Kamers

A recent project, directly inspired by the client's visit to House No. 19, is the cultural building, De Kamers ('The Rooms'), Amersfoort (Figure 17.7). The building is situated in Vathorst, a new suburb near Amersfoort. Vathorst is one of the many low-rise monofunctional suburbs that have been built in the Netherlands since the early 1990s. These suburbs usually lack any social or cultural infrastructure of their own.

17.7
De Kamers, Amersfoort, exterior

Photo: Stefan Müller

De Kamers is a private project initiated by a vicar and an artist. Both regarded the pioneering years of the new suburb as a challenging social and cultural period, and saw an important task for themselves. They jointly decided to create a place for 'sociability, inspiration and expression' in the area, with the generous support of many sponsors and the municipality of Amersfoort. The building and its activities are meant to grow with its growing surroundings over time, to offer space for various cultural activities and events such as theatre, film and creative education. Its heart is the *huiskamer*, a public 'living room', meant to be a hospitable space for everybody.

The design consists of simple wooden volumes with cubic shapes and varying dimensions. These rooms are loosely collected in a casual, almost improvised composition that allows for multifunctional use and future changes. Special attention has been paid to the spatial character of each of the rooms, their proportions, materiality and use of daylight.

The extremely tight privately funded budget led to an architectural decision to give priority to the interior (Figure 17.10) rather than the exterior. This time we made use of two different, similarly sophisticated, timber-building systems. All 'rooms' have been constructed in timber. For the walls we used solid timber panels; the floors and roofs, however, are made of timber hollow-core elements that we imported from Switzerland to achieve larger spans than the solid panels would allow. The prefabricated elements guarantee a clear, simple and sustainable structure with high-quality finishes and good spatial and acoustic properties.

The exterior is clad with stained heat-treated timber boards, which is a new, environmentally sound procedure to make European softwood more durable. The plinth has been designed for advertising, as an ever-changing band of hand-decorated panels covered with artwork, graffiti, posters and texts made by the users of the building.

17.8
De Kamers, ground floor

Photo: Mechthild Stuhlmacher

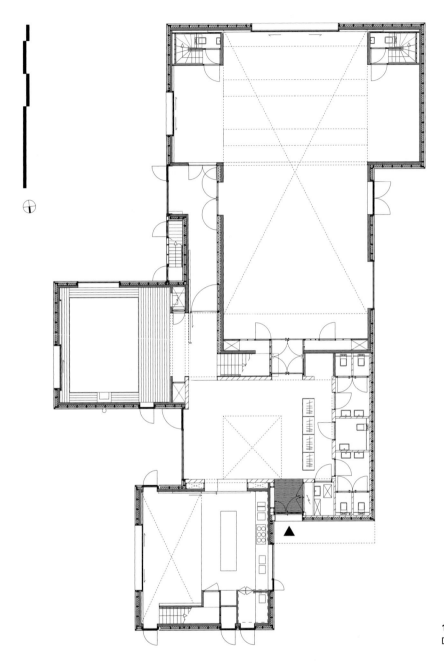

17.9
De Kamers, first floor

The composition of cubes implies the semi-enclosure of outdoor spaces. These 'garden rooms' are regarded as just as important as the indoor spaces and are used as outdoor stages, gardens and terraces. Here the colourful painted plinth turns into a wainscot of self-made wallpaper. The large sliding doors emphasize the direct relationship between indoors and outdoors and the inviting and open character of the project as a whole.

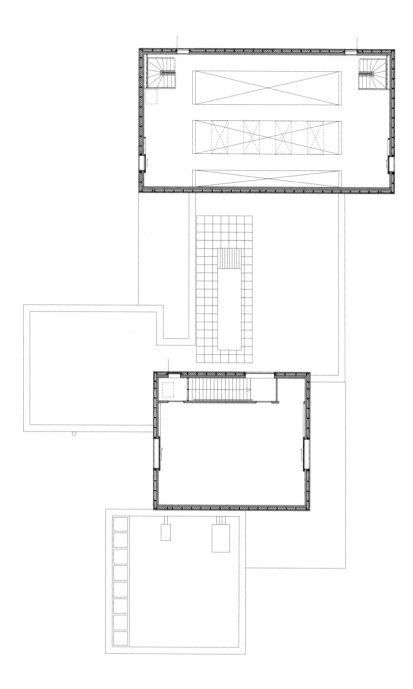

17.10
De Kamers, interior

Photo: Stefan Müller

Conclusion

These projects and our reflections on them are just beginnings. We founded our office in 2001 when the general public in the Netherlands, even more than in other European countries, was still not ready (or willing) to make the link between global realities and personal behaviour. Even though awareness has improved in recent times, the recent economic crisis, strangely enough, has

diminished the very basis of architectural culture and, therefore, the possibilities for our profession. After eight years of practice it seems harder than ever to find clients who are willing to take risks and truly explore the architectural possibilities of sustainability thinking.

To counteract this frightening development we conclude that, despite all efforts, we have failed to communicate our concerns in a way that reaches all the people that matter. We feel that now, more than ever, we should concentrate on our 'main task', very much in keeping with the description of 'the ideal architect' in the introduction: the design of healthy, beautiful, durable and comfortable spaces. Sustainable architecture is something that should be within the reach not only of a cultural elite but also of everybody else. Project De Kamers was a first important step in a promising direction as it combines our technical concerns with our cultural ambitions. Furthermore, it is a hospitable building that many, very different people can visit and enjoy. But much more needs to be done. The ubiquitous call and urgent need for sustainability is not just a technical issue to be solved. It is a serious cultural task that needs our full attention, despite the all-determining rules of a risk-avoiding and hesitant market.

Sustainable Subtropical City

An Architecture of Timber-framed Landscapes

Brit Andresen

The urgent challenge is: How can we develop distinctive, sustainable constructional forms that complement our landscape, trees, climate, myths and socio-cultural values? The solution is exemplified in the 'Queenslander' house, its set of rooms surrounded by a fringe of timber posts forming thresholds to the landscape, offering potential for variety and interpretation, i.e. cultural as well as environmental sustainability. This chapter explores that solution; use of timber is a recurring motif in the work of Andresen O'Gorman Architects.

Queensland architecture

The primary frames of buildings designed by Andresen O'Gorman Architects are constructed from Australian hardwood, which is a common regional building material in the coastal subtropics. The eucalypts' material properties have in turn formed our architectural intentions, particularly those ideas that explore the expressive capacity of construction and the potential for interaction with the natural environment.

Wood has been used for construction throughout much of the world since ancient times. The tree, with its hierarchy of parts and capacity for yielding dimensional variation, inspires ways of building as diverse as weaving with fibres, layering and bending with lathes, framing networks of posts and beams and 'lafting' with logs laid horizontally. Trees, landscape, climate, myth and socio-cultural values contribute to the development of distinct constructional forms of timber dwellings to such an extent that Norberg-Schulz (1998: 8) claims, 'The Nordic people still dream of wooden caves, while the Japanese live in a world of penetrated layers.'

Generations of Australians, mainly in the north-east regions of the country, have been born into a world of the timber pavilion set in a tropical garden. Australian writer David Malouf (1990: 264) grew up in Brisbane and, playing as a child in the family's wooden house, discovered his:

> first sensual experiences in the world of touch; the feel of tongue and groove boards, the soft places where they have rotted, the way the paint flakes and the wood underneath will release sometimes, if you press it, a trickle of spicy reddish dust.

In these recollections Malouf (1990: 266) reveals the sensuousness of wood as the essence of the Brisbane house. He describes the creaking and yielding of its timber structure, the darkness among its forest of stumps and the openness of the nested interior – a place made more secure by the surrounding frame of the veranda – itself opening onto a garden tending to overgrown wilderness.

Furthermore, the landscape of the Brisbane hills and gullies, filled with Moreton Bay fig trees and flowering shade trees, form a grand subtropical garden and the timber houses are 'in this place, so utterly of it, both in form and substance. Open wooden affairs, they seem often like elaborated tree-houses, great grown-up cubby-houses hanging precariously above ground' (Malouf (1990: 262)).

This delight in coherence between the subtropical house, the garden and its environment owes much to the generous building allotments, the material qualities of wood, and a recurring 'filtered openness' made possible by the timber-frame construction.

The simple 'Queenslander' house, with its set of rooms surrounded by a fringe of timber posts forming thresholds to the landscape, offers potential for variety and interpretation and is a recurring pattern in our work.

Native timber

Plentiful supply, improved technology and a powerful timber industry ensured that wood became the dominant building material during European settlement of south-east Queensland. With the ready availability of local, native pines (particularly hoop pine), softwood became the preferred construction material until timber supplies from extensive forests were exhausted:

> Once these softwood forests had been comprehensively cleared and burnt, they did not regenerate naturally. Instead they were replaced by the open eucalypt forests, which now appear to be the original natural environment of the region, as for example the re-growth on Mt Coot-tha.
>
> (Watson 1985: 12)

The *Eucalyptus* genus supplied the bulk of the hardwoods for building and was highly valued for its quick growth, strength, colour range, grain, figuring and other physical properties. Much of the world that Malouf writes about was built from quality hardwood timbers together with hoop pine and imported timbers, such as oregon.

The commercial value of *Eucalyptus* hardwood was well established by the early twentieth century. Richard Baker (1919: xiii), forestry lecturer at the University of Sydney, claimed:

Australia has among the largest variety of hardwood in the world. Generous nature has given us a good soil and a perfect tree climate over a vast extent of country. Reafforestation of our fast disappearing varieties of timber should be the watchword of every Australian.

Despite conservation efforts, the Eco-Design Foundation estimates that almost half of all Australian native forests have been cleared for agriculture over the past 200 years and that almost three-quarters of the native forest currently harvested is exported as woodchips. Timber for the construction industry accounts for significantly less. Willis and Tonkin (1998: 15–21) write: 'As a percentage of the total harvest, building products made from native forest timbers account for slightly over 10 per cent.'

By the mid twentieth century, demand for wood had escalated and plantation softwoods of introduced species, such as *Pinus radiata*, were increasingly established, thus creating further ecological problems in terms of land clearing and impoverished fauna habitat. With the post-war introduction of alternative building materials, hardwood's range of use for construction was limited primarily to hard-wearing flooring and mass framing where hardwoods were concealed in the cavities of floors and stud walls.

The emergence of ecologically sustainable native forest management and increasing Australian hardwood plantations has contributed to the supply of hardwood for building and to the prospects of protecting old growth forests. Australian hardwood, however, remains a scarce resource to be valued for its inherent qualities, to be used sparingly and appropriately. With the widespread availability of timber for building in south-east Queensland since European settlement, it is surprising that Australian hardwood has so rarely been explored in architectural terms and found few, contemporary, artistic expressions.

Eucalyptus tectonic and timber frames expressing the architectural idea

Andresen O'Gorman Architects has had a long-term interest in using local eucalypt hardwood and exploring its possibilities for architectural expression. Most species of hardwood offer magnificent material for domestic building. Strong and durable, the timber is capable of playing a significant role in exterior expression. Most eucalypt timbers, however, display characteristics that mean that they should not be used like North American or European softwoods are. The inherent hardness when dry usually requires that the Australian hardwood is used while still 'green' (containing high water content) for easier workability. Cut from logs with a pronounced spiral growth, and a high variability of moisture from heartwood to sapwood, the material usually continues to dry within the building.

The timber is also subject to inconsistent shrinkage, warping, twisting and cupping across the grain. This, and that it remains an active material after construction has occurred, are traditional criticisms. To overcome this, we use a simple lamination tactic. Forming components out of pairs of members, matched in opposing grain formation, so setting the movement of one

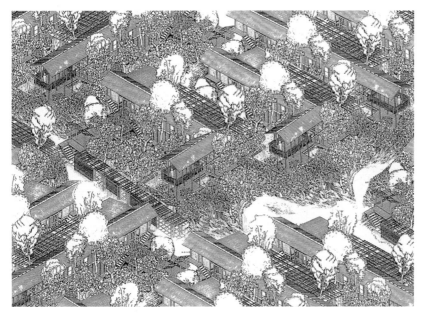

18.1
Mooloomba City: architecture of timber-framed landscapes for the future subtropical city

Source: Andresen O'Gorman Architects

component against the other, it is possible to counteract warping and twisting. This strategy started with a house at Redbank Plains (1970) and has been used more recently in work, such as Mooloomba House (1995–1999).

Having 'tamed' the material in this way, it may be freed from being hidden inside the stud wall. Exposed to take advantage of its durability and strength, the hardwood is available to contribute to the expressive form of the building in which it plays such a physical part. With the release of the timber

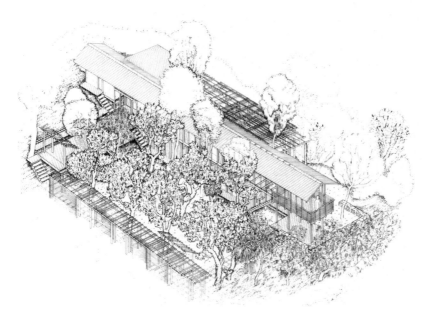

18.2
Mooloomba House: timber-framed house and landscape

Source: Andresen O'Gorman Architects, drawing by Michael Barnett

18.3
Mooloomba House:
transparency in house and
landscape

Photo: Anthony Browell

18.4
Mooloomba House: permeable
tectonic structure with people
and landscape scale

Photo: Anthony Browell

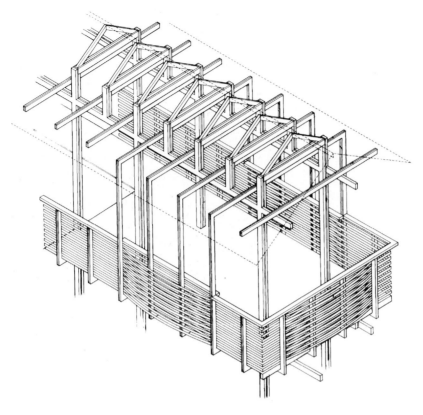

18.5
Mooloomba House:
axonometric drawing of
belvedere timber construction

Source: Andresen O'Gorman
Architects

18.6
Mooloomba House: exterior
view of belvedere timber with
landscape

Photo: John Gollings

Brit Andresen

frame from concealment in the stud wall a number of architectural opportunities are possible. Our work since the 1970s has included exploring this very simple notion. With each house, we attempt to translate the abstract architectural idea into a physical (constructional and structural) interpretation derived from the exposed frame. Over the years these attempts have been developed, refined and adapted through various projects to include a set of working principles involving interactions between the frame and ideas for patterning, visual dynamic, transparency, spatial interaction and formal character.

Expressed frames affect the building's visual pattern

The first, simplest and, in some ways, most profound of these working principles is the technical concept determining the visual patterning of the building. This, of course, is true of any technique of building. The implication of legible order is helped by the articulation of the parts: the primary frame, the secondary frame and the membrane or 'skin', which in turn is a consequence of the exposed frame. As with the ancients, there is some effort to describe the relationship of parts of the building through abstract qualities of scale and proportion to convey fundamental architectural qualities, which include the simple visual pleasures of basic proportions: the square and the double square, for example, or the 'divine ratio' of 1:1.618. Others involve figurative and metaphorical qualities (as discussed below), yet more involve visually registering the 'skeleton' frame that makes the 'demas' ('the human mind and body as a unity') embody a relationship analogous to life and nature.

In our work we look for the opportunity to 'humanize' the larger form by a geometric subdivision measured to the body. The skeletal frame extends an opportunity to register scale relations to interrelate body, building and setting. The traditional timber house of Japan, for example, recalls the body in the tatami mat, approximately $1 \times 2\,\text{m}$ and, in that way, gives the house an expression of human presence. The traditional Japanese timber house offers other insights into the qualities inherent in the timber frame and continues to influence our work.

The visual dynamic of the timber frame

The visual dynamic of the timber frame provides a qualitatively distinct construction system. Christian Norberg-Schulz (1998: 8) describes how a timber post contrasts with a stone column:

> The [stone] column opposes the draw and destructive power of gravity, it has remained the most significant expression of victory and durability. While the [timber] post does recall echoes of this relation, its primary motion is its ascension and dissolution into the network of beam, ribs and rafters that make up the roof. Wood architecture represents another form of durability. Static durability is replaced by dynamic life, where death simply represents unceasing new beginnings.

Later in the essay, he continues: 'This is the result of wood's ability ... which allow[s] a dynamic whole to emerge.' The three-dimensional timber frame is perceived as a conceptual whole comprising interconnected components, as in the ancient definition of 'harmonica'. Each part has a logical and dynamic relation with the others in overlapping systems so parts are simultaneously individual and belong to a whole. A dynamic dual reading of the parts and their relations to the whole is fundamental to life and art.

Transparency

Timber's capacities to bear compression and tension (consequently bending), its workability and possibilities for dimensional variation, allow its use over a wide range, from furniture to log churches. Its capacity to carry loads, in bending over medium spans, and a variety of jointing possibilities with simple tools contributes to timber's long-standing application to domestic buildings. These characteristics lead naturally to the tectonic frame, a conceptual form of construction, where a building is made up of many parts locked together in some logical cage of structure.

An inevitable consequence of the tectonic nature of the material is the opportunity for transparency, to see past one layer of construction to whatever lies beyond. Transparency, always an interesting characteristic of buildings, will permit layers of space to be seen simultaneously, for example: inside and outside, higher and lower spaces, space and threshold. Traditional Japanese timber buildings exhibit the essential transparency that the frame permits. The walls do not close off the exterior and a house receives nature filtered by the frame of the walls. There is no fixed point and space is unfolded layer after layer.

Experiencing this spatial layering has a lot to do with the demarcation of light and shadow, which is among the most basic conditions that can trigger

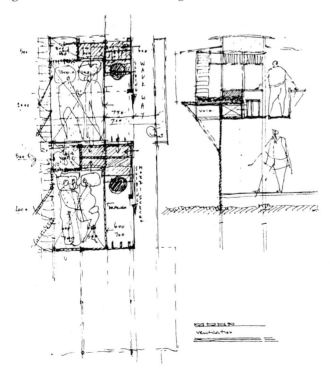

18.7
Mooloomba House Studio:
transverse section study – early
sketch

Source: Andresen O'Gorman
Architects

Brit Andresen

human memory, such as the memory of sitting under a tree in cool shade, looking out from deep shadow onto sunlit grass. The temperate climate of coastal north-east Australia with its rich, subtropical play of light and shadow provides wonderful opportunities to layer space between indoors and outdoors, to layer subtle gradations of light and shade and to extend spatial experience.

In Australian landscapes, detail comes to the fore and then retreats into the definition of the background. Unlike the trees of other countries, eucalypts are transparent. The tree structure, comprising the trunk, branch and twig, is clearly visible whether standing alone or clustered into a greater whole. Eucalypts appear as a haze of colour in a green-grey continuum with seasonal spicy and floral scents. We like to think that the graded layers and tectonic transparency of our architecture have such spatial qualities relating the building to its place.

Correlation between a spatial concept and a framing concept

Architecture in Australia is located in many different landscapes and climate zones. In our work we look for interactions with the surrounding local landscape, usually through small spatial gestures in constant interplay. This includes the articulation of the building form to provide views onto, into and through the natural environment. The variety of scales made possible by the timber frame allows us to identify spatial sub-components as units of structural clarity and to use these to articulate the larger form.

There are, of course, many ways of organizing sub-clusters of space. Conceptual orders based on the arrangement of social territories and sequences of experience abound in the work of architects. Louis Khan's ordering of 'served' and 'servant' spaces is a well-known example. Our work seeks to identify related activities in a programme clustering subsets by use or spatial experience. These may be for primary activities (such as cooking, sleeping, bathing) or for transitional uses (part of the relationship between subsets or with the garden and larger setting).

The design process requires a creative leap to conceptually integrate spatial and technical concepts. Our aim is for an articulated form of defined spatial zones identified as simple, but useful, skeletal zones (such as 'spines', 'cages', 'nets' or a grid). Through the frame's expression opportunities for rhythms, directions, character associations and scale arise.

Contributing qualities of place to experiences of a building

Cornelis van de Ven (1987: 5) explains the difference between 'stereotomic' and 'tectonic' forms. Stereotomic forms create architectural space as if carved out of solid material (such as stone, concrete or clay) essentially evoking the memory of a sheltering cave. Tectonic forms build space from articulated assemblies, stick on stick, characterized in tree-houses. These spatial types define prototypical shelters, places of cave and bower. While they are generally associated with either 'massive' or 'skeletal' structural systems, both have potential expression in timber construction. Cave and bower spaces recur in

18.8
Mooloomba House: view from
sitting room 'cave' to studio
'bower'

Source: Andresen O'Gorman
Architects

our work, including houses at Indooroopilly, Tomsgate Way, Mooloomba and
Rosebery.

A skeletal system is defined through distinctions between bounding
surfaces and support elements. Support elements are usually posts and beams,
often recurring both as primary and secondary elements, which offer a wide
range of possible combinations and, consequently, a wide range of potentially
different characters and expressions.

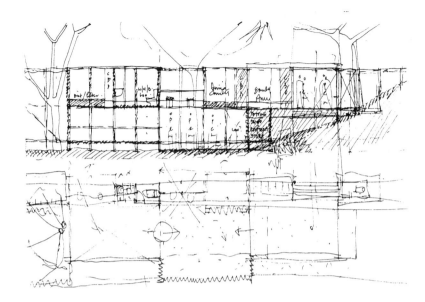

18.9

Mooloomba House: longitudinal
section study – early sketch

Source: Andresen O'Gorman
Architects

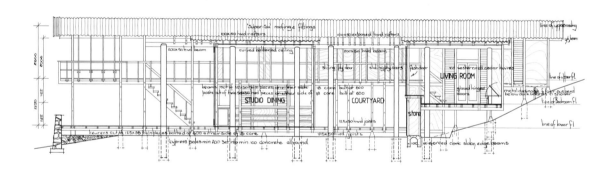

SECTION A-A

18.10

Mooloomba House: longitudinal
section

Source: Andresen O'Gorman
Architects

Since the Renaissance, when architects sought the greater articulation offered by skeletal forms, massive systems have been transformed into composite technics with otherwise solid walls articulated by integrating primary and secondary structural systems. Of course, the Renaissance developed the technique of the superimposed expressive pilaster frame into a highly articulate scenographic contribution to the setting of the building. In this way, the solidity of the 'massive' wall could appropriate the figurative architectural expression of the 'tectonic' structure.

In terms of understanding the full palette of opportunity in this simplest of design choices, the corollary is also true: that, if the architectural idea suggests the suppression of the figurative expression externally, this is possible by reversing the frame exposure from outside to inside (Tomsgate Way, 1990). If the ambiguity of the inside–outside condition is sought, the wall can be

18.11
Mooloomba House: studio room
in the afternoon

Source: Andresen O'Gorman
Architects

designed to expose the frame on both the interior and the exterior, as in the Mooloomba House construction.

Also developed in Renaissance times, and much loved by modernists, is the abstraction of segregating free-standing expressive elements (as much as structural necessities permit). Separation of elements further supports opportunities for visual layering and 'phenomenal transparency', as well as levels of richness through overlapping conditions of scale, colour, texture, light, different materials and so on. The opportunities offered for separating the open frame and the potential for expressing both literal and phenomenal transparency provided in subtropical north-east Australia is a great advantage.

Material contributes character and a visual grammar of forms

Possessing adaptability in jointing, and the opportunity for expression of different scales, skeletal timber frames have always offered architectural potential. Significantly, details of the whole assist in grammatical clarity, as shown in traditional Japanese houses. These timber buildings were produced not by architects, as we know them in the West, but rather by master builders. As apprentices, builders were trained to acquire knowledge of jointing systems that, in turn, would allow the proportional discipline and dimensional coordination of the 'mats' system in the frames.

Japanese master builders made considerable efforts to develop a method of jointing timber that would transfer loads and make the visual form of the primary frame continue around corners and into the third dimension, although timber lent itself to stacking beam on beam. Clearly, for Japanese master builders, the consistency of human scale and the continuous height of the openings warranted the more difficult integrated joints at the three-dimensional nodes of the primary frame. This shows the importance of detail in fulfilling architectural intention.

However, architectural character becomes less conservative, more dramatic and more abstract if the primary and secondary elements are 'stacked on one another' around the corner. This effect might well be the desired result. The visual articulation of the order of what might otherwise be a physically competent cage of structural sub-components can be altered dramatically by suppressing or expressing particular physical characteristics of those subsets. The issue raised here is of a spectrum of possible architectural characters from the classical to the organic, as describing an open-endedness through growth patterns. In Mooloomba House the simultaneous coexistence of both classical and organic characters exaggerates the dynamic further.

David Malouf raises the interesting, if self-evident, truth that buildings tend to be experienced as a sequence. Experiencing a place involves memory and gives buildings one of their most powerful characteristics: potential to evoke experience through metaphor. Any exposed frame made of components reliant on each other for support (membrane to sub-frame to primary frame) will result in a 'textural grain' to the building. This dimensional weave in the structural system offers a wide range of possible options for establishing openness or closure, for example, making buildings rich in metaphorical opportunities.

David Malouf's memory of his childhood home is suffused with recollections of the feel of warmth and textured hoop pine boards, the taste, sound and smell of the open wooden house that formed his first experiences of the world. In wood there is also depth and signs of its origins and working, a 'frozen history' and 'life force', which are recurring themes in writing, including poetry. Whatever its origins, human beings' associations with wood can hold almost mystical connotations.

References

Baker, R.T. (1919) *The Hardwoods of Australia and Their Economics*, Sydney: NSW Government.

Malouf, D. (1990) 'A first place: The mapping of a world', in J. Tulip (ed.) *Johnno, Short Stories, Poems, Essays and Interviews*, Brisbane: University of Queensland Press.

Norberg-Schulz, C. (1998) 'Treverk', in *Arkitekturhefte 1*, Oslo: Trelastindustriens Landsforening.

Van de Ven, C. (1987) *Space in Architecture*, Assen Maastricht: Van Gorcum.

Watson, D. (1985) 'An overview of the Brisbane House', in *Brisbane: Housing, Health, The River and The Arts*, Brisbane: Brisbane History Group.

Willis, A.-M. and Tonkin, C. (1998) *Timber in Context: A Guide to Sustainable Use*, Sydney: Construction Information Systems Australia Pty Ltd.

Beyond the EcoEdge

John Fien and Esther Charlesworth

Introduction

The case studies in this book highlight three urgent design challenges in building sustainable cities. These are, first, the need for urban politicians, managers and designers to recognize the interlocking dimensions of urban design, infrastructure and architecture as mutually dependent dimensions of planning for sustainable cities, and, second, the importance of social development and equity amidst the greening of environmental sustainability. Unfortunately, by omission, they also point to a third and, perhaps, most significant challenge: the need to overcome the tendency to view sustainability instrumentally, as a policy or set of tools designed to achieve certain, albeit desirable, ends instead of as a frame of mind that enables people to live, play and work sustainably. This last chapter reviews these urgent design challenges. It begins with a brief overview of the first two challenges. The chapter then turns to the critique of instrumental views of sustainability. This third section examines the implications of viewing sustainability as a frame of mind and the notion of a 'sustainable learning city' that results from this.

Urgent design challenge 1: the mutuality of urban design, infrastructure and architecture

In her introductory chapter of this book, *EcoEdge* editor Esther Charlesworth pointed to the gap between rhetoric and reality in building sustainable cities. She highlighted the preponderance of 'greenspeak' in architectural and design discourse in contrast to the relatively few examples in the built realm. Passive solar design, water recycling, energy efficiency and low-carbon materials are all possible in the design of homes, apartments, offices, factories and public buildings, as illustrated in case studies of sustainable architecture in the third part of this book. Infrastructure, too, can play a role in building sustainability into our cities, whether it is through the integrated philosophy and interventions of 'ecopolis' described by *EcoEdge* author Paul Downton, the recycling of a whole quarter of downtown Savannah described by *EcoEdge* author Scott Boylston, or the establishment of a 'green edge' in China outlined by *EcoEdge* author Neville Mars. Opportunities to expand water-sensitive urban design, locate employment opportunities in and between residential neighbourhoods and promote public transport are further examples of the potential of sustainable infrastructure. These may all be seen as responses to current and impending population growth and climate change on cities also, as are the case study examples of sustainable urban design in the first section of this book.

The urgent design challenge now is to build commitment in, and capacity for, integrating urban design, infrastructure and architecture into a coherent vision, policy framework and action plan for our cities. As *EcoEdge* author Scott Drake argues on several occasions in his chapter, the challenge is not merely technological; it is typological, and invites government and corporate shapers of the city to look to new typologies of urban form. Several examples of this are to be found among the case studies of, for example, Melbourne in Australia, Thu Thiem in Vietnam, South Bank in the United Kingdom, Xin Yu City in China and Savannah in the United States. And the interesting thing about these examples is that it does not matter whether one's starting point is urban design, infrastructure or architecture; successfully meeting an urgent design challenge in building sustainable cities is to see these different dimensions as mutually dependent.

Urgent design challenge 2: ensuring social development and equity amidst the greening

Far too many books and treatises on sustainable urbanism adopt a very narrow view of sustainability as pertaining to the natural world and the efficiency of resource use only. Michael Sorkin traces this, at least in part, to the progressivist Darwinian influences on Patrick Geddes and the way his Garden City 'redescribed urbanism as a sheltering activity with a prominently biological basis' (Sorkin 2005). Thus, he said, abundance of greenery in cities will be the mark of their efficiency and progress in the future. Sorkin (2005: 233) went on to argue that:

> For virtually every issue our cities confront, nature has an answer. Our new urban gardens – ubiquitous on every horizontal – will supply us with oxygen, sequester carbon dioxide, control our temperatures, provide habitat for our fellow creatures, offer us food, grow construction materials, calm our gaze, and instrumentalize our autonomy. This condition must become the default. Our lives depend on it.

As important as urban greening is, a comprehensive view of sustainability gives equal emphasis to the cultural, social and economic dimensions of urban life. Thus, numerous case studies in this book emphasize the importance of quality of life issues and 'the local' – as well as 'the green' – in integrating work and home life in our cities. The case studies by *EcoEdge* authors Wim Hafkamp, Sheela Nair and Chrisna Du Plessis provide insights into urban sustainability that are simply not found elsewhere in the architectural literature.

Hafkamp's account of urban violence rising from the increasing ethnic mix of modern cities poses urgent challenges for city managers. In her research on 'Divided Cities' with Jon Calane, *EcoEdge* editor Esther Charlesworth argued that urban sustainability depends on city managers and citizens maintaining the urban contract of civility through fair, equal and transparent access to services, employment and the other benefits of urban life. All cities are located on a continuum of adherence to the urban contract – and divided cities such as Beirut, Belfast and Jerusalem, which have flared into widespread violence and partition, are just closer to the negative end of the continuum than others (see Calame and Charlesworth 2009). Hafkamp's case study of the sudden flaring of ethnic urban violence in the Netherlands provides new arenas of social sustainability in which architects and designers may work.

The same is true of the provision of potable drinking water and sanitation in Sheela Nair's case study of the urgent design challenge in Indian cities. With access to water and sanitation being a basic human right – not commodities to be traded and purchased – this case study illustrates the role of designers as guardians of human rights and the contributions they can make to social equity and public health. Yet, we wonder, where were the architects in the designs in her case study? What roles did they play in the design of water tanks and rainwater harvesting systems in Chennai? Or in the design of eco-pans and outhouses for personal hygiene, health and river health in Musiri? If architects can design teapots for Alessi and chairs for the rich, where were the architects when Sheela Nair was organizing 'display villages' of alternative outhouse designs? In his introduction to Cynthia Smith's (2007) *Design for the Other 90%*, Paul Polak wrote, 'The majority of the world's designers focus all their efforts on developing products and services exclusively for the richest 10% of the world's customers. Nothing less than a revolution in design is needed to reach the other 90%.'

The emphasis on social sustainability in design and infrastructure in these two case studies encourages us to look beyond the ordered landscapes of rational urban planning to recognize that 'the edge of chaos is the natural state of cities', as *EcoEdge* author Chrisna Du Plessis argues in her case study of Johannesburg. In accord with Scott Drake and other *EcoEdge* authors, she said, 'Urban sustainability is not necessarily about making "correct" choices in technology or social and economic ideologies, or finding solutions to a range of pre-determined ... problems.' As part of social sustainability, Du Plessis writes about the need for 'participating effectively in the natural evolution of the city' or what Sheela Nair called 'community co-management' of the city and its resources. *EcoEdge* author Brit Andresen also writes of the need for architecture to complement not only the natural environment but also our 'myths and socio-cultural values' while *EcoEdge* author John Worthington noted that managing behavioural change in cities was emerging as the primary concern in successful design for sustainability. Or, as *EcoEdge* editor Rob Adams argues, it is necessary to 'stimulate a shift in societal expectations and behaviour' if the goals of sustainable urbanism are to be met.

Urgent design challenge 3: towards sustainable learning cities

The third urgent design challenge arises from some of the contradictions highlighted in the previous sections. While the *EcoEdge* authors who were cited agree that public involvement is necessary to meet the urgent design challenge of sustainable cities, there is much difference of opinion over what forms such involvement should take. Sheela Nair and Chrisna Du Plessis seem to lean towards participatory democracy and Adams towards urban politicians, planners and architects as designers of the spaces and infrastructure that will encourage changes in community behaviour that can lead to more sustainable outcomes, or what *EcoEdge* author Ralph Horne describes as a socio-technical approach.

However, missing from most chapters is an understanding that the root causes of unsustainable development are prevailing values and social (economic, political, cultural) arrangements. *EcoEdge* author Melanie Dodd comes closest to this position when she writes that 'our cities are not neutral vessels, capable of being acted on by top-down policy towards sustainability'. In this statement, she was saying that most approaches to urban sustainability are pervaded by an instrumental rationality that overlooks the fact that the root causes of unsustainable development are to be found not in regulations, technologies and social practices but in prevailing attitudes and values in society. Viewing sustainability as a policy or set of technologies precludes recognition of the diversity and complexity of meanings and values in society. More significantly, it fails to question the learned attitudes of mind that sanction the continued exploitation of nature and maintenance of inequality in which design is complicit.

Rather than viewing sustainability as policy designed to achieve a certain state of affairs, Michael Bonnett (2002) suggested that sustainability be viewed as a frame of mind that involves respect for human and non-human nature with each seeking fulfilment through a process of co-evolution. This would involve, in his words, engaging:

> in those kinds of enquiry which reveal the underlying dominant motives that are in play in society; motives which are inherent in our most fundamental ways of thinking about ourselves and the world. That such a metaphysical investigation will be discomforting for many seems unavoidable, but it promises to be more productive in the long term than proceeding on the basis of easy assumptions about the goals of sustainable development as though it were a policy whose chief problems are of implementation rather than meaning.
>
> (Bonnett 2002: 19)

This is essentially a learning-based approach to social change, and is not new to studies of urbanism although it is to considerations of sustainable cities. However, cities have long been centres of the kinds of learning that can help people and their communities assess, think about and change their realities. The innovations in agricultural productivity that freed an increasing percentage of the population from daily food production and enabled the growth of cities also enabled artisans, priests, scholars and citizens to debate and discuss issues pertaining to the quality of life in, and the future of, the settlements they called home.

A 'learning city' has been described as one that 'mobilizes all its resources in every sector to develop and enrich all its human potential for the fostering of personal growth, the maintenance of social cohesion, and the creation of prosperity'. In other words:

> A Learning City is any city, town or village that strives to learn to renew itself in a time of extraordinary global change. Using lifelong learning as an organising principle and social goal, Learning Cities promote collaboration of the civic, private, voluntary and education sectors in the process of achieving agreed upon objectives related to the twin goals of sustainable economic development and social inclusiveness.
>
> (Learning City Network 1998)

An OECD (2001) report stressed the link between such socio-economic development and learning but it is only recently that the Learning Cities movement has begun considering sustainability in its integrated, holistic sense. Thus, reflecting a triple bottom line perspective (Figure 19.1), Ron Faris argued that a learning city is founded on:

- the enhancement of human and social capital that comes from lifelong learning and which underpins economic vitality;
- the development of social capital and social cohesion that comes from lifelong learning, especially non-formal and adult learning;
- learning respect for the Earth and the interdependence of humans and the physical environment that comes from active involvement in environmental programmes.

A key aspect of a sustainable Learning City is the development of a *sense of place* and *sustainability ethics* as central objectives, not just because these can help conserve the natural environment or make people feel better

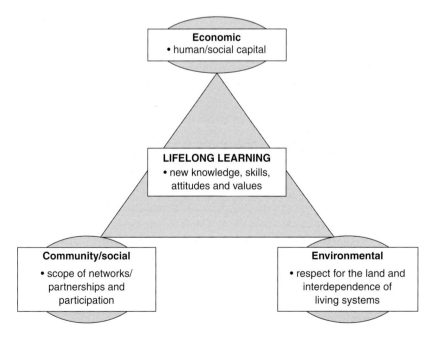

19.1
Lifelong learning and the triple bottom line of sustainability

Source: Adult Learning Australia

John Fien and Esther Charlesworth

feeling at home in a known and loved locale, but because they are also central to the long-term economic vitality of a community and to the quality of life that its members enjoy. Thus, success in building sustainable cities depends on:

- a healthy environment in equilibrium with its natural milieu;
- education as a basis for economic progress and wealth generation;
- values of equity, tolerance and inclusiveness;
- high levels of citizen control and self-determination;
- a culture that looks beyond adaptation and, instead, looks to anticipate and achieve;
- cooperative partnerships and social interaction as a means of bringing people together to facilitate social action and change (Morris 2001).

However, the goal of a sustainable learning city will not be achieved without leadership from government. As the levels of government closest to the everyday sustainability needs of people, city councils are particularly important to develop the infrastructure and processes that embed learning for sustainability, not just as an aspiration but as a process of governance. It is here that deliberative forms of democracy that enhance (and renew) local participation in decision-making need to be developed and trialled (Gastil and Levine 2005). Extensive guidelines and examples of how to do this are now widely available. Figure 19.2 is a brief list of some of the most accessible and useful of these.

Central to all of the strategies for deliberative democracy in these resources is the concept of *place*, the need for urban managers and community groups and members to recognize the often taken-for-granted bioregional dimensions of city life and the responsibilities that everyone has for the resources they consume and the impacts of this on all other parts of human and non-human nature. Coming to an understanding of this ever-present reality of city life and developing the commitment and capacity to live and work in sure knowledge of this reality is what 'learning our way out' means, and which ties the interdependent development of social capital, learning and the protection of natural capital together as the key challenge in building sustainable cities.

19.2 Tools for deliberative democracy (source: the authors)

- The Citizen Science Toolbox: www.coastal.crc.org.au/toolbox/index.asp
- The Community Planning Handbook and Website: www. communityplanning.net
- The New South Wales iPlan Community Engagement Essentials: www. iplan.nsw.gov.au/engagement/essentials/index.jsp
- The Victorian Effective Engagement Kits and downloadable Effective Engagement Planning Tool: www.dse.vic.gov.au/dse/wcmn203. nsf/0/8A461F99E54B17EBCA25703 40016F3A9?open
- USA Opportunities to Participate in Community Engagement Strategies: www.health.state.mn.us/communityeng/disparities/strategies.html

References

Adult Learning Australia (2005) *Hume Global Learning Village Learning Together Strategy 2004/2008*, Canberra: Adult Learning Australia.

Bonnett, M. (2002) 'Education for sustainability as a frame of mind', *Environmental Education Research*, 8, 1: 9–20.

Calame, J. and Charlesworth, E. (2009) *Divided Cities: Beirut, Belfast, Jerusalem, Nicosia and Mostar*, Philadelphia: University of Pennsylvania Press.

Gastil, J. and Levine, P. (eds) (2005) *The Deliberative Democracy Handbook: Strategies for Effective Civic Engagement in the Twenty-First Century*, San Francisco: Jossey-Bass.

Learning City Network (1998) *Learning Communities: A Guide to Assessing Practice and Progress*, London: Department of Education and Science.

Morris, P. (2001) *Learning Communities: A Review of Literature*, Working Paper 01-32, Research Centre for Vocational Education and Training, Sydney: University of Technology Sydney.

OECD (2001) *Cities and Regions in the New Learning Economy*, Paris: Organisation for Economic Cooperation and Development.

Smith, C.E. (2007) *Design for the Other 90%*, Paris: Editions Assouline, pp. 2–3.

Sorkin, M. (2005) 'From New York to Darwinism: Formulary for a sustainable urbanism', in E. Charlesworth (ed.), *CityEdge: Case Studies in Contemporary Urbanism*, Oxford and Burlington, Mass.: Architectural Press, pp. 226–233.

Index

Abalos, I. 14
accessible programmes, networks cities 134–5
activity centres, development around 34–5
Adams, R. 33
adaptive capacity, characteristics determining 56
Adelaide, Christie Walk 96–102
affordable housing: Savannah 82–3; South Africa 46, 57
Agenda 21, China 105
air conditioning 14–15, 16–17
air quality 8, 12–18
Ajax soccer grounds, Amsterdam 24–5
Alberti, M. 53
Amersfoort, De Kamers 166–9
Amin, A. 8
Amsterdam: Ajax soccer grounds 24–5; architectural heritage project 27–8; Dapperbuurt restoration project 27–8
Anderies, J.M. 54
Anderson, W. 63
Andresen O'Gorman Architects 171, 183
apartheid 50
apartments, China 110–12
architects: impact of 117–18; role of 158–9
architectural culture, Netherlands 163–5
architectural heritage project, Amsterdam 27–8
architectural set pieces 150–1
architecture: mutuality with urban design and infrastructure 184–5; overview 117–20; Queensland 171–2
argumentative cities 120
Arup 143
Australia Research Council 15–16
Australia: Christie Walk 96–102; National Australia Bank 15–18; timber-framed buildings 171–83

Bailey, M. 150
Baker, Herbert 31

Baker, Richard 172–3
BAU (Brearley Architects and Urbanists) 133, 140, 143
Bauman, Z. 8
Beach Institute, Savannah 87
Beall, J. 50
behavioural habits 8
behavioural change management 9
Beijing, public transport 112
BikvanderPol 165
biofuels 88
biogeochemical activity 93–4
Birkeland, J. 90
Bond, P. 50
Bonner, P. 50
Bonnett, M. 187
Bookchin, M. 95
Boyden, S. 14, 91, 94
Brand, S. 12, 155, 156
BREEAM (Building Research Establishment Environmental Assessment Method) 42
Bremner, L. 50, 55
'brickification' 109
Brown, P. 42
Brugmann, J. 30
building densities 9; China 106–7, 108–9, 144–6; Christie Walk 101; Thu Thiem 129
building materials, recycling 82–3, 84
building process, Netherlands 163–5
Burke, M. 86
Burke, S. 96

Calame, J. 186
Cambridge Futures 43–5
Cambridge Past, Present and Future 45
Cambridge, sustainable growth 43–5, 48–9
Cambridgeshire Quality Charter 44–5
canal district, Thu Thiem 125–7
car parking project, Shanghai 112–13
Carolin, Peter 43
Carrier, Willis 14
case studies overview 1–2
centralized water supply systems 71–2, 75

Centre for Urban Ecology, Australia 96–7
Cerda, Ildefonsa 119–20
Certeau, Michel de 10
Charlesworth, E. 186
Chatham Area Transit 88
Chatham Environmental Forum (CEF) 88
Chengdu East city extension 137–40
Chennai Metropolitan Area Ground Water Regulation Act (1987) 72
Chennai Metropolitan Water Supply and Sewerage Board 72, 73
Chennai, water management 71–5
China: breaking the rules 108–12; dynamic density 106; economic growth 103–4; green consumers 107–8; green edge 106–7; green imaginaries 105–6; leapfrog development 104–5; networks cities 133–47
Chinese Communist Party (CCP) 107–8
Christie Walk, Adelaide: awareness 100–1; community energy 96–7; organization and design strategy 97–100; research and education 97; as urban fractal 101–2
city business districts (CBDs), China 108–10, 139, 144
City Improvement Districts, Johannesburg 55
city planners, China 146
climate change, reprogramming cities for 30–7
co-management of infrastructures 68
coalition politics, Netherlands 23–4
Coin Street Community Builders (CSCB) 152–3, 155, 156, 157
commercial network, Chengdu East 140
Commission for Architecture and the Built Environment (CABE) 42–3
community compost toilets 77–9
community energy 96–7
community latrines 75, 76
community-driven projects 96–102
competitions, city design 124, 145–6

complex adaptive systems (CASs), cities as 54–5
complex systems approach to sustainability 9–10, 54, 57
composting, human waste 77
Confederation of British Industries 48
County Hall, London 149
Cowan, George 55
Crescent Boulevard, Thu Thiem 128–9, 130
Crescent Park, Thu Thiem 127
Cross, C. 57
Cultural Revolution, China 146

D-rail, Beijing 112
Dagenham Dock Sustainable Industries Park 46–7
daily life, relationship with urban form 7–8
Daniell, K.A. 101
Dansereau, P. 91
Dapperbuurt, Amsterdam 27–8
Davis, Llewellyn 155
Day, P. 118
De Kamers, Amersfoort 166–70
De Landa, M. 10
dead cities 93, 94–5
Deaderick, John 84
Deakin, M. 53
decentralized waste disposal systems 75–9
decentralized water supply systems 72–5
default planning formula, China 133
deliberative democracy, tools for 189
design challenges 184–9
Design for London 46
design strategy, Christie Walk 97–100
designer denial 2–3
developer-led approach, housing 36
development indicators 52–4
dispersed programmes, networks cities 134–5
Dixon Jones 48
Dodson, J. 31
'doorstep urbanization' 109
Douglas, I. 91, 95
Douglas, M. 13
Downton, P.F. 91, 96
Drake, S. 15
drought-flood cycles, Tamil Nadu 71–5
Du Plessis, C. 54
Duffy, Frank 14
Durrett, C. 96
Dynamic City Foundation 105
dynamic density (DD) 106
dynamic city 63, 65

dynamic systems approach, sustainability 42–3

E_tree, Shanghai 112–13
Earthcraft community 84
Earthcraft sustainability standards 82
eco-corridor networks 136–7, 141–3
Eco-Design Foundation 173
ecological meta-networks 135
ecological strategy, Thu Thiem peninsula 125, 126
economic efficiency, expansion strategies 43–5
economic growth, China 103–4, 107
ecopolis 90–102
EcoSan compost toilets 76–9
ecosystems, cities as 54
edge-of-chaos urbanization 50–7
Einstein, Albert 3, 31
elevators 14
Elmqvist, T. 56
'emergence' concept of 55
Emergent Structures Project, Savannah 82–3
energy policy, key drivers 41
energy use 13–15
environmental imaginaries 105–6
environmental quality, expansion strategies 43–5
equity, ensuring 185–6
Erickson, D. 135
ethnic tensions 21–3
Eucalyptus 171–9
European cities, evolution of 151–2
European Union, city transformations 32
Evans, Walter O. 88
existing infrastructure, reprogramming cities around: new approach 31–2; potential for transformation 32–6; residential intensification 36–7
expansion strategy: Cambridge 43–5; China 106–7; Thames Gateway 45–7

Fanger, Ole 15
Farmer, J. 90
Farr, D. 96, 97, 99
Farrell, T. 45, 46
fast-track design/approval, China 144–6
Festival of London 149, 156
Finco, A. 53
flexible housing 154–5
Fortuyn, Pim 21, 22, 23, 24
framing concept, correlation with spatial concept 179

Fretton, T. 119
fringes, locating new communities on 31, 32, 33
Frogtown condominiums, Savannah 84–5, 88
Fuerst, F. 41–2

Gaian ecosystem 94
Gandelsonas, M. 119
Garden City movement 33
Gastil, J. 189
gated communities/office parks, China 133, 139, 144
Geddes, P. 91
Geels, F.W. 67–8
Gehl Architects 32
Gehl, J. 94–5
Gell-Mann, Murray 55
ghetto-city planning, China 143–6
Giddens, A. 63
Gillespie, R. 14
Girardet, H. 63
Gore, Al 103
Gotts, N.M. 55
Goubert, J.-P. 13
Greater London Council 152–3
Green Building Council of Australia 15
green consumption, China 107–8
green imaginaries 105–6
green networks 136–7, 138, 139, 141–3
greenhouse gas emissions 30
greenspeak 2
Greenwich Peninsula, London 149
ground-up vs. top-down urban design 151–2
groundwater recharge, Chennai 71–5
Gunderson, L.H. 56
Gutman, R. 117

Harris, K. 31
Harrison, P. 50, 55
Hawthorne Effect 14
Hayward Gallery, London 148, 150
health and water 13
Healy, E. 67
Herreros, J. 14
Herty Foundation Advanced Materials Development Center 88
hidden city 63, 64–5
high-density housing 33–7
high-rise office buildings: energy use 14–15; mixed-mode spaces 15–18
high-tech companies, Cambridge 43
Hilton, A. 48
Hirshi Ali, Ayaan 21, 24
historic buildings, re-use of 84, 86–7
Holling, C.S. 55, 56

Hoogvliet, regeneration project 160–1
Hornsby, A.108
Hough, M. 91
House No. 19, Utrecht 165–6
household-centred EcoSan toilets 76
Housing and Communities Agency,
    UK 46
housing challenges, Savannah 81–2
housing laws, Rotterdam 23–4
Hub, London 47–8
Hungerford railway bridge, London
    155–6
hutong, China 110, 111
hybrid cells, networks cities 140–1

imaginaries 105–6
imaginary city 64, 65–6
immigration issues: Netherlands 21–4;
    South Africa 54–5
incremental change 40
industrial clusters 46–7
infrastructure: mutuality with urban
    design and architecture 184–5;
    overview 63–8; tensions facing
    66–7; three dimensions of 63–5
inhabited cities 93, 94–5
innovation, risks of 18
Institute for Sustainability (IfS) 46
instrumentally driven approach to
    planning 40–2
integrated approaches, urban planning
    42–9
integration issues, Netherlands 23–4,
    28–9
International Council for Local
    Environmental Initiatives 87
International Panel on Climate
    Change (IPCC) 68
International Urban Ideas
    Competition, Thu Thiem
    peninsula 124
Investment and Construction
    Authority (ICA), Thu Thiem New
    Urban Area 123–5
Islam 24
Ito, T. 134

Jacobs, Greg 84
Jacobs, J. 53, 151
Japanese timber houses 177, 178, 182–3
Johannesburg: complex systems
    approach 54–5; post-apartheid
    urban experiences 51–2; resilience
    thinking 55–7; sustainability
    challenge 52–4
Johnson, Stephen 151
Jupiter, T. 40

Kaliski, J. 10
Kemp, R. 67
Kenworthy, J. 63
Khan, Louis 179
King's Cross station, London 47–9
King's Place, London 48
Klangkörper pavilion 161
Koch, Robert 13
Koetter, F. 118–19, 151
Kohler, N. 53
Koolhas, R. 10
Kronquest, S. 81

L-building, China 110–12
Lacan, J.-M.-E. 105
Lacaton, Anne 158–9
land reclamation 21–2
land regeneration 47–8
land use program, Thu Thiem 130
land use zones, China 133–47
Landman, K. 50, 55
Landry, C. 8
Landscape Design Associates 46
Lapo, A.V. 93
Latour, B. 14, 63
LDS 153, 155–6
Le Corbusier 90
leach pit latrines 75, 76
'leapfrog development', China 104–5
Leatherbarrow, D. 12
LEED (Leadership in Energy and
    Environmental Design) 42, 82;
    projects in Savannah 84–8
Levine, P. 189
Life between buildings (Gehl) 94–5
Lifschutz Davidson Sandilands 148
localized collection and use of energy
    18
localized collection and use of water
    13
London: land regeneration 47–8; South
    Bank regeneration 148–57; Thames
    Gateway Parklands Vision 45–7
long-term holistic sustainability 40–2
Lovelock, James 93, 94
Lucan, J. 134
Lucas, C. 55

Maastricht, traffic artery tunnel
    project, 25–7
Mabin, A. 50, 55
McAllister, P. 41–2
McCamant, K. 96
McCartney, Danielle 101
McLeod, C. 101
Magnaghi, A. 93
Malouf, David 172, 183

Manzini, E. 8
Margulis, Lynn 93
Marias, J. 117
market-driven unintentional
    development (MUD) 106, 108
Mars, N. 108
Martin Luther King Jr Drive, Savannah
    88
Martin, R. 14
Marx, C. 57
'massive' structural systems 179–81
master builders, architects as 158–9
Mau, B. 10
Maylam, P. 50
Meadows, D. 53, 54
Medway towns 46
Meili Peter Architekten 161
Melbourne: reprogramming for
    population growth and climate
    change 30–7; workplace air quality
    12–18
Millennium Dome, Greenwich 149
mixed mode office spaces 15–18
mixed use approach to cities 37–8
mixed use development: London 47–8,
    152–4; Savannah 84–8; Thu Thiem
    121–32
modernism 33, 106–7, 143, 156, 182
Mooloomba House, Queensland 173–9
Morris, P. 189
Mostafavi, M. 12
Mouffe, Chantal 118
multiculturalism 8–9, 28–9
multiple use structures 153–4
multiplier effect, energy policy 41
Mumford, L. 92, 95
Munday, R. 120
Munnell, A.H. 63
Murcutt, Glenn 160
Museum of South Vietnam 121, 127,
    128
Musiri Town Panchayat, in situ waste
    management 70, 75–9

Napier, M. 57
National Australia Bank, Melbourne
    15–18
National Theatre, London 148, 150
natural ventilation 15–18
Netherlands: prefabricated buildings
    158–70; socio-political dimensions
    of cities 20–9
networks cities, China 134–5; Chengdu
    East 137–40; Symbiotic City 140–3;
    urban planning formula 143–6; Xin
    Yu 136–7
Newman, P. 63

Nijkamp, P. 53
Norberg-Schulz, Christian 177–8
not-for-profit principle 152–3

O'Connor, K. 67
Odell, J. 54
Office of Government Commerce
    (OGC), UK 42
Oliphant, M. 100
Olsson, P. 68
Oosterscheldedam, Netherlands 22
organizational arrangements, Christie
    Walk 97–100
Oxo Building 154, 155, 157
Oxo Tower Wharf, London 149, 153–4

Parasite Las Palmas 159, 165
'Parasites' exhibition project
    (1999–2006) 159–61
parkland networks, China 135, 144–5
Parnell, S. 51
Partnership for a Sustainable Georgia
    87–8
pattern-book housing 154–5
pedestrian orientation, Thu Thiem
    125–7
People's Party for Freedom and
    Democracy, Netherlands 23
People's Urbanity of China (PUC)
    108–10
Peyroux, E. 50, 55
ping fang, China 110
Pinkerton, C.C. 86
place, qualities of 179–82
planning formula, Chinese ghetto-
    cities 143–6
planning process, Thu Thiem
    peninsula 123–5
planning regulations, China 108–12
planning schemes, need for new
    approaches 36–7
poldering 21–2
pollution, human waste 75–6
Popper, Karl 118
population growth 9; reprogramming
    cities for 30–9
post-war planning policies, London
    South Bank 148–9
prefabricated buildings 158–70
prestige building, London 150–1
productive suburbs, development
    around 34–5
Proud of the Netherlands 23
psychological benefits of water 13
public awareness programs: Christie
    Walk 100–1; rainwater harvesting
    73–4

public buildings: London South Bank
    148; Thu Thiem 130
public realm improvements, London
    South Bank 155–6
public spaces, Thu Thiem 125–7
public tendering system, Netherlands
    26–7
public transport: Beijing 112;
    development around 32, 34–5;
    Savannah 81, 88; Thu Thiem 130

Queenslander houses: architecture
    171–2; contributing qualities of
    place to experiences of a building
    179–82; correlation between a
    spatial concept and a framing
    concept 179; material contributing
    character and a visual grammar of
    forms 182–3; tectonic and timber
    frames expressing the architectural
    idea 173–9; use of native timber
    172–3

railway lands redevelopment 47–8
rainwater harvesting 71–5
Ravilious, K. 118
recycling: building materials 82–3, 84;
    human waste 77–9
Rees, W.E. 94
Regent Quarter, London 47–8
regimes of care 118–19
Reid, D. 7
relocation strategies 32
Renaissance 181, 182
research and development projects
    97
residential intensification 33–5; public
    perceptions 35; strategies for 36–7;
    visualizing 35–6
resilience thinking 55–7
response diversity 56
responsive cities 148–57
Richardson, K. 90
right-wing movements, Netherlands
    23–4
Rip, A. 67
Risselada, M. 143
Rittel, H.W.J. 53
rooftop rainwater harvesting systems
    73–4
Rotterdam, Parasite Las Palmas 159,
    165
Rowe, C. 118–19, 151
Royal Festival Hall, London 148, 149,
    150
Royston, L. 57
rural cells, networks cities 140–1

safety issues, Netherlands 23
Saigon River 121–2, 125, 126, 127,
    128–30, 131
St Pancras station, London 47–8
Salt, D. 55–6
Sandercock, L. 8
Sasaki Associates 122, 124
Savannah College of Art and Design
    (SCAD) 82, 86–7; Historic
    Preservation Department 84
Savannah Historic Foundation 86
Savannah, Georgia: emergent
    structures project 82–3; LEED
    projects 84–8; Starland Design
    District 83–4; water, transport and
    housing challenges 81–2
Schienke, E. 105
Schönteich, M. 55
Schot, J. 67–8
SCOPE 76, 77
seismic change 40
Seitz, H. 63
septic tank latrines 75, 76
Sexton, R. 32
Shane, D.G. 119
Shanghai, car parking project 112–13
shelter, need for 91–2
short-term sustainability targets 42–3
Shove, E. 8, 13, 67
silos 3
Sipe, G. 31
'skeleton' structural systems 177,
    179–81, 182–3
small-scale sustainability: De Kamers
    166–9; House No. 19 165–6;
    Parasite Las Palmas 165; 'Parasites'
    exhibition project 159–61; role of
    architect 158–9; solid timber
    construction 161–5
Smart Growth Network 84
Smith, Cynthia 186
Snow, John 13
social change 96–102
social development, ensuring 185–6
social equity, expansion strategies 43–5
social planners, sanitation challenges
    80
social spaces, office buildings 16
social sustainability, China 110–12
social-ecological systems (SESs), cities
    as 10, 54–7
socio-political dimensions of cities 8–9;
    dissatisfaction and conflict 22–3;
    solutions and ways forward 24–5;
    sustainability off the agenda 23–4;
    turning point 21–2
socio-technical transitions 67–8

SOHO (single occupant home office / small office home office), China 144
soil-based composting toilets 77–9
solid timber construction buildings 161–5
Soria y Puig, A. 119
Sorkin, Michael 118, 185
South Africa, post-apartheid urban experiences 51–2
South Bank Employers Group 155
South Bank, London: big event blight 149; building for prestige 150; early development 148–9; mixed use and adaptability 153–4; monument and fabric 150–1; pattern-book housing 154–5; planning and profit 152–3; public realm improvements 155–6; responsive city 156–7; top-down vs. ground-up urban design 151–2
Southface Institute 82
spatial concept, correlation with framing concept 179
spontaneous urban development 151–2
Stalker, C. 1
Starland Design District, Savannah 83–4
Steele, C. 7
stereophonic forms 179–81
Stott, J. 101
street culture, Johannesburg 51–2
subtropical cities 171–83
sustainability agenda, UK: case studies 43–9; challenge ahead 42–3; designing for a world of paradox 40; zero carbon agenda 40–2
sustainable cities, attributes of 42
Sustainable Fellwood 84–5
sustainable learning cities 186–9
Symbiotic City, Hangzhou Xia Sha 140–3
system behaviour, optimization of 56–7
Szokolay, S.V. 94

Tainter, J.A. 14
Tamil Nadu Agricultural University of Coimbatore 77
tectonic frames 173–9
temporary buildings 159–61, 165–6

Terreblanche, S. 50
territorial control 92–3
Thames Gateway Parklands Vision 45–7, 48–9
Thames River 148–9, 153–4, 156
thermal comfort, models of 15
Thrift, N. 8
Thu Thiem peninsula development: implementation of plan 130–1; land use program 130; peninsula 121–3; plan elements 125–9; planning process 123–5
Tianjin city business district 108–10
timber housing construction 158–70
timber-framed housing 171–83
timber, jointing 182–3
Tonkin, C. 173
top-down vs. ground-up urban design 151–2
traffic artery tunnel project, Maastricht 25–7
Transforming Australian cities (Adams) 33
transparency, timber-framed buildings 178–9
transport challenges, Savannah 81–2
transport linkages, Thu Thiem 128
transport networks, China 141
transport routes: development along 33–5, 37; London South Bank 155–6
Trubka, R. 31

UK, sustainability agenda 39–49
United Nations: development and environment programmes 105; development indicators 52–3
University of Cape Town 31
urban cells, networks cities 140–1
urban corridors, development around 34–5
urban delta, Thu Thiem 125, 126
urban design: mutuality with infrastructure and architecture 184–5; overview 7–10
Urban Ecology Australia 96–7
urban fractals 96–102
urban heat islands 12, 142
Urban Initiatives 47
Urban Planning Institute (UPI), Ho Chi Minh City 123–5, 131

urban renewal challenges, Savannah 81–9
urbanism as a living system 90–6; Christie Walk 96–102
Usable Buildings Trust 41
Utrecht, House No. 19 165–6

van de Ven, Cornelius 179–80
van den Dobbelsteen, Andy 40, 41
van den Heuvel, D. 143
Van Gogh, Theo 21, 24
Venturi, Robert 118
Verdonk, Rita 23–4
Victorian Department of Transport 32
Vigarello, G. 13
visual dynamic, timber frames 177–8
visual patterning, expressed frames 177

Waldrop, M.M. 54, 55
Walker, B.H. 55–6
Wang, Qishan 107
waste management, Murisi Town Panchayat 75–9
water challenges, Savannah 81–2
water management: Chennai 71–5; networks cities 135, 139; Thu Thiem peninsula 125
water quality 72, 73
water, demand and supply 12–13
Waterloo station, London 149
Watson, D. 172
Webber, M.M. 53
Whitford, Steve 133, 140
Wilber, K. 54
Wilders, Geert 24
Willis, A.-M. 173
Willis, C. 14
work practices, changes in 40
workplace air quality 12–18
Worthington, John 14, 40
Wrangham, R. 13

Xin Yu Networks City 136–7

Yeang, K. 118

zero carbon agenda 40–2
zoning bands 134
zoning networks 134